The International Responsibility of the European Union

When is the European Union (EU) responsible under international law? Is the EU a 'special case' international organization? The United Nations General Assembly's adoption of the International Law Commission (ILC) articles on the International Responsibility of International Organizations was only the catalyst for debate on this topic. In this book, the author examines the legal personality of the EU, how – if at all – its responsibility under international agreements is shared between Member States and how the international responsibility of the EU relates to its internal responsibilities under EU law. By exploring how, in practice, such legal regimes as the ILC, the United Nations Convention on the Law of the Sea and the World Trade Organization have held the EU responsible, this book provides an innovative analysis of a fundamental aspect of the relationship between the EU and international law.

Andrés Delgado Casteleiro is a senior research fellow at the Max Planck Institute Luxembourg for International, European and Regulatory Procedural Law. Prior to that, he was a lecturer at Durham Law School and co-director of its European Law Centre (DELI). Andrés holds a PhD in law from the European University Institute (Florence, Italy) and is a member of the Madrid Bar Association.

Cambridge Studies in European Law and Policy

This series aims to produce original works which contain a critical analysis of the state of the law in particular areas of European law and set out different perspectives and suggestions for its future development. It also aims to encourage a range of work on law, legal institutions and legal phenomena in Europe, including "law in context" approaches. The titles in the series will be of interest to academics; policy-makers; policy formers who are interested in European legal, commercial and political affairs; practising lawyers, including the judiciary; and advanced law students and researchers.

Books in the Series

Frontex and Non-Refoulement: The International Responsibility of the EU
Roberta Mungianu

The International Responsibility of the European Union: From Competence to Normative Control
Andrés Delgado Casteleiro

Gendering European Working Time Regimes: The Working Time Directive and the Case of Poland
Ania Zbyszewska

EU Renewable Electricity Law and Policy: From National Targets to a Common Market
Tim Maxian Rusche

European Constitution
Kaarlo Tuori

Brokering Europe
Antoine Vauchez

Services Liberalization in the EU and the WTO
Marcus Klamert

Referendums and the European Union: A Comparative Enquiry
Fernando Mendez, Mario Mendez, Vasiliki Triga

The Allocation of Regulatory Competence in the EU Emissions Trading Scheme
Jospehine Van Zeben

The Eurozone Crisis
Kaarlo Tuori and Klaus Tuori

International Trade Disputes and EU Liability
Anne Thies

The Limits of Legal Reasoning and the European Court of Justice
Gerard Conway

New Governance and the Transformation of European Law: Coordinating EU Social Law and Policy
Mark Dawson

The Lisbon Treaty: A Legal and Political Analysis
Jean-Claude Piris

The Ethos of Europe: Values, Law and Justice in the EU
Andrew Williams

The European Union's Fight Against Corruption: The Evolving Policy Towards Member States and Candidate Countries
Patrycja Szarek-Mason

State and Market in European Union Law
Wolf Sauter and Harm Schepel

The European Civil Code: The Way Forward
Hugh Collins

Ethical Dimensions of the Foreign Policy of the European Union: A Legal Appraisal
Urfan Khaliq

Implementing EU Pollution Control: Law and Integration
Bettina Lange

European Broadcasting Law and Policy
Jackie Harrison and Lorna Woods

The Transformation of Citizenship in the European Union: Electoral Rights and the Restructuring of Political Space
Jo Shaw

The European Convention on Human Rights: Achievements, Problems and Prospects
Steven Greer

The Constitution for Europe: A Legal Analysis
Jean-Claude Piris

Social Rights and Market Freedom in the European Constitution: A Labour Law Perspective
Stefano Giubboni

EU Enlargement and the Constitutions of Central and Eastern Europe
Anneli Albi

The International Responsibility of the European Union

From Competence to Normative Control

Andrés Delgado Casteleiro

Max Planck Institute Luxembourg for International, European and Regulatory Procedural Law

CAMBRIDGE
UNIVERSITY PRESS

CAMBRIDGE
UNIVERSITY PRESS

University Printing House, Cambridge CB2 8BS, United Kingdom

Cambridge University Press is part of the University of Cambridge.

It furthers the University's mission by disseminating knowledge in the pursuit of education, learning, and research at the highest international levels of excellence.

www.cambridge.org
Information on this title: www.cambridge.org/9781107090545

First published 2016

A catalogue record for this publication is available from the British Library.

ISBN 978-1-107-09054-5 Hardback

Contents

Series Editors' Preface

The international responsibility of the European Union is a veritable minefield, with many an unexpected surprise for the unwary. One of the great strengths of Delgado Castelerio's study is that he plots a sure path through the minefield of how different international bodies understand the relationship between the European Union and its Member States in establishing responsibility for breach of an international agreement directly caused by the implementation of EU law.

After exposing the divisions even within the Court of Justice on international responsibility, and looking at the EU's normative control in this area, the author critically reviews the International Law Commission's Draft Articles on International Responsibility of International Organizations. The weaknesses of declarations of competence are then exposed, particularly in view of the evolutionary nature of EU law and competence: mere declarations offer the appearance of certainty, but not the reality. The study then discusses the EU's international responsibility in three areas: environmental law (UNCLOS and the Aarhus Convention Compliance Committee), the WTO Dispute Settlement Mechanism and International Investment Law.

On the basis of this study, the author argues that normative control should have some consequences in the international sphere, especially as concerns attribution of responsibility, so that the EU should in most areas be responsible for the acts of its Member States in their implementation of EU law, although in relation to actions falling under the EU's Common Foreign and Security Policy, joint responsibility would be appropriate.

This study covers an often neglected aspect of EU law, but one which is of major importance, both in the EU's international relations and in the relationship between the EU and its Member States. It is a major scholarly contribution to the literature on the international responsibility of the Union, and is written accessibly, and stimulatingly. For all these reasons, we very much welcome it as a most timely and opportune addition to *Cambridge Studies in European Law and Policy*.

Laurence Gormley
Jo Shaw.

Acknowledgements

This monograph is a revised version of my PhD dissertation defended at the European University Institute in 2011 and re-written while on research leave at Durham University. I would have never completed this book without help and support from many colleagues and friends, to whom I am extremely grateful.

I am especially indebted to my supervisor, Marise Cremona, for her guidance and continuous support over the years. I would also like to thank the members of my examining board, Giorgio Gaja, Esa Paasivirta and Ernst-Ulrich Petersmann, for their helpful comments in their reports and during the viva.

I also had the great luck of discussing different aspects of this book with Pekka Aalto, Bruno De Witte, Angelos Dimopoulos, Alexis Galán Avila, Gleider Hernández, Frank Hoffmeister, Joris Larik, Gracia Marín Durán, Greg Messenger, Aoife O'Donoghue, Martina Spernbauer, Nikos Skoutaris, Robert Schütze and Bart Van Vooren. Special thanks are due to Verity Adams for her invaluable assistance during the last and most tedious parts of the writing process.

This book would not have been possible without the financial support of the following institutions: Agencia Española de Cooperación Internacional y Desarrollo, Ministerio de Ciencia e Innovación, Ministerio de Educación, Fundación Española para la Ciencia y la Tecnología, the European University Institute and Durham University. I am also very grateful to the staff at Cambridge University Press, and specially to Elizabeth Spicer, for coping with me during the whole editorial process.

Finally, I would like to thank my parents, Ricardo y Lola, and my sister, Alicia, for reminding me how lucky I am to work on what I always wanted to work on. Last but not least, the two most important people all along this period have been Paulina, whose never-ending patience and support have made this book possible, and our son Pablo, who was born in the late stages of writing this book.

Introduction

1 International Organizations as Subjects of International Law

In 1950, Eagleton explored the possibility of whether international subjects other than states could bear international responsibility.[1] In the aftermath of the Opinion of the International Court of Justice (ICJ) on the *Reparations of Injuries Suffered in the Service of United Nations*, Eagleton wondered about the implications of the ICJ's holding that the United Nations was a 'subject of international law and capable of possessing international rights and duties, and that it had capacity to maintain its rights by bringing international claims'.[2] For Eagleton, International Organizations (IOs) had not only rights but also duties towards the rest of International society,[3] including the possibility of incurring responsibility under international law.[4] The issues of which specific rights and duties can be inferred from IOs' legal personality[5] and the extent to which IOs bear responsibility for their own acts continue to be a matter of debate in international legal discourse.[6] However, since 1950 the panorama has change drastically. Nowadays, as Brölmann highlights, 'Organisations are involved in almost all fields of human cooperation, where they present themselves not only as institutional fora for states, but also as

1 Clyde Eagleton, 'International Organization and the Law of Responsibility' [1950] 76(1) *Recueil de Cours de la Académie du Droit International* 316, 325.

2 *Reparation for Injuries Suffered in the Service of United Nations* (Advisory Opinion) [1949] ICJ Rep 174, 179.

3 Eagleton, (n 1) 345.

4 Jan Klabbers, *An Introduction to International Institutional Law* (Cambridge University Press 2009) 272.

5 José E Alvarez, *International Organizations as Law-makers* (Oxford University Press 2005) 134.

6 Klabbers, (n 4) 271.

independent international actors'.[7] As well as this, IOs conclude international agreements, adopt internal autonomous measures that affect individuals, trade goods, solve international disputes and buy and sell property.[8] In other words, IOs have over the years developed new powers that they use to achieve the objectives for which they were created.[9] Likewise, the logical consequence of this increasing relevance of IOs in the international scene is the increasing possibility for IOs to breach international law.

Yet, the emergence of IOs as subjects of international law is constrained by the State-centric structure of international law. The common narrative concerning IOs describes them as an aggregation of states that create a new international subject to achieve certain objectives. States confer the IO with certain powers to carry out the necessary functions for the achievement of these objectives.[10] Therefore, when an IO cannot or will not meet its international obligations, the issue of the IO's responsibility will bring to fore the complex relation with its Member States and their responsibility for the actions of the IO.[11]

It is against this backdrop that the debates on the joint and/or subsidiary responsibility of an IOs' Member States take place. While there are very sensible policy considerations supporting the contention that the Member States of an IO might bear responsibility for the actions of the latter,[12]

7 Catherine Brölmann, *The Institutional Veil in Public International Law: International Organisations and the Law of Treaties* (Hart 2007) 1.

8 Alvarez, (n 5) 136.

9 Eric Stein, 'External Relations of the European Community: Structure and Process' [1990] Collected Courses of the Academy of European Law 115, 130.

10 This is the traditional functionalist narrative regarding IOs. For a critique of this approach see: Jan Klabbers, 'The Emergence of Functionalism in International Institutional Law: Colonial Inspirations' [2014] 25(3) European Journal of International Law 645.

11 Jan Klabbers, 'The Transformation of International Organizations Law' [2015] 26(1) European Journal of International Law 9, 63.

12 Jean D'Aspremont, 'Abuse of the Legal Personality of International Organizations and the Responsibility of Member States' [2007] 4 International Organizations Law Review 91; Ian Brownlie, 'The Responsibility of State for the Acts of International Organizations' in Maurizzio Ragazzi (ed), *International Responsbility Today: Essays in Memory of Oscar Schachter* (Martinus Nijhoff 2005); Chittaranjan Felix Amerasinghe, 'Liability to Third Parties fo Member States of International Organizations: Practice, Principle and Judicial Precedent' [1991] 85(2) American Journal of International Law 259; Cedric Ryngaert, 'Oscillating between Embracing and Avoiding Bosphorus: The European Court of Human Rights on Member State Responsibility for Acts of International Organisations and the Case of the EU' [2014] 39(2) European Law Review 176; Sienho Yee (ed), *The Responsibility of States Members of an International Organization for Its Conduct as a Result of Membership or Their Normal Conduct Associated with Membership* (Martinus Nijhoff 2005).

it is unclear whether international law would support such a functional view of IOs.[13]

2 The EU and International Responsibility

No other IO has developed more powers or evolved as fast as the EU. Since its inception as the European Coal and Steel Community (ESC), to its actual configuration established in the Treaty of Lisbon, the EU has completely changed its image, both internally and externally. The EU is no longer an IO with the mission of 'contributing to economic expansion, the development of employment and the improvement of the standard of living in the participating countries through the institution, in harmony with the general economy of the Member States, of a common market',[14] but something else entrusted with a great variety of objectives which range, for example, from establishing an internal market[15] to the eradication of poverty and the protection of human rights, in particular the rights of the child.[16]

The EU's evolutionary dynamics are specially embedded in the way it relates to the wider world. For instance in 1991, Stein, when analysing how the classic four components of the external powers of a state were present in the then European Community's external relations, noted that three out of the four components – communication and diplomacy, international autonomous acts and treaty-making power – were present in the EU's external powers.[17] According to Stein the European Community had delegations in third countries; adopted international autonomous measures like the Common Customs Tariffs and international sanctions; and had concluded international agreements.[18] However, in relation to the fourth component – i.e. international responsibility – Stein pointed to the dearth of practice on the topic.[19] Nowadays, international bodies increasingly deal with issues concerning the international responsibility of the European Union.

For a critique see: Esa Paasivirta, 'Responsibility of a Member State of an International Organization: Where Will It End? Comments on Article 60 of the ILC Draft on the Responsibility of International Organizations' [2010] 7 International Organizations Law Review 49.

13 Klabbers, (n 11) 63. Klabbers argues that there is no rule in international law that would support the responsibility of a Member State jointly or subsidiarily for the actions of the IO. On the contrary, the ILC argues that there might be. See article 60 ARIO.

14 Article 2 of the Treaty constituting the European Coal and Steel Community.

15 Article 3 (3) TEU.

16 Article 3 (5) TEU.

17 Stein, (n 9) 131.

18 Ibid.

19 Ibid.

This study addresses the question of when the EU is internationally responsible. More precisely, it examines the extent to which the EU and its Member States bear responsibility for violations of international agreements committed as a consequence of the implementation of EU law. The specific features of the multi-level system implementation of EU law pose a series of very interesting questions as regards the EU's relations with its Member States and their responsibility under international law. The EU primarily implements its law through its Member States' authorities. As such, should the EU bear responsibility for a violation committed by a Member State organ because it was implementing EU law? Should a Member State that, in complying with a piece of EU legislation, violated an international obligation be held liable?

3 The EU's Responsibility Conundrum

In the same way that international law has not made its mind up on the issue of the joint responsibility of IOs, it appears the Court of Justice of the EU (CJEU) has not either. In *Parliament v Council* the Court seemed to support the idea that the EU and its Member States are jointly responsible for the implementation of the Cotonou Agreement.[20] Yet as it will be shown, the Court's approach is far from clear.[21] Moreover, different Advocate Generals (AG) have taken very different positions regarding the EU's international responsibility. For instance, AG Tesauro, in *Hèrmes*, in relation to the EU's obligations within the World Trade Organization (WTO) noted:

[20] Case C-316/91 *Parliament v Council* [1994] ECR I-661, para. 29. Cf. ILC, 'Second Report on Responsibility of International Organizations, by Giorgio Gaja, Special Rapporteur' (2 April 2004) UN Doc A/CN.4/541; Martin Björklund, 'Responsibility in the EC for Mixed Agreements' [2001] 70 Nordic Journal of International Law 373; Allan Rosas, 'International Responsibility of the EU and the European Court of Justice' in Malcolm D. Evans and Panos Koutrakos (eds), *The International Responsbility of the European Union European and International Perspectives* (Hart 2013); Christian Tomuschat, 'The International Responsibility of the European Union' in Enzo Cannizazaro (ed), *The European Union as an Actor in International Relations* (Kluwer Law International 2002).

[21] See Chapter 1. Cf. Marise Cremona, *External Relations of the EU and the Member States: Competence, Mixed Agreements, International Responsibility, and Effects of International Law* (2006) 14; Pieter Jan Kuijper, 'International Responsibility for EU Mixed Agreements' in Christophe Hillion and Panos Koutrakos (eds), *Mixed Agreements Revisited: The EU and Its Member States in the World* (Hart 2010); Pieter Jan Kuijper and Esa Paasivirta, 'EU International Responsibility and Its Attribution: From the Inside Looking Out' in Panos Koutrakos and Malcolm D. Evans (eds), *The International Responsibility of the European Union European and International Perspectives* (Hart 2013).

> [t]he Member States and the [Union] constitute, vis-à-vis contracting non-member States, a single contracting party or at least contracting parties bearing equal responsibility in the event of failure to implement the agreement.[22]

For AG Tesauro, the joint responsibility of the EU and its Member States relied on two elements. On one hand, unless it is expressly provided, both the EU and its Member States are bound by the whole agreement they have concluded with a third party. On the other, the division of competences is a purely internal issue that should not play a role when establishing the responsibility of the EU internationally.[23]

By contrast, AG Mischo in *Commission v Ireland*, argued that the fact that both the EU and its Member States are bound by the whole agreement does not necessarily mean they are jointly responsible in the event of breach.[24] It might very well mean the contrary:

> the very fact that the [Union] and its Member States had recourse to the formula of a mixed agreement announces to non-member countries that that agreement does not fall wholly within the competence of the [Union] and that, consequently, the [Union] is, a priori, only assuming responsibility for those parts falling within its competence.[25]

The debate within the CJEU focuses, perhaps in excess, on how the division of competences might a priori affect the international responsibility of the EU. However, it does not further articulate how the exercise of that competence plays out in relation to the attribution of responsibility. By focusing only on the division of competences, the CJEU disregards how the constitutional architecture of the EU determines the relationship between the EU and its Member States.[26]

The contradictory views on the EU's international responsibility also extend to the EU's recent treaty-making practice. The EU seems to be favouring joint responsibility as the default rule in the European

22 Case C-53/96 *Hermès* [1998] ECR I-3603, para. 14 (Opinion of the AG).

23 Ibid.

24 Case C- 13/00 *Ireland v Commission (Berne Convention)* [2002] ECR I-2943, para. 30 (Opinion of the AG).

25 Ibid.

26 On the discussion on how the special features of the EU should inform its international responsibility: Stefan Talmon, 'Responsibility of International Organizations: Does the European Community Require Special Treatment?' in Maurizzio Ragazzi (ed), *International Responsibility Today: Essays in Memory of Oscar Schachter* (Martinus Nijhoff 2005); Kuijper and Paasivirta, (n 21); Esa Paasivirta and Pieter-Jan Kuijper, 'Does One Size Fit All? The European Community and the Responsibility of International Organizations' XXXVI Netherlands Yearbook of International Law 169.

Convention on Human Rights (ECHR). The now failed draft agreement on the EU's accession to the ECHR[27] provided in its article 3 (7) that:

> If the violation in respect of which a High Contracting Party is a co-respondent to the proceedings is established, the respondent and the co-respondent shall be jointly responsible for that violation, unless the Court, on the basis of the reasons given by the respondent and the co-respondent, and having sought the views of the applicant, decides that only one of them be held responsible.

Conversely, in relation to the responsibility stemming from International investor-State arbitration, joint responsibility is not the general rule. Instead, the financial responsibility regulation[28] links the responsibility of the EU to the factual scenario that gave rise to the breach of international law.[29]

This study tries to contribute to these debates in a two-fold manner. First, it submits that the EU's constitutional architecture and, especially, the articulation of the exercise of the EU's competences in practice run against the idea of joint responsibility when Member States implement EU law. Second, international bodies seem to recognize this fact and so far have preferred to hold the EU solely responsible for those breaches committed by its Member States when implementing EU law, instead of jointly responsible with the Member State that breached the international obligation.

4 Scope and Structure of This Monograph

This monograph sets out to examine how the special features of the EU influence its international responsibility by examining how international bodies approach the issue.[30] Logically, this analysis entails focusing on

27 The draft Agreement and its Explanatory Report can be found in the Council of Europe Doc 47+1 (2013) R008, available at: www.coe.int/t/dghl/standardsetting/hrpolicy/Accession/Meeting_reports/47_1(2013)008_final_report_EN.pdf.

28 Regulation (EU) 912/2014 of the European Parliament and of the Council of 23 July 2014 establishing a framework for managing financial responsibility linked to investor-to-state dispute settlement tribunals established by international agreements to which the European Union is party, [2014] OJ L 257.

29 For an in-depth analysis, see Chapter 7. Also: Angelos Dimopoulos, 'The Involvement of the EU in Investor-State Dispute Settlement: A Question of Responsibilities' [2014] 51(6) Common Market Law Review 1671.

30 Cf. Frank Hoffmeister, 'Litigating against the European Union and Its Member States – Who Responds under the ILC's Draft Articles on International Responsibility of International Organizations?' [2010] 21(3) European Journal of International Law 723.

disputes brought against either the EU or its Member States by third countries on issues covered by EU law. Thus far, those disputes have only arisen in matters relating to compliance with multilateral agreements, and in areas covered by what had previously been considered the first pillar.

Consequently, insofar as there has not been any international dispute brought against the EU or its Member States on issues covered by the EU's Common Foreign and Security Policy (CFSP), the monograph does not discuss the issues that would be raised in the event of a breach of an international obligation stemming from an act adopted under the CFSP. Overall, the monograph provides an analysis of the EU's international responsibility with reference to the most relevant case law on the topic. The only case law concerning the responsibility of the EU that is not analysed in greater detail is the European Court of Human Rights (ECtHR),[31] though it does not mean that the relevant ECtHR case law is not briefly examined.[32] The decision to exclude ECtHR was based on the critical point at which relations between the EU and the ECtHR find themselves at this moment. Even though by virtue of article 6 (2) TEU, the EU is supposed to accede to the ECHR and, as such, the way in which the ECtHR deals with the EU's responsibility would change drastically, the negative stance of the Court of Justice of the European Union (CJEU) in *Opinion 2/13*[33] has cast a shadow of doubt over the current draft agreement.[34] Therefore, as it is unclear which parts of the draft agreement will survive the next round of negotiations, this study does not rush to make conclusions as to how

[31] E.g. ECtHR, *Bosphorus Hava Yollari Turizm Ve Ticaret Anonim Şirketi v Ireland* [2006] 42 EHRR 1; ECtHR, *Senator Lines GmbH v Austria, Belgium, Denmark, Finland, France, Germany, Greece, Ireland, Italy, Luxembourg, the Netherlands, Portugal, Spain, Sweden and the United Kingdom* [2004] 39 EHRR SE3. On the topic see: Andrew Clapham, 'The European Union before the European Court of Human Rights' in Laurence Boisson de Chazournes, Cesare Romano and Ruth Mackenzie (eds), *International Organizations and International Dispute Settlement: Trends and Prospects* (Trasnantional 2002); José Manuel Cortés Martín, 'Adhesión al CEDH y Autonomía del Derecho de la Unión: Legitimación pasiva de la Unión y sus miembros y compatibilidad material' [2010] 22 Revista General de Derecho Europeo 53; Jean Paul Jacqué, 'Communauté européenne et Convention européenne des droits de l'homme' in Louis' Edmond Pettiti, Emmanuel Decaux and Pierre-Henri Imbet (eds), *La Convention européenne des droits de l'homme Commentaire article par article* (Economica 1999).

[32] See Chapters 2 and 3.

[33] Case Opinion 2/13 *Re: Accession of the European Union to the ECHR* [nyr] ECR.

[34] For a critical examination of the current mechanism to deal with the EU's responsibility in the ECHR see: Andrés Delgado Casteleiro, 'United We Stand: The EU and Its Member States in the Strasbourg Court' in Vasiliki Kosta, Nikos Skoutaris and Vassilis P Tzevelekos (eds), *The EU Accession to the ECHR* (Hart 2014).

the responsibility of the EU will change was the EU to ever acceded to the ECHR.

This book starts by analysing in Chapter 1 how the EU becomes bound by international law and how the relations between the EU and its Member States determine the way in which they comply with the international obligations binding upon them. The chapter first focuses on the EU's powers to conclude international agreements, its practice in that regard and the effects those agreements have on the EU and its Member States. It seeks to outline the circumstances under which the EU is bound by an international agreement and can consequently be responsible for its eventual violation. Furthermore the chapter addresses the effects that these agreements have on EU Member States. The chapter analyses to what extent EU Member States are bound by agreements concluded by the EU and vice versa. Only by understanding when the EU and its Member States are bound by an international agreement, and on what grounds, will it be possible to know when their international responsibility will arise. The second part of Chapter 1 examines how EU law is implemented. Given that this monograph examines the EU's international responsibility stemming from the implementation of EU law, it is necessary to establish how EU law is implemented. The chapter describes how the EU's executive federalism operates, and to what extent Member States are obliged to implement EU law.[35] In other words, this chapter examines the extent to which EU Member States enjoy autonomy when implementing EU law. The chapter argues that the principles and institutional design of the EU's executive federalism, and more specifically the way the EU exercises its normative control over its Member States, clearly limits EU Member States' autonomy, and argues that this fact should have an external projection when addressing the breach of an international obligation committed by an EU Member State when implementing EU law.

Chapter 2 and 3 examine how the EU's normative control is taken into account by the international law of responsibility. More specifically, Chapter 2 analyses how the ILC Articles on the Responsibility of International Organizations (ARIO) approach the issue of attribution of conduct, while Chapter 3 focuses on other rules which can lead to the responsibility of the EU.[36] The ILC is a subsidiary organ of the General Assembly of the

[35] Cf. Robert Schütze, 'From Rome to Lisbon: "Executive Federalism" in the (New) European Union' [2010] 47(5) Common Market Law Review 1385; Kuijper, (n 21).

[36] ILC, 'Report of the International Law Commission on the Work of Its 61ST Session' (4 May–5 June and 6 July–7 August 2009) UN Doc A/64/10.

United Nations,[37] entrusted with the task of promoting the progressive development of international law and its codification.[38] The ARIO responds to this mandate and enshrines a series of rules concerning the responsibility of IOs and their Member States for the commission of an internationally wrongful act. These two chapters examine how these rules would apply to the EU and to what extent they provide solutions to the problems and specificities that the EU and its Member States pose as regards their international responsibility.

Chapters 4 and 5 focus on the main mechanism used by the EU to deal with its international responsibility. More specifically they address the question of whether the division of competence is a good way to establish the EU's responsibility under an international agreement. To do so, these chapters examine to what extent the externalization of their internal division of competences solves the question of the apportionment of responsibility in those multilateral agreements signed by the EU and its Member States.

Chapter 4 critically approaches the examination of the main techniques used by the EU to establish its responsibility within an agreement by linking it to the EU's division of powers.[39] In other words, the chapter examines a mechanism by which the EU attempts, through a declaration annexed to the agreement, to limit its responsibility by linking the agreement to the division of competences between the EU and its Member States. The chapter provides an overview of these declarations, categorizing them and analysing their effectiveness.

Chapter 5 continues with the analysis of these declarations. More specifically, it analyses their practical relevance and effectiveness by looking into their application by international bodies. In this regard, Chapter 5 examines how these declarations have been applied in practice to establish to what extent competence is a good way to establish the EU's responsibility for the violation of an agreement.

Chapter 6 puts forward the example of the Dispute Settlement System of the WTO. The chapter shows how WTO panels attribute the commission

[37] Ian Brownlie, *Principles of Public International Law* (7th edn, Oxford University Press 2008) 29.

[38] UNGA Res 174 (II) (21 November 1947) UN Doc A/RES/174(II), Annex Statute of the International Law Commission, Article 1. Most scholars, and the ILC itself, agree that the differentiation between progressive development and codification are indissolubly linked. See: Alvarez, (n 5) 306; Brownlie, (n 37) 29.

[39] A previous version of this chapter was published in: Andrés Delgado Casteleiro, 'EU Declarations of Competence to Multilateral Agreements: A Useful Reference Base?' [2012] 17(4) European Foreign Affairs Review 491.

of internationally wrongful acts to the EU, and the extent to which the EU bears responsibility for EU Member States' acts in implementing EU law.

Chapter 7 looks at the issue of the EU's normative control and Member States' responsibility. The chapter examines the extent to which EU Member States bear responsibility for the violation of international agreements committed under the EU's normative control. The chapter examines this situation within the framework of International investment arbitration. The chapter shows how in situations in which the EU is not bound by the international obligation which a Member State act has breached while implementing EU law, rules of normative conflict would still apply.

Finally, the conclusions comment on the extent to which the EU constitutes a special case and the implications the notion of normative control has on the EU's nature, especially in areas not discussed in this study, such as the CFSP.

1 The EU's Normative Control and International Responsibility

1.1 Introduction

Whereas article 47 TEU might have put to rest the discussions on the international legal personality of the EU,[1] its scope continues nevertheless to be contested given its limited nature.[2] This becomes especially clear in relation to the debates on the EU's international responsibility.[3] The extent to which the EU can be considered an autonomous international subject seems to rest on its responsibility under international law.[4] Therefore, because the EU's international responsibility is inextricably linked to its international personality, it is necessary to analyse certain aspects of the latter to fully comprehend how the former should be articulated. More specifically, it is fundamental to understand how the EU assumes an international obligation, and how it implements it.

By examining how the EU becomes bound by an international obligation and the consequences that follow from it, this chapter hopes to draw a picture of how the relations between the EU and its Member States

[1] Panos Koutrakos, *EU International Relations Law* (2nd edn, Hart 2015) 14.

[2] On the limited nature of the personality of the EU and other individual organizations (IOs): Henry G. Schermers and Niels M. Blokker, *International Institutional Law: Unity within Diversity* (4th edn, Martinus Nijhoff 2003) 993 – 'to be an international person means only to be capable of bearing rights and duties. No answer is given to the question of what rights and duties individual organizations have.' Cf. Jan Klabbers, *An Introduction to International Institutional Law* (Cambridge University Press 2009) 50.

[3] Gleider I. Hernández, 'Beyond the Control Paradigm? International Responsibility and the European Union' [2014] 15 *Cambridge Yearbook of European Legal Studies* 643, 648. Ottavio Quirico, 'The International Responsibility of the European Union: A Basic Interpretative Pattern' [2013] 63 *Hungarian Yearbook of International and European Law* 63.

[4] Daniel Müller, 'Union Européenne et Responsabilité International' in Myriam Benlolo-Carabot, Ukas Candas and Eglantine Cujo (eds), *Union Européenne et Droit International En l'honneur de Patrick Dlaillier* (Pedone 2012) 340.

influence their international responsibility. In other words, if first we understand when and to what extent the EU and its Member States are bound by the international obligation they have violated, it will be easier to understand when the EU, in implementing its law, simultaneously breaches an international obligation binding upon on it.

For that reason, this chapter is divided into four sections. The first section sets up the debate by entering into the general discussion on the international legal personality of the EU and the consequences both for the EU and its Member States. The second section focuses on how the EU becomes bound by international agreements and the effects that those agreements have within the EU legal order. The third section examines how the EU's multi-level system of implementation operates, because only by understanding how EU law is implemented will it be possible to comprehend how the rules of attribution should work when confronted by an EU and/or a Member State's breach of an international agreement. The fourth part of this chapter provides some concluding thoughts on the EU's responsibility in light of its international personality as described in the previous sections.

1.2 The International Legal Personality of the EU and Its Member States

1.2.1 The EU as a Person under International Law as a Possible Way to Establish the International Responsibility of the EU

Like most IOs,[5] the EU's legal personality can be described as a sort of transparent veil[6] that leaves its institutional structure with its Member

[5] In *Opinion 2/13*, while the CJEU recognized that the EU is, under international law, precluded by its very nature from being considered a state, it has still to provide a positive definition of what the EU might be if not a state, *Opinion 2/13* Re: Accession of the European Union to the ECHR [nyr] ECR para. 156. Van Vooren and Wessel argue that, in principle, it should be considered an IO, Bart Van Vooren and Ramses A. Wessel, *EU External Relations Law: Text, Cases and Materials* (Cambridge University Press 2014) 4. Klabbers mentions how the EU is often defined as the most developed form of IO, Jan Klabbers, 'Contending Approaches to International Organizations: Between Functionalism and Constitutionalism' in Jan Klabbers and Asa Wallendahl (eds), *Research Handbook on the Law of International Organizations* (Edward Elgar 2011) 24. Cf. Marjorie Beulay, 'L'Union européenne comme organisation international' in Myriam Benlolo-Carabot, Ulas Candas and Eglantine Cujo (eds), *Union européenne et Droit international* (Pedone 2012) 95; Pierre Klein, *La responsabilité des organisations internationales dans les ordres juridiques internes et en droit de gens* (Bruylant 1998) 6. By contrast, De Baere argues that 'the European Union is unique as a polity organized along federal lines but with fully fledged States as its component political entities. The tension between the self-consciousness of the Member States and their constitutional relationship within the

States partially visible to third parties.[7] Depending on how the relationship between the EU and its Member States is construed, the EU's veil will be more transparent or opaque. The more transparent the veil is, the less autonomy the IO would have from its Member States. By contrast, the opaquer the veil of the legal personality is, the more autonomous the IO will be, and consequently a stronger case for its sole responsibility under international law could be made. Therefore, which elements must be present in an IO so as to make its legal personality more opaque and, consequently, more independent from its Member States?

The explicit endowment of that legal personality in the constituent instrument could be seen as a useful guideline in this respect. Inasmuch as the Member States of an IO have granted the latter with personality, this would indicate that they wished to create an entity separate from them, and that may play a role when deciding whether the former should be held responsible for the activities of the IO.[8] The granting of international legal personality to an IO would mean that its institutional veil would allow

Union is specially pronounced in the foreign policy field', Gert De Baere, *Constitutional Principles of EU External Relations* (Oxford University Press 2008) 1. Similarly, Schütze argues that the EU is a federation of states, Robert Schütze, *Foreign Affairs and the EU Constitution* (Cambridge University Press 2014) 46. The international practice of the EU is not of much help in establishing its international nature either. On one hand, the EU has contributed to the works of the ILC in relation to the responsibility of IOs since it holds that the outcome of the ILC's works may have particular relevance to its own activities (56th sess., 25 June 2004) UN Doc A/CN.4/545, 5. On the other hand, in its day-to-day practice, the EU does not refer to any international instrument regulating the conduct of IOs. For instance, it refers to the 1969 Vienna Convention on the Law of the Treaties between States (VCLT) and not to the 1989 Vienna Convention on the Law of the Treaties between States and International Organizations or between International Organizations (VCLT II). It is noteworthy that the CJEU explains that it applies the VCLT insofar as the rules are an expression of general international customary law. Yet, it avoids referring to the EU as an IO: 'the fact that the Vienna Convention does not apply to international agreements concluded between States and *other subjects of international law* [emphasis added] is not to affect the application to them of any of the rules set forth in that convention to which they would be subject under international law independently of the convention,' Case C-386/98 Brita GmbH v Hauptzollamt Hamburg-Hafen [2010] ECRI-01289 para. 40. See Jan Klabbers, *The European Union in International Law* (Pedone 2012), 7.

[6] Cf. Catherine Brölmann, *The Institutional Veil in Public International Law: International Organisations and the Law of Treaties* (Hart 2007), Prosper Weil, 'Le droit international en quête de son identité: cours général de droit international public' [2015] 237 *Recueil de Cours de la Académie du Droit International* 370.

[7] Catherine Brölmann, 'International Organizations and Treaties' in Jan Klabbers (ed), *Research Handbook on International Organizations: Contractual Freedom and Institutional Constraint* (Edward Elgar 2011) 286.

[8] Klabbers, (n 2) 50; C. F. Amerasinghe, *Principles of the Institutional Law of International Organizations* (Cambridge University Press 2005) 68.

the IO to bear responsibility in certain circumstances. On the contrary, the absence of legal personality would indicate that the IO's Member States could be liable for the actions of the IO. Consequently, taking into account that article 47 TEU confers the EU legal personality and that it entails the capacity to establish contractual links with third countries,[9] the EU would logically also be held responsible for breaching those links.

Yet, while undoubtedly the EU's responsibility under international law stems from the fact that it has been vested with a legal personality,[10] its precise scope cannot be established on the basis of its international legal personality alone.[11] By way of example, the EU, like any other IO, requires that Member States carry out its mission due to the limited capabilities and resources put at its disposal.[12] In an nutshell, EU law is mainly implemented by EU Member States and not by the EU itself.[13] As a result, any lack of conformity between a piece of EU law and an international obligation will more likely be evident when EU Member States are implementing that piece of EU law. Consequently, should the EU Member States bear responsibility for acts committed when implementing EU law? The mere fact that the EU has an international legal personality does not answer that question. It is necessary to establish the scope of that personality by analysing the relationship between the EU and its Member States when implementing EU law.

Moreover, there are situations where the subjective nature of an IO (its consideration as an independent international actor from its members) may compete with the nature of its legal system.[14] Regardless of its legal personality, the EU continues to be a forum wherein its Member States co-operate intensively to pursue a set of common objectives.[15] For instance, the Council, one of the EU's legislative bodies, is constituted of representatives of the Member States.[16] Member States acting as the Council can adopt legislation that could violate their international

[9] *Case 22/70 Commission v Council (ERTA)* [1971] ECR 263 para. 14.

[10] Article 2 ARIO seems to support this idea. See Chapter 2.

[11] See Chapter 2. Cf. José Manuel Cortés Martín, *Las Organizaciones Internacionales: Codificación y Desarrollo Progresivo de su Responsabilidad Internacional* (Instituto Andaluz de Administración Pública 2008) 79; Antoni Pigrau Solé, 'La Responsabilidad Internacional de la Comunidad Europea' in Fernando M. Mariño Menéndez (ed), *Acción exterior de la Unión Europea y comunidad internacional* (Boletín Oficial del Estado 1998) 173.

[12] Cf. Klabbers, (n 2); Schermers and Blokker, (n 2).

[13] See Chapter 2.

[14] Catherine Brölmann, 'A Flat Earth? International Organizations in the System of International Law' [2001] 70 *Nordic Journal of International Law* 319, 320.

[15] Klabbers, (n 2) 25.

[16] Article 16.2 TEU.

obligations. In such situations, the question of the responsibility of the EU or its Member States could revolve around the issue of the *volonté distincte* of the EU and the extent to which the Member States' control of the EU's machinery, and not around whether the EU is an international legal person.[17] In fact, the discussion would concern the possibility of EU Member States hiding behind the EU's personality to avoid their responsibility under international law.[18] Whereas such a scenario, where the EU is no more than the concerted will of its Member States,[19] is difficult to argue in the current state of the EU's integration process, it shows nonetheless how the constitutional relationship between the EU and its Member States plays a fundamental role in understanding the precise scope of the EU's international responsibility and, by extension, its international personality.[20]

17 Jan Klabbers, 'The Changing Image of International Organizations' in Jean-Marc Coicaud and Veijo Heiskanen (eds), *The Legitimacy of International Organizations* (United Nations University Press 2001) 226. Rosalyn Higgins, 'Report for Institute de Droit International: The Legal Consequences for Member States of the Non-fulfilment by International Organizations of Their Obligations toward Third Parties' in Rosalyn Higgins (ed), *Themes and Theories: Selected Essays, Speeches, and Writings in International Law*, vol 2 (Oxford University Press 2009) 841. Brölmann, (n 6) 253.

18 See Chapter 3.

19 Cf. Robert Schütze, 'On "Federal" Ground: The European Unions as an (inter)National Phenomenon' [2009] 46 *Common Market Law Review* 1069.

20 By virtue of how this relationship is articulated, the EU is often defined as sui generis both from the perspective of the EU as a legal system (Bruno Simma, 'Of Planets and the Universe: Self-Contained Regimes in International Law' [2006] 17 *European Journal of International Law* 483, 516; Alain Pellet, 'Les fondements juridiques internationaux du droit communautaire' [1994] V(2) *Collected Courses of the Academy of European Law* 201, 249; Bruno De Witte, 'The Emergence of European System of Public International Law: The EU and Its Member States as Strange Subjects' in Jan Wouters, André Nollkaemper and Erika De Wet (eds), *The Europeanisation of International Law* (T. M. C. Asser Press 2009) 40) and from the perspective of an international subject (Allan Rosas, 'The European Court of Justice and Public International Law' in Jan Wouters, André Nollkaemper and Erika De Wet (eds), *The Europeanisation of International Law* (T. M. C. Asser Press 2009) 71; Christian Timmermans, 'EU and International Public Law' [1999] 4 *European Foreign Affairs Review* 181, 182). Yet, the sui generis label does not help in understanding how international law should deal with the special features of the EU (Eileen Denza, *The Intergovernamental Pillars of the European Union* (Oxford University Press 2002) 1; Schütze, (n 5) 34). Regardless of whether the EU does or does not fit easily into traditional international law classifications (Rosas, 'The European Court of Justice and Public International Law' 71), or whether it is the only Regional Economic Integration Organization (REIO) (De Witte, 'Emergence of European System ' 40), there is no doubt that the EU is an international subject with its own legal personality that, by virtue of the powers conferred to it, can be bound by international law, breach it, and be held responsible for those breaches where the extent of the EU's responsibility would boil down to how its relationships with its Member States are characterized.

1.2.2 *An Examination of the EU's Treaty-Making Power as a Way to Establish the Scope of the EU's Responsibility under International Law*

The limited and functional nature of the EU's personality shows how the responsibility of the EU under international law is inextricably linked to the division of competences between the EU and its Member States.[21] In other words, the EU can be responsible inasmuch as it has competence. This is an expression both of the limited nature of the EU's legal personality and of the principle of conferral as enshrined in article 5 (2) TEU. As the CJEU put it in *Opinion 2/94*, 'the [Union] is to act within the limits of the powers conferred upon it'.[22] The principle of conferral obviously entails a limitation to the powers of the EU,[23] and to a certain extent, it could be seen as useful to delineate the external contours of the EU's personality.[24] Yet, could an examination of the EU Treaties shed any light on the extent of the EU's international responsibility?

Given that the ability of the EU to conclude international agreements is one of the basic expressions of its capacity of representation on the international plane,[25] and that it is also a pre-requisite for international responsibility to arise, it seems rather obvious to note that the EU's treaty-making power arises only when the competence to enter into international agreements exists.[26] Furthermore, since the Lisbon Treaty introduced a

21 Jean-Victor Louis, 'La personnalité juridique internationale de la Communauté et de l'Union Européenne' in Jean-Victor Louis and Marianne Dony (eds), *Commentaire J Megret Le Droit de la CE et de l'Union Européenne Relations Exterieures*, vol 12 (Université de Bruxelles 2005) 41.

22 Case *Opinion 2/94 Re: Accession to the ECHR* [1996] ECR I-1759 para. 23.

23 Article 5.2 TEU: '. . . the Union shall act only within the limits of the competences conferred upon it by the Member States in the Treaties to attain the objectives set out therein'.

24 Giorgio Gaja, 'How Does the European Community's International Responsibility Relate to Its Exclusive Competence?' in *Studi di Diritto Internazionale in Onore di Gaetano Arangio-Ruiz*, vol II (Editoriale Scientifica 2004) 747; Allan Rosas, 'International Dispute Settlement: EU Practices and Procedures' [2003] 46 *German Yearbook of International Law* 284. See Chapter 4.

25 *Case 6/64 Costa v ENEL* [1964] ECR 583 para. 3. Eric Stein, 'External Relations of the European Community: Structure and Process' [1991] 1 *Collected Courses of the Academy of European Law* 115, 131. In this same vein, the ICJ, when analysing the legal personality of the United Nations, stated that 'whereas a State possesses the totality of international rights and duties recognized by international law, the rights and duties of an entity such as the [United Nations] Organization must depend upon its purposes and functions as specified or implied in its constituted documents and relevant practice.' From this perspective, the EU, as any other IO, can enter into international agreements only to the extent that it has competence to do so, *Reparation for Injuries Suffered in the Service of United Nations (Advisory Opinion)* [1949] ICJ Rep 174.

26 Alan Dashwood, 'Implied External Competence of the EC' in Martti Koskenniemi (ed), *International Law Aspects of the European Union* (Kluwer Law International 1998) 120.

catalogue of EU competences, the answer to the EU's international responsibility could be found in that catalogue.[27] Yet, the scenarios in which this competence arises are not as straightforward as *Opinion 2/94* or article 5 (2) TEU might convey.[28] Instead, as it will be shown, the articulation of the EU's treaty-making power is far from clear in practice.

In this regard, article 216 TFEU would be the perfect expression of the inherent complexity of the EU's treaty-making powers. The provision identifies four situations by which the EU can enter into an international agreement: (1) where the Treaties so provide (constitutional express powers); (2) where the conclusion of an agreement is necessary to achieve, within the framework of the Union's policies, one of the objectives referred to in the Treaties (external flexibility clause); (3) where it is provided for in a legally binding Union act (WTO Doctrine); or (4) where it is likely to affect common rules or alter their scope (ERTA-type implied powers). Out these four scenarios, two of them could be considered to be two very different manifestations of the principle of conferral (1 and 3) while the other two (2 and 4) would be expressions of the doctrine of implied powers.

1.2.2.1 EU Express Powers

The inherent logic of the constitutional principle of conferral entails that the EU's power to conclude an international agreement stems from the Treaties. However, that does not necessarily require the existence of a one-stop shop for the EU's treaty-making competences. Any reading of article 216 TFU makes that clear: there is not a single legal basis for the EU to conduct its external relations. The EU Treaties adopt a sectoral approach to its treaty-making power, in which the Treaties expressly confer on the EU the competence to act externally as regards certain policy areas.[29] By virtue of these legal bases, the EU can enter into international agreements and, in the case of a breach, can be subject to international responsibility:

- CFSP: Article 37 (ex Article 24) TEU;
- European neighbourhood policy: Article 8 (2) TEU;
- Common customs tariffs: Article 32 (a) (ex Article 26) TFEU;
- Agriculture: Article 40 (2) (ex Article 34.2) TFEU;

[27] For a critical analysis of the catalogues, see Lucia Serena Rossi, 'Does the Lisbon Treaty Provide a Clearer Separation of Competences between EU and Member States?' in Andrea Biondi, Piet Eeckhout and Stefanie Ripley (eds), *EU Law after Lisbon* (Oxford University Press 2012) 102.

[28] Robert Schütze, 'Lisbon and the Federal Order of Competences: A Prospective Analysis' [2008] 33 *European Law Review* 709, 722.

[29] De Baere, (n 5) 11.

- Capital and payments: Article 63 (ex Article 57) TFEU;
- Asylum: Article 78 (2) (g) TFEU;
- Monetary policy: Article 138 (ex Article 111.4) TFEU;
- Education: Article 165 (3) (ex Article 149.3) TFEU;
- Vocational training: Article 166 (3) (ex Article 150.3) TFEU;
- Culture: Article 167 (3) (ex Article 151.3) TFEU;
- Public health: Article 168 (3) (ex Article 152.3) TFEU;
- Trans-European networks: Article 171 (3) (ex Article 155) TFEU;
- Research and technical development: Article 180 (ex Article 164) and Article 186 (ex Article 170);
- Environment: Article 191 (4) (ex article 174) TFEU;
- Common commercial policy: article 207 (ex article 133) TFEU;
- Development cooperation: article 209 (2) (ex article 177) TFEU;
- Economical and financial cooperation with third countries: article 212 (3) (ex article 181 A) TFEU;
- Humanitarian aid: article 214 (4) TFEU;
- Relations with other IOs: article 220 (ex articles 302–304 TEC) TFEU;
- Association agreements: article 217 (ex article 310 TEC) TFEU.

However, although at first sight, this list could be seen as a useful guideline to understanding where the EU can be held responsible under international law, a closer look at the inner workings shows otherwise. The common commercial policy (CCP) constitutes a good example of how the existence of an EU external competence does not settle per se the question on the competence to conclude an international agreement. Article 207 TFEU identifies the areas covered by the CCP competence like the 'the conclusion of tariff and trade agreements relating to . . . foreign direct investment'.[30] Yet the exact scope of these areas is not that clear.[31] For instance, the definition of foreign direct investment (FDI) would call for three different interpretations on its scope. A first possible way to approach the concept of FDI as enshrined in article 207 TFEU is to understand that the framers have coined a new, autonomous and very broad concept of foreign direct investment. This new definition of FDI would cover all aspects linked to investment protection covering FDI

[30] For an in-depth analysis of the interplay between investment arbitration and EU responsibility, see Chapter 7.

[31] Piet Eeckhout, *EU External Relations Law* (2nd edn, Oxford University Press 2011) 63.

sensu stricto as well as portfolio investment, dispute settlement and even expropriation.[32]

A second possible interpretation of the definition of FDI would follow the international definition of FDI that excludes portfolio investments from its scope. This definition of FDI can be found in multiple Organisation for Economic Co-operation and Development and International Monetary Fund instruments.[33] Moreover, it would also be in consonance with the definition of direct investment that the CJEU has developed in its internal market case law.[34] This reading of the FDI competence would entail that not all aspects of investment protection would be covered by the CCP. Therefore, those parts not covered by the CCP would be covered either by other EU implied powers or by EU Member States' competences.

The third possible understanding of the scope of the FDI as enshrined in the CCP is the most restrictive one of the three. Based on a literal reading of article 206 TFEU, it would argue that the EU's exclusive competence does not cover all aspects related to FDI but instead only covers the issue of admission of FDI. Article 206 TFEU provides that among the CCP objectives, the progressive abolition of restrictions on international trade and on foreign direct investment is the aspect of FDI that has been entrusted to the EU.[35] Consequently, post-admission measures would fall outside the scope of the CCP. This narrow reading of FDI under the CCP would very much restrict the EU's powers in the field of FDI. This discussion shows how, even in areas in which the Treaties provide express treaty-making powers to the EU, there might still be plenty of uncertainties as regards those powers. Therefore, it seems rather improbable to understand the extent of the EU's international responsibility just by knowing which external powers have been conferred to the EU in the Treaties. In fact, even if the CJEU delimits the scope of certain competence, the uncertainties will still remain.[36]

32 The Commission seems in favour of this position given its recent request for an Opinion to the CJEU on the scope of the competence to conclude a free trade agreement with Singapore. See www.statewatch.org/news/2015/feb/eu-com-fta-cjeu-com-8218-14.pdf.

33 Eeckhout, (n 31) 64.

34 For an in-depth analysis, see Angelos Dimopoulos, *EU Foreign Investment Law* (Oxford University Press 2011).

35 Jan Asmus Bischoff, 'Just a Little Bit of "Mixity"? The EU's Role in the Field of International Investment Protection Law' [2011] 48(5) *Common Market Law Review* 1527.

36 See, for instance, the different ways in which the Court delimited the intersection between trade and environment as regards the conclusion of international agreements in these three cases: *Opinion 2/00 Re: Cartagenal Protocol* [2001] ECR I-09713, *Case C-94/03*

Moreover, article 216 (1) TFEU accepts that legislative acts can also provide the EU with power to conclude international agreements. From a constitutional point of view, there is a fundamental conceptual difference between Treaty powers and those provided in a legislative act. Express Treaty powers correspond to the traditional conception of conferral by which the EU can only expand its competences by virtue of a Treaty change. By contrast, those powers envisaged in a Union legislative act would not correspond to that traditional understanding of the principle of conferral.[37]

Moreover, this provision seems to codify the 'WTO doctrine'[38] by which, whenever the EU has, in its internal legislative acts, expressly conferred on its institutions powers to negotiate with non-member countries, it acquires exclusive external competence in the spheres covered by those acts.[39] Though undoubtedly this provision does not give carte blanche to the EU institutions as regards the possibility to conclude international agreements,[40] it nevertheless shows the broad express treaty-making powers that the EU enjoys.[41] Moreover, it adds another layer of complexity in the exercise of a priori identifying when the EU can bear responsibility under international law based on the powers it has.

1.2.2.2 The Dynamic Nature of the EU's Treaty-Making Powers

Furthermore, article 216 (1) TFEU recognizes the shortcomings that the conferred nature of the EU can have when pursuing the objectives for

Commission v Council (Rotterdam Convention) [2006] ECR I-1, *Case C-178/03 Commission v Parliament and Council (Dangerous Chemicals Regulation)* [2006] ECR I-107. Cf. Panos Koutrakos, 'Case C-94/03, Commission v. Council, Judgment of the Second Chamber of 10 January 2006 [2006] ECR I-1; Case C-178/03, Commission v. Parliament and Council, judgment of the Second Chamber of 10 January 2006, [2006] ECR I-107' [2007] *Common Market Law Review* 171.

37 See Schütze, (n 5) 311. 38 Ibid.

39 *Opinion 1/94 Re: Competence of the Community to conclude international agreements concerning services and the protection of intellectual property* [1994] ECR I-05267 para. 95.

40 Marise Cremona, 'Who Can Make Treaties? The European Union' in Duncan B. Hollis (ed), *Oxford Guide to Treaties* (Oxford University Press 2012) 101.

41 A. G. Kokott has argued in favour of a broad approach to this treaty-making power in *UK v Council*. The case concerned the Council's decision to introduce, in its Association Agreement with Turkey, certain provisions on the coordination of social security systems which draw upon the rules applying within the EU and the legal basis required for the adoption of that act. Kokott argued that inasmuch as the Association Agreement with Turkey and its Additional Protocol are two agreements concluded by the EU, they are to be regarded as 'legally binding Union acts' within the meaning of in Article 216(1) TFEU. Therefore, recourse to provision where the conclusion of an international agreement is provided in another international agreement is conceivable. This broad reading of Article 216 (1) TFEU was not addressed by the CJEU, which remained silent in the whole discussion. *Case C-81/13 UK v Council* [nyr] ECR, Opinion of the AG, para. 108.

which it was created. Even though the EU's functional nature is based on the conferral or attribution of competence, the EU's powers are not all expressly enshrined in Treaties or in Union legislative acts. As Schermers and Blokker point out, implied powers are a logical consequence of the way in which IOs are designed: 'It is never possible to lay down an exhaustive list of powers of the organization in a constitution, inter alia because any organization needs to respond to developments in practice which cannot be foreseen when it is created.'[42] Therefore, article 216 (1) TFEU provides a constitutional legal basis for the conclusion of an internal agreement whenever there is the need to fill a gap where an EU objective needs to be attained in the absence of a specific provision of the Treaties that confers on the EU express competences to act.[43]

a The External Flexibility Clause

The external flexibility clause could be seen as an attempt to constitutionalize the doctrine of parallelism (*in foro interno in foro externo*) as developed by the Court in *Opinion 1/76*.[44] The classical formulation stated,

> Whenever [EU] law has created for the institutions of the [Union] powers within its internal system for the purpose of attaining a specific objective, the [EU] has authority to enter into the international commitments necessary for the attainment of that objective even in the absence of an express provision in that connexion.[45]

However, the constitutionalization of that doctrine seems to be too broad in its scope by reproducing part of the language of article 352 (ex article 308) TFEU;[46] the Treaties seem to decouple the necessity of having an internal power as a precondition from the application of this clause.[47] It signals that the EU may conclude an international agreement when it is

[42] Schermers and Blokker, (n 2) 177. [43] De Baere, (n 5) 30; Klabbers, (n 2) 59.

[44] Cf. Alan Dashwood, 'Mixity in the Era of the Lisbon Treaty' in Christophe Hillion and Panos Koutrakos (eds), *Mixed Agreements Revisited: The EU and Its Member States in the World* (Hart 2010) 360. Theodore Konstadinides, 'EU Foreign Policy under the Doctrine of Implied Powers: Codification Drawbacks and Constitutional Limitations' [2014] 39(4) *European Law Review* 511, 515.

[45] *Opinion 1/76 Re: Inland Waterways* [1977] ECR 741, para. 3.

[46] Article 352 (ex Article 398) TFEU: 'If action by the Union should prove necessary, within the framework of the policies defined in the Treaties, to attain one of the objectives set out in the Treaties, and the Treaties have not provided the necessary powers, the Council, acting unanimously on a proposal from the Commission and after obtaining the consent of the European Parliament, shall adopt the appropriate measures. Where the measures in question are adopted by the Council in accordance with a special legislative procedure, it shall also act unanimously on a proposal from the Commission and after obtaining the consent of the European Parliament.'

[47] Schütze, (n 5) 310; Cremona, (n 40) 101.

necessary to achieve one of the Treaty objectives regardless of whether there is an internal competence.

In *Opinion 1/13*, the Court had the opportunity to further define the scope of the external flexibility clause as regards the competence to conclude the 1980 Hague Convention on Child Abduction. Yet, the Court decided not to focus on the wording of article 216 (1) TFEU when addressing the question of the existence of an EU competence. Instead, the Court referred to its previous case law and acknowledged that it is now contained in article 216 (1) TFEU.[48] It seems reasonable to understand that the statement of the CJEU on the existence of an EU competence based on the external flexibility clause of article 216 (1) TFEU must be read in conjunction with the rest of *Opinion 1/13*. More specifically, because the question being asked to the Court revolved around the exclusive nature of an external competence and the extent to which this stemmed from Regulation 2201/2003, there was no doubt that there was an internal power and that, in fact, that power had already been exercised.[49] Therefore, the question of whether, in the absence of that internal power, the external flexibility clause could nevertheless apply still remains unanswered.

Be that as it may, the lesson that can be extracted from *Opinion 1/13* is that regardless of whether the wording of the external flexibility clause seems to expand the EU's external powers, the external flexibility clause of article 216 (1) TFEU renders it even more difficult to ascertain a priori the external competences of the EU. The inherent uncertainty of the doctrine of parallelism continues to persist after its codification. Moreover, the expansion of its scope of application seems to increase the uncertainty exponentially.

b The ERTA Doctrine and the Existence of Implied Powers

The final part of article 216 (1) TFEU again attempts to replicate the language used by the CJEU to interpret the scope of the EU's treaty-making powers: in the last part of the provision, it is the latest developments of the ERTA doctrine which are codified into the Treaty. The CJEU in its ERTA judgment acknowledged the existence of other kinds of competences besides the ones expressly conferred by the Treaties to the EU. The Court affirmed that

48 *Opinion 1/13 Re: Hague Convention of 25 October 1980 on the Civil Aspects of International Child Abduction* [nyr] para. 67.

49 Council Regulation (EC) 2201/2003 of 27 November 2003 concerning jurisdiction and the recognition and enforcement of judgments in matrimonial matters and the matters of parental responsibility, repealing Regulation (EC) No 1347/2000 [2003] OJ L 338, p. 1.

> to determine in a particular case the [Union]'s authority to enter into international agreements, regard must be had to the whole scheme of the Treaty no less than to its substantive provisions.... Such authority arises not only from an express conferment by the Treaty...but may equally flow from other provisions of the Treaty and from measures adopted, within the framework of those provisions, by the [Union] institutions.[50]

The Court understood that the EU also had other powers that could be implied from certain provisions of the Treaties. Likewise, this quote from the ERTA case shows the complexity that underlies the EU competence system and, consequently, the implementation of international agreements. The CJEU seems to be aware of the impossibility of laying down an exhaustive list of EU competences.[51] Although it is not the purpose of this section to analyse the developments and implications of the doctrine of implied powers as it has been built up by the Luxembourg Court,[52] it is necessary to identify which of the different versions of the doctrine of implied powers the framers had in mind when they included the reference 'is likely to affect common rules or alter their scope' in article 216 (1) TFEU.[53]

The constitutionalization of the ERTA doctrine calls for two comments. First, given the broad wording of the external flexibility clause already enshrined in this provision, it is difficult to envisage a situation in which an international agreement should be concluded because it is likely to affect common rules, and yet, the external flexibility clause would not be triggered as well.[54] For instance, in *Opinion 1/13*, the Court applied the external flexibility clause to ascertain the existence of EU competence in relation to the 1980 Hague Convention on Child Abduction, and the ERTA doctrine (its variant of article 3 (2) TFEU)[55] to establish the exclusive nature of that competence.[56]

Second, the language used in the provision points to questions linked to the nature of implied powers to conclude an agreement, instead of addressing the preliminary question of the existence of those implied powers. As can be seen in article 3 (2) TFEU, the possibility that an

50 *Case 22/70 Commission v Council (ERTA)* para. 15.

51 However, it appears that the framers of the Treaties are not that aware of the possibility given the list of competence envisaged in Articles 2–6 TFEU.

52 For an in-depth analysis of the doctrine of implied powers, see Dashwood, (n 26); Panos Koutrakos, (n 1) 77; Piet Eeckhout, (n 31) 58.

53 Dashwood, (n 26). De Baere makes a completely different reading, De Baere, (n 5) 16.

54 Cremona, (n 40) 101.

55 Eeckhout, (n 31) 113.

56 *Opinion 1/13 Re: Hague Convention of 25 October 1980 on the Civil Aspects of International Child Abduction* paras. 67 and 71.

agreement may affect common rules is one of the three situations by which an EU competence becomes exclusive.[57] Regardless of the confusion between the existence and the nature of EU competence that can be found throughout CJEU's case law, the fact that common rules are likely to be affected relates to the nature of the competence and not the recognition of its existence in the first place.[58] In this regard, *Opinion 1/03* would be a very useful guide in understanding the difference between implied competences or powers and the nature of those powers.[59] The opinion first focuses on the existence of implied powers in the EU legal system:

> The competence of the [Union] to conclude international agreements may arise not only from an express conferment by the Treaty but may equally flow implicitly from other provisions of the Treaty and from measures adopted, within the framework of those provisions, by the[Union] institutions.[60]

Subsequently, the Court acknowledges that those implied powers do not always have (as with any other power conferred to the EU) the same nature:

> That competence of the [Union] may be exclusive or shared with the Member States.... Where common rules have been adopted, the Member States no longer have the right, acting individually or even collectively, to undertake obligations with non-Member countries which affect those rules. In such a case, the [Union] also has exclusive competence to conclude international agreements.[61]

The wording of article 216 (1) TFEU is a good illustration of the problems linked with trying to capture the extent of the EU's external powers. The complexity of understanding when the EU has an implied power to conclude an agreement could cast some doubts on the extent to which it is bound by the agreement in practice and to a certain extent its responsibility under international law in the event of a breach.

[57] Ibid; *Case C-66/13 Green Network* [nyr] ECR; *Case C-114/12 Commission v Council (Broadcasting Rights Convention)* [nyr] ECR; *Opinion 1/03 Re: Competence of the Community to conclude the new Lugano Convention on jurisdiction and the recognition and enforcement of judgments in civil and commercial matters* [2006] ECR I-01145 para. 121.

[58] *Case C-466/98 Commission v United Kingdom (Open Skies)* [2002] ECR I-09427 para. 108. Cf. Koutrakos, (n 1) 123.

[59] *Opinion 1/03 Re: Competence of the Community to conclude the new Lugano Convention on jurisdiction and the recognition and enforcement of judgments in civil and commercial matters* [2006] ECR I-1145.

[60] Ibid. [61] Ibid.

1.2.3 On the Nature of EU Competences and Its Impact on EU Member States' External Action: EU Member States as Strange Subjects of International Law

While there is no doubt that granting of legal personality to the EU entails that it can exercise the basic legal features inherent to its consideration as an international legal subject (treaty making, representation, immunities and responsibility),[62] it is unclear whether the international legal subjectivity of EU Member States might be affected by the creation of the EU. EU Member States are not like other states. Even though states continue to be at the centre of international law (they do not have their treaty-making powers limited, they can freely act within international law, and they are completely responsible for their acts), when speaking about EU Member States, those facts are not that clear. The complex relationship between the EU and its Member States manifests in its external action more than anywhere else.[63] In this regard, it could be argued that EU Member States, due to their membership, have become 'strange subjects' of international law.[64]

This becomes apparent when analysing how the EU's treaty-making power influences the capacity of EU Member States to conclude international agreements. The degree to which the EU's external power curtails EU Member States' external powers is exceptional when compared with other IOs.[65] Although undoubtedly this is clear when speaking about EU exclusive competences,[66] it can also be seen in most shared competences.[67]

[62] Pierre D'Argent, 'La personalité juridique international de l'organisation internationale' in Evelyne Lagrange and Jean-Marc Sorel (eds), *Droit des organisations internationales* (LGDJ 2013) 454; Koutrakos, (n 1) 14; Stein, (n 25) 131.

[63] Andrea Ott and Ramses A. Wessel, 'The EU's External Relations Regime: Multilevel Complexity in an Expanding Union' in Steven Blockmans and Adam Lazowski (eds), *The European Union and Its Neighbours: A Legal Appraisal of the EU's Policies of Stabilisation, Partnership and Integration* (T. M. C. Asser Press 2006) 20.

[64] De Witte, (n 20) 43. De Witte argues that EU Member States 'have accepted more or less deliberately, to curtail their own capacity to act on the international plane in favour of, precisely, the [EU]'.

[65] Dan Sarooshi, *International Organizations and Their Exercise of Sovereign Powers* (Oxford University Press 2005) 54; J.H.H. Weiler, 'The Transformation of Europe' [1991] 100 *Yale Law Journal* 2403, 2414.

[66] Even though this was a question far from settled at the beginning: *Opinion 1/75 Re: Understanding on a Local Cost Standard* [1975] ECR 1355; Schütze, (n 5) 212.

[67] The different types of competences, as codified in Article 2 TFEU, can be broadly classified as exclusive or shared. Article 2 TFEU also speaks about complementary

In relation to the first category, to consider that a competence is exclusive entails that only the Union may legislate and adopt legally binding acts. As a matter of EU law, Member States could only act insofar as the EU authorizes them to do so. Consequently, an external exclusive competence would, in theory, exclude Member States from concluding agreements falling under such a classification, unless the EU authorized them to do so.[68] For instance, going back to the example of the definition of the scope of the FDI as enshrined in the CCP,[69] given that article 3 TFEU envisages the exclusive nature of the CCP, a broad definition of FDI would entail extending the reach of EU's exclusivity more than if a narrow definition of FDI were to be adopted. Moreover, the EU's exclusive competence over FDI entails that EU Member States now need an authorization if they have to act within this policy field.[70] Consequently, it could be argued that in terms of international responsibility, the EU would incur international responsibility insofar as it has exclusive competence over the subject matter of the breach.[71] Therefore, by examining which competences are listed in article 3 TFEU, the areas in which the EU would bear international responsibility could be established. If there is an exclusive competence, the EU should bear exclusive responsibility. Conversely, it could be argued that where the EU and its Member States share a competence, the responsibility should be shared as well.[72]

The internal workings of shared competences, however, show that the dynamic nature of the EU legal order is constrained not only to the implicit development of new competences but also to the competences'

competence, coordination and competence on CFSP. All these categories can be considered shared, to the extent that they allow both the EU and its Member States to act on areas covered by the competence. On the different types of EU external competences, see Marise Cremona, 'External Relations and External Competence of the European Union: The Emergence of an Integrated Policy' in Paul Craig and Gráinne de Burca (eds), *The Evolution of EU Law* (2nd edn, Oxford University Press 2010), 220.

68 On the practice of Member States' agreements authorized by the EU, see Marise Cremona, 'Member States as Trustees of the Community Interest: Participating in International Agreements on Behalf of the European Community' [2009] 17 *EUI Working Paper Law* 20.

69 See note 29.

70 Regulation (EU) 1219/2012 of the European Parliament and of the Council of 20 December 2012 establishing transitional arrangements for bilateral investment agreement between Member States and third Countries [2012] OJ L 351, pp. 40–46.

71 Gaja, (n 24) 747; Rosas, (n 24) 284.

72 The main authority supporting that view would be an obiter dictum in a CJEU case: *Case C-316/91 Parliament v Council* [1994] ECR 661 29. Rosas, (n 24).

progressive transformation from shared to exclusive. Shared competences provide that both the Union and the Member States may legislate and adopt legally binding acts within the same area. Even though shared competences are the general rule within the EU, their articulation in practice is much more complex than it might first appear, especially within the realm of external competences. According to article 2 (2) TFEU, the Member States shall exercise their competences to the extent that the Union has not exercised its competence. This could be seen as a manifestation of the principle of primacy of EU law.[73] In other words, when the Union has exercised its competence in a given area, Member States are pre-empted or excluded from exercising their competences in that same area.[74]

The exclusionary effect of the principle of pre-emption has very important consequences as regards the nature of the EU's treaty-making powers. According to the CJEU, the exercise of a competence internally by the EU can render it exclusive externally.[75] Leaving aside the constitutional theory questions that equating constitutional exclusivity with pre-emption raises, the practical consequence of the exercise of an EU shared competence encompasses an exclusionary effect that resembles the effects of constitutional exclusivity.[76] Member States would not be able to conclude agreements in those areas where the EU has exercised its shared pre-emptive competence. This was last confirmed in *Opinion 1/13*; the CJEU's recognition of an implied exclusive power as regards the conclusion of the 1980 Hague Convention on Child Abduction means that EU Member States cannot individually make separate declarations accepting third-state accessions to the Convention.[77] They could only do that jointly after the EU had authorized them.[78]

Consequently given the importance that the exercise of EU shared competences entails in the external realm, the actual delimitation of the area within which pre-emption will take place has been the object of plenty of litigation[79] now poorly codified in article 3 (2) TFEU.[80] This provision

[73] Alan Dashwood and Joni Helikoski, 'The Classic Authorities Revisited' in Alan Dashwood and Christophe Hillion (eds), *The General Law of EC External Relations* (Sweet and Maxwell 2000) 6.

[74] Van Vooren and Wessel, (n 5) 109.

[75] *Opinion 2/91 Re: Convention No 170 of the International Labour Organization concerning safety in the use of chemicals at work* [1993] ECR I-1061 para. 9.

[76] Schütze, (n 5) 272.

[77] *Opinion 1/13 Re: Hague Convention of 25 October 1980 on the Civil Aspects of International Child Abduction* para. 89.

[78] Ibid. [79] For analysis of this case law up until Lisbon see: De Baere, (n 5)s 43.

[80] Cremona, (n 40) 101; Schütze, (n 28).

identifies three situations in which the exercise of a shared competence encompasses its exclusive external nature. First, the 'WTO Doctrine'[81] by which the EU would not only have an external competence if provided in a legislation act but also this new competence, would be exclusive. Second, article 3 (2) enshrines the 'Necessity doctrine' by which the EU would have external competence as long as it is necessary to enable the Union to exercise its internal competence. Finally, the provision constitutionalized the ERTA pre-emption rule by which the EU would have an exclusive treaty-making power insofar as its conclusion may affect common rules or alter their scope.

Moreover, when approaching the scope of this implied exclusivity, the CJEU, especially after the Lisbon reform, has adopted a broad approach.[82] For instance, in *Opinion 1/13*, the Court reaffirmed that it was not necessary to have a complete and overall overlap between the internal EU legislation and the external competence to trigger the exclusivity of the latter. Just a partial overlap between the policy area and the international agreement is enough as long as the latter may affect the former.[83] Therefore, even in situations in which the EU Treaty has provided that the EU and the Member States might share the competence, externally that might not be the case and EU Member States' treaty-making powers will be restricted accordingly. Furthermore, the analysis that the CJEU carries out is characterized for its high unpredictability.[84] The CJEU has applied different versions of what kind of pre-emption is necessary for a shared competence to become an external exclusive competence, and even after the consolidations of its doctrine in the Lisbon Treaty, and in *Opinion 1/13*, it continues to slightly adapt it.[85]

It should be mentioned nonetheless that although shared pre-emptive competences are the majority of shared competences, there are other

81 See note 38.

82 Opinion 1/13 *Re: Hague Convention of 25 October 1980 on the Civil Aspects of International Child Abduction; Case C-114/12 Commission v Council (Broadcasting Rights Convention)*; Case C-66/13 *Green Network*.

83 *Opinion 1/13 Re: Hague Convention of 25 October 1980 on the Civil Aspects of International Child Abduction* para. 83. Andrés Delgado Casteleiro, 'Opinion 1/13: on the scope of the EU's exclusive competence after the Lisbon Treaty' [2015] 51 *Revista de Derecho Comunitario Europeo* 669.

84 Raas Holdgard, *External Relations Law of the European Community: Legal Reasoning and Legal Discourses* (Wolter Kluwer 2008) 115; De Baere, (n 5)s 50.

85 Compare its appliaction in *C-114/12 Commission v Council (Broadcasting Rights Convention); C-66/13 Green Network Opinion 1/13 Re: Hague Convention of 25 October 1980 on the Civil Aspects of International Child Abduction.*

categories of shared competences to which the principle of pre-emption would not apply. Three relevant examples of this type of non-pre-emptive competences would be development cooperation, humanitarian aid[86] and the CFSP.[87] Yet, despite the fact that EU Member States may still retain the powers to conclude international agreements in these areas, they still have to comply with certain obligations vis-à-vis the EU. Article 21 TEU imposes an obligation of coherence in the EU's external action that is crucial in the formulation of these policies.[88] Moreover, the principle of loyalty envisaged in article 4 (3) TEU would also apply to EU Member States' actions regardless of the competence involved.[89] Therefore, even within these competences, the EU Member States' treaty-making powers are also to a certain extent restricted by virtue of EU law.

All in all, these limits imposed by EU law on EU Member States' external powers raise a series of questions concerning their ability to bear responsibility under international law. If EU Member States can no longer act freely in the international scene, to what extent should they be responsible for acts committed when acting under the scope of EU law? Moreover, given the dynamic nature of the division of competences, it is too difficult to use it as a benchmark to better understand how the relationship between the EU and its Member States influences their respective responsibility under international law.

To sum up, while undoubtedly the issue of the division of competences between the EU and its Member States is inextricably linked to the establishment of responsibility for violations of international law, the articulation of that link in practice is not an easy exercise. The implied nature of the EU's powers raises questions as to the possibility of using the existence of a competence as way to attribute responsibility to the EU. It is difficult to know when the EU would be competent by examining the EU Treaties. By contrast, it could be argued that the EU's international responsibility could be established by examining the nature of EU competence instead of the existence of that competence: EU exclusive competence would entail the exclusive responsibility of the EU, and shared competence would

86 Article 4 (4) TFEU: 'In the areas of development cooperation and humanitarian aid, the Union shall have competence to carry out activities and conduct a common policy; however, the exercise of that competence shall not result in Member States being prevented from exercising theirs.'

87 Article 2(4) TFEU.

88 Bart Van Vooren, *EU External Relations Law and the European Neighbourhood Policy: A Paradigm for Coherence* (Routledge 2012) 14.

89 Ibid.

entail shared or joint responsibility. However, the articulation of implied exclusive powers make the possibility of shared responsibility based on the shared competence a little bit more elusive.

1.3 The EU and International Agreements: An Enquiry into Its Legal Effects

Having seen how the complex competence system renders the exercise of linking the EU's responsibility to its division of competences almost impossible, the following two sections add a different perspective on the link between competence and responsibility.[90] The delimitation of the EU's external competence as way of understanding the scope of the EU's international legal personality has shown how it is quite difficult to pin down the size of the EU's veil, as the implied powers doctrine shows. Instead, the examination of how the veil restricts Member States in practice seems a more logical pathway to better understand how the EU's international responsibility should be articulated. Moreover, to consider how the EU's veil acts as a straightjacket on EU Member States, the next two sections will mirror the two main requirements needed for international responsibility to arise.[91] First, this section focuses on when the EU is bound by an international agreement and to what extent. International law requires for the responsibility arise that the subject breaching an international obligation must be bound by it. It is thus necessary to understand the extent to which the EU and its Member States are bound by the international agreements they have signed. The examination of the legal effects of international agreements in the EU provides very useful insights as to the way the EU and its Member States comply with international law, and the obligations that the EU imposes on its Member States when the former is bound by international law. Unlike other IOs, the federal structure of the EU clearly influences the effects of international law within the EU. Rules of international law become a part of the EU legal order and can benefit from the principles, procedures and mechanisms set up to ensure compliance with EU law.[92]

The next section instead will focus on whether the actions of Member States can be considered actions of the EU by examining the extent to which the EU controls them when they implement EU law.

90 For an illustration in practice see: Chapter 5.

91 See article 2 of the Articles on State Responsibility.

92 André Nollkaemper, 'The Role of National Courts in Inducing Compliance with International and European Law – A Comparison' in Marise Cremona (ed), *Compliance and Enforcment of EU Law* (Oxford University Press 2012) 159.

1.3.1 The Legal Effect of Union Agreements

Over the years the EU has developed its treaty-making practice on an impressive scale.[93] The EU (throughout its different incarnations) has signed over 700 bilateral international agreements since the creation of the ESC, and over 200 multilateral agreements.[94] Out of these 900 international agreements, more or less, the vast majority have been concluded by the EU alone (Union agreements).

In theory, Union agreements can cover areas relating to both exclusive and/or shared competences. In practice, Union agreements usually cover areas that fall under exclusive competence. There are few examples of international agreements concluded solely by the EU based on shared competence, and all of them concern areas covered by shared competences of a complementary and bilateral nature.[95] However, the possibility of the EU concluding an agreement that falls under shared competence cannot be discounted.

1.3.1.1 International Legal Effects

The logical starting point from which to address the international effects of the agreements concluded by the EU is article 26 VCLT.[96] This provision – as well as its twin in the VCLT II – establishes that the parties to an agreement are bound by it as matter of international law. Therefore, in

93 Klabbers, (n 2) 257.

94 The numbers are taken from the European Commission's Treaty Office Database: http://ec.europa.eu/world/agreements/default.home.do.

95 Council Decision (EC) 94/578/EC of 18 July 1994 concerning the conclusion of the Cooperation Agreement between the European Community and the Republic of India on Partnership and Development [1994] OJ L 223, p. 23; Council Decision (EC) 2006/964/EC of 18 December 2006 on the conclusion of the Agreement between the European Community and the government of Canada establishing a framework for cooperation in higher education, training and youth [2006] OJ L 397, p. 14; Council and Commission Decision (EC) 2004/112/EC of 22 December 2003 on the signature on behalf of the European Community and of the European Atomic Energy Community of the Agreement on Scientific and Technological Cooperation between the European Community and the European Atomic Energy Community, of the one part, and the Swiss Confederation, of the other part [2004] OJ L 32, p. 22.

96 'Every treaty in force is binding upon the parties to it and must be performed by them in good faith', Vienna Convention on the Law of Treaties (adopted 23 May 1969, entry into force 27 January 1980) 1155 UNTS 331. Cf. Article 26 of the Vienna Convention on the Law of Treaties between States and International Organizations or between International Organizations (adopted 21 March 1986) A/CONF.129/15. See 'Official Records of the United Nations Conference on the Law of Treaties between States and International Organizations or between International Organizations, vol II' (Vienna 18 February–21 March 1986) UN Doc A/CONF.129/16.

principle, responsibility for the breach of an international agreement will arise for only those who have entered into the agreement.

Consequently, when speaking about Union agreements (i.e. those concluded between the EU and third states), only the EU and not its Member States would be bound by the agreement. International law seems to discount the possibility that the special character of the relations between an IO and its Member States might extend the binding force of the international obligations accepted by one of them. The VCLT II conceptualized IOs as independent legal persons, with an autonomous will different from that of its Member States, capable of entering into agreements and being bound by them, and consequently responsible for any breach they might commit. Article 34 VCLT II specifically addresses this issue and provides that: 'A treaty does not create either obligations or rights for a third State or a third organization without the consent of that State or that organization'. Therefore, given that Member States would not be internationally bound by the agreement, in principle it would very difficult to argue that they would be nevertheless responsible for any violation of the agreement.[97]

1.3.1.2 Internal Legal Effects of Union Agreements

Nevertheless, by virtue of article 216 (2) TFEU, EU Member States still have to comply with Union agreements regardless of whether they have signed them.[98] The CJEU has established the scope of this provision in numerous cases.[99] In *Haegeman* the CJEU argued that 'the provision of [an] agreement . . . form[s] an integral part of [EU] law',[100] imposing on the Member States an obligation to implement the international agreements concluded by the EU as a matter of EU law.[101]

One of the main implications of this interpretation of the legal effects of international agreements revolves around their implementation. By taking a monistic approach the CJEU establishes that the provisions of a Union agreement do not need be incorporated into a Union act to be part of the EU legal order and to be implemented within the

[97] Yet, the question of secondary or subsidiary responsibility could arise nevertheless: see article 62 ARIO and its discussion in Chapter 4.

[98] Article 216.2 TFEU: 'Agreements concluded under the conditions set out in this Article shall be binding on the institutions of the Community and on Member States.'

[99] For a comprehensive analysis of this case law see: Mario Mendez, *The Legal Effects of EU Agreements* (Oxford University Press 2013).

[100] Case 181/73 *Haegeman* [1974] ECR 449 para. 5.

[101] Koutrakos, (n 1) 185.

EU.[102] Therefore, when the EU concludes an international agreement on its own it not only binds the EU as matter of international law, but also EU Member States as a matter of EU law.

Moreover, the binding force of Union agreements has very important consequences in terms of compliance. The institutional structure set up by the EU institutions to ensure compliance with EU law, gets extended to Union agreements. Not even most federal states have such a strong enforcement mechanism. Most federations cannot control the state's compliance with international obligations assumed by the federation.[103]

1.3.2 The Legal Effects of Mixed Agreements

International agreements can cover not only issues in which the EU has competence or the Member States have competence, but also others in which the competence remains or is shared with the Member States. This is usually the case in relation to multilateral conventions. In those cases, the EU and its Member States can jointly conclude the agreement.[104] These agreements are often denominated as mixed agreements and, as Eeckhout has stated, 'have always occupied a central position in the [EU] external relations law'.[105] It is not the purpose of this section to carry out an in-depth analysis of the mixed agreements but simply to characterize them briefly.[106]

There are many reasons to support the conclusion of a mixed agreement. There are political considerations underpinning the election of the mixed formula. Either Member States want to enter into the agreements or third parties to the agreement demand the participation of both the EU and its Member States regardless of whether they have competence on the

102 Eeckhout, (n 31) 328.

103 Pieter Jan Kuijper and Esa Paasivirta, 'EU International Responsibility and Its Attribution: From the Inside Looking Out' in Panos Koutrakos and Malcolm D. Evans (eds), *The International Responsibility of the European Union European and International Perspectives* (Hart 2013) 39.

104 Joni Heliskoski, *Mixed Agreements as a Technique for Organizing the International Relations of the European Community and Its Member States* (Kluwer Law International 2001) 7; C. D. Ehlermann, 'Mixed Agreements: A List of Problems' in David O'Keeffe and Henry G. Schermers (eds), *Mixed Agreements* (Kluwer Law and Taxation 1983) 11. Gaja, (n 24); Pierre Pescatore, 'Les Relations extérieures des Communautés européennes' [1961] 103 Recueil de Cours de la Académie du Droit International 9.

105 Piet Eeckhout, *External Relations of the EU and the Member States Competence, Mixed Agreements, International Responsibility, and Effects of International Law* 212.

106 For in-depth analysis, see: Eleftheria Neframi, *Les Accords Mixtes De La Communauté Européenne: Aspects Communautaires Et Internationaux* (Bruylant 2007); Heliskoski, (n 104).

issue.[107] But mostly there are pragmatic reasons such as the inconvenience of signing separate agreements,[108] the '*prima facie* legal justification . . . is that parts of the agreement do not come within the EU's competence, and that conclusion of the agreement therefore requires joint action by the [EU] and its Member States',[109] or the fact that the issues covered by the agreement fall within their shared competence.[110] Be that as it may, there are no clear guidelines to determine when an agreement must take a mixed form, so the necessity of having a mixed agreement is decided on a case-by-case basis.[111]

Regardless of the particular reason which might justify the use of the mixed formula in a particular case, the complexities surrounding the division of competences and the EU's treaty-making power underlies any justification for recourse to mixed agreements.[112] Mixed agreements leave any question regarding the powers of the EU or its Member States to enter into an agreement in a vacuum, unanswered.[113] Furthermore, by avoiding the competence question through joint participation in an agreement, the EU and its Member States externalize a 'domestic' European affair.[114]

Even though some scholars have expressed concerns over the constitutional validity[115] of this form of arrangement of the external relations of the EU, and particular criticisms have been aimed at the underlying justification for the conclusion of mixed agreements,[116] the CJEU has accepted

[107] Ehlermann, (n 104) 28. [108] Stein, (n 25) 161. [109] Eeckhout, (n 31) 190.

[110] Opinion 2/91 *Re: Convention No 170 of the International Labour Organization concerning safety in the use of chemicals at work* para. 12. Cf. Opinion 1/08 *Re: GATS [2009] ECR I-11129; C-316/91 Parliament v Council.*

[111] Frank Hoffmeister, 'Curse or Blessing? Mixed Agreements in the Recent Practice of the European Community and Its Member States' in Cristophe Hillion and Panos Koutrakos (eds), *Mixed Agreements in EU Law Revisited: The EU and Its Member States in the World* (Hart 2010) 253.

[112] Robert Schütze, 'Federalism and Foreign Affairs: Mixity as a (Inter)national Phenomenon' in Christophe Hillion and Panos Koutrakos (eds), *Mixed Agreements Revisited: The EU and Its Member States in the World* (Hart 2010) 81.

[113] Koutrakos, (n 1) 152; Allan Rosas, 'Mixed Union–Mixed Agreements' in Martti Koskenniemi (ed), *International Law Aspects of the European Union* (Kluwer Law International 1998) 145; Heliskoski, (n 104) 13.

[114] Schütze, (n 112) 81. [115] Stein, (n 25) 160.

[116] Jean Groux, *The European Communities in the International Order* (Commission of the European Communities 1985) 68. Javier Roldán Barbero, 'La CEE y el Convenio sobre Derecho del Mar de 1982: consideraciones sobre la relación entre el Derecho de Comunitario y el Derecho Internacional' Revista de Instituciones Europeas 551. Joseph H. H. Weiler, 'External Legal Relations of Non-Unitary Actors' in Joseph H. H. Weiler (ed), *The Constitution of Europe: Do the New Clothes Have an Emperor?* (Cambridge University Press 1999).

this practice within the EU legal order. As early as in *Opinion 1/78*,[117] the Court already 'appeared much more accommodating towards mixity',[118] and by *Opinion 1/94*,[119] it had fully embraced it.

Within mixed agreements the relationship between Member States and the EU is completely different from the relationship established by an agreement concluded solely by the EU. Whereas in the latter there is a vertical relation, whereby the Union agreement binds the EU and becomes part of EU law, and EU law binds the Member States, in the former we have a sort of triangular relationship whereby the EU and its Member States stand at the same level with the mixed agreement between them.[120]

1.3.2.1 International Effects

The logical consequence of the horizontal relationship between the EU and its Member States is that, by virtue of the *Pacta Sunt Servanda* principle, in mixed agreements both the EU and the Member States that have concluded the agreement are internationally bound by it. Consequently, *prima facie* both of them would be responsible for any breach; however, the extent to which they are bound is unclear. Should the EU and its Member States only be bound to the extent that they retain competence over the provision being violated? Should it be understood that both are bound by the whole agreement regardless of whether they have competence over that part of the agreement?

On one hand, the EU has tried to apportion the international obligations envisaged in mixed agreements to clarify the extent to which it is bound by the agreement.[121] On the other, in the absence of any instrument that would effectively apportion the provisions between the EU and its Member States, both are bound by the whole agreement. In this regard, the fact that both are *prima facie* responsible for the agreement raises the question of whether the special relationship between the EU and its Member States

117 Opinion 1/78 *Re: International Agreement on Natural Rubber* [1979] ECR 2871.

118 Eeckhout, (n 31) 195.

119 Opinion 1/94 *Re: Competence of the Community to conclude international agreements concerning services and the protection of intellectual property*.

120 Nanette A. Neuwahl, *Mixed Agreements: Analysis of the Phenomenon and Their Legal Significance* (PhD thesis, European University Institute 1988) 118. Kuijper and Paasivirta speak of a vertical and a horizontal dimension of the implementation of international obligations by the EU, Pieter Jan Kuijper and Esa Paasivirta, 'Further Exploring International Responsibility: The European Community and the ILC's Project on Responsibility of International Organizations' [2004] 1 International Organizations Law Review 111, 115.

121 See infra Chapter 4.

should play any role in the event that either of them breaches the mixed agreement.[122]

As a consequence of the horizontal relationship added to the vacuum in which the mixity leaves the division of competences, the question of the legal certainty of third parties to the agreement logically arises.[123] Moreover, given that the division of competences does not help in apportioning the agreement, it has been argued that in this scenario the EU and its Member States should be joint regardless of the specific circumstances leading up to the breach.[124] However, while there is no doubt that joint responsibility would preserve legal certainty that someone would eventually be responsible, it would undermine the division of competences.[125] The EU could be held responsible for acts for which it has no competence conferred, and EU Member States for actions of the EU in which they had no involvement whatsoever.

1.3.2.2 Internal Effects

While externally the relationship between the EU and its Member States might be characterized as horizontal in relation to mixed agreements, this relationship has been shifting over the years towards a more vertical one from an internal perspective.[126] Initially, some kind of horizontal relationship between the EU and its Member States towards third parties was also recognized as regards Union agreements. In *Kupferberg*, the Court recognized the horizontal nature of the relationship by acknowledging that,

> in ensuring respect for commitments arising from an agreement concluded by the [Union] institutions the Member States fulfil an obligation not only in relation to the non-member country concerned but also and above all in relation

122 See Chapter 3 for the discussion on the link between apportionment and responsibility.

123 Eeckhout, (n 31) 262; Martin Björklund, 'Responsibility in the EC for Mixed Agreements' [2001] 70 Nordic Journal of International Law 373; Eleftheria Neframi, 'International Responsibility of the European Community and of Member States under Mixed Agreements' in Enzo Cannizzaro (ed), *The European Union as an Actor in International Relations* (Kluwer Law International 2002).

124 See Chapter 2 for an in-depth discussion.

125 Marise Cremona, *External Relations of the EU and the Member States: Competence, Mixed Agreements, International Responsibility, and Effects of International Law* (2006) EUI Law Working Paper 2006/22, http://ssrn.com/abstract=963316, 21; Heliskoski, (n 104) 141.

126 For an overview of the evolution see: Eleftheria Neframi, 'Mixed Agreements as a Source of European Union Law' in Enzo Cannizazaro, Paolo Palcehtti and Ramses A. Wessel (eds), *International Law as Law of the European Union* (Martinus Nijhoff 2012).

to the [Union] which has assumed responsibility for the due performance of the agreement.[127]

Yet, in subsequent cases, references to the third party to the agreement were dropped,[128] reinforcing the vertical relationship between the EU and its Member States. Nowadays, even when speaking about mixed agreements, the CJEU has established that EU Member States fulfil an obligation towards the EU when complying with a mixed agreement.[129]

Moreover, that special obligation towards the EU boils down to equating mixed agreements with Union agreements as regards their legal effects. In *Étang de Berre*, the Court held that mixed agreements 'concluded by the [EU], its Member States and non-member countries have the same status in the [EU] legal order as purely [Union] agreements in so far as the provisions fall within the scope of [EU] competence'.[130]

Therefore, EU Member States not only have an international obligation to comply with agreements they have signed, they also have an EU obligation to comply with the agreements because of their mixed character, at least in those parts where there is EU competence.[131] Yet the CJEU's broad understanding as to when a provision falls within the scope of Union competence[132] seems to favour not only an expansive reading of the binding force of mixed agreements as a matter of EU law but more importantly entails an expansion of the scope of the institutional mechanisms (including the CJEU's jurisdiction) to ensure that Member States comply with their international obligations.[133]

127 Case 104/81 *Kupferberg* [1982] ECR 3641 para. 13.

128 Allan Rosas, 'International Responsibility of the EU and the European Court of Justice' in Malcolm D. Evans and Panos Koutrakos (eds), *The International Responsibility of the European Union: European and International Perspectives* (Hart 2013) 152.

129 Case 12/86 *Demirel* [1987] ECR 3719 para. 11; Case C-13/00 *Ireland v Commission (Berne Convention)* [2002] ECR I-2943 para. 15; Case C–239/03 *Commission v France (Ètang de Berre)* [2004] ECR I- 9325 para. 26.

130 Case C-239/03 *Commission v France (Ètang de Berre)* para. 25.

131 Cremona, (n 125) 15.

132 The EU law obligation arises when the field in general is covered in large measure by EU legislation, Case C-239/03 *Commission v France (Ètang de Berre)* para. 29. As Cremona highlights, the language used by the Court recalls that used to address the exclusive nature of a competence, instead of focusing on the existence of a competence, Cremona, (n 125) 16. Cf. Rosas, (n 24) 284. On the interpretation of mixed agreements by the Court: Panos Koutrakos, 'Intepretation of Mixed Agreements' in Christophe Hillion and Panos Koutrakos (eds), *Mixed Agreements Revisited: The EU and Its Member States in the World* (Hart 2010).

133 Eeckhout, (n 31) 277.

The expansive reading that the Court does of its own jurisdiction in relation to mixed agreements is not constrained to those situations in which the provision falls within the scope of Union competence. The CJEU has also recognized its jurisdiction in relation to situations falling within the realm of Member States' shared competence and imposed on national courts an obligation of consistent interpretation of those agreements which would further connote how the CJEU seems to have the last word on the legal effects of mixed agreement within the EU.

A good example of the expansive reach of the CJEU's jurisdiction as regards mixed agreements concerns the interpretation of procedural provisions enshrined in mixed agreements such as article 50 TRIPS[134] or article 9 (3) Aarhus Convention.[135] These provisions impose an obligation on the administrations of each the contracting parties of the mixed agreement to adapt its internal procedures so as to meet the standard laid down in the agreement. Consequently, inasmuch as the EU has not laid down common rules on the issue, it only has competence to adapt its own procedures, these provisions fall within the scope of both EU and national law.[136] In theory, when complying with procedural provisions, Member States would not be under an EU law obligation to adapt their national procedures, and the national courts would be competent under their national rules to examine the compatibility of those procedures with the obligations laid down in the international agreement. Yet, the Court recognized that in such situations it had jurisdiction as to the interpretation of those provisions even when the matters at hand felt outside the scope of EU law because

> it is clearly in the interest of [Union law] that, in order to forestall future differences of interpretation, that provision should be interpreted uniformly, whatever the circumstances in which it is to apply.[137]

The expansive reach of the CJEU's jurisdiction as regards international agreements has as one of its main consequences their 'Europeanization'.

[134] Case C-53/96 *Hermès* [1998] ECR I-3603; Case C-300/98 and C 392/98 *Parfums Christian Dior and Others* [2000] ECR I-11307.

[135] Case C-240/09 *Lesoochranárske zoskupenie VLK v Ministerstvo zivotného prostredia Slovenskej republiky* [2011] ECR I-01255; Case C-401/12 P, C-402/12 P, C-403/12 P *Vereniging Milieudefensie and Stichting Stop Luchtverontreiniging Utrecht* [nyr] ECR; Case C-404/12, C-405/12 *Council and Commission v Stichting Natuur en Milieu and Pesticide Action Network Europe* [nyr] ECR.

[136] For a discussion: Koutrakos, (n 132).

[137] Case C-240/09 *Lesoochranárske zoskupenie VLK v Ministerstvo zivotného prostredia Slovenskej republiky* para. 42.

Mixed agreements transform into EU law notably in relation to their uniform application and interpretation.[138] By virtue of article 216 (2) TFEU inasmuch as an international agreement becomes an integral part of EU law[139] it would benefit from the same normative pull that any other EU rule would get as regards their control of compliance by the EU institutions.[140]

1.3.3 Member States Agreements

Member States Agreements are binding under international law only on those Member States which have signed them. In principle, the EU is not internationally bound to comply with agreements signed by its Member States.

Internally, the vertical relation established through the primacy of EU law, in principle precludes Member States Agreements from having any effects on the EU level.[141] However, there are certain situations in which agreements concluded by Member States have effects over the EU and its legislation, subverting to a certain extent the principle of primacy. These situations stem from two specific contexts.

First, the EU can be bound by an agreement even though it cannot or decides not to accede to the agreement. The Convention on International Trade in Endangered Species of Wild Fauna and Flora (CITES) constitutes an example of an international agreement signed by Member States that binds the EU.[142] In this respect, the binding force of the agreement arises from its inclusion on a piece of secondary legislation. Article 1 of Regulation 338/97 [143] reads as follows: 'This Regulation shall apply in compliance with the objectives, principles and provisions of the Convention'.[144]

138 Nollkaemper, (n 92) 157.

139 Case C-61/94 *Commission v Germany (International Dairy Arrangement)* [1996] ECR I-3989.

140 Nollkaemper, (n 92) 194.

141 Case C- 308/06 *The Queen on the Application of Intertanko and Others v Secretary of State for Transport* [2008] ECR I-4057.

142 Cremona, (n 68) 9. This is no longer the case as the EU has finally joined CITES. See: Council Decision (EU) 2015/451 of 6 March 2015 concerning the accession of the European Union to the Convention on International Trade in Endangered Species of Wild Fauna and Flora (CITES) [2015] OJ L 75, pp. 1–3.

143 Council Regulation (EC) No 338/97 of 9 December 1996 on the protection of species of wild fauna and flora by regulating trade therein [1996] OJ L 61, pp. 1–69.

144 The previous version of the regulation highlighted in a clearer way the binding force of the CITES: 'The Convention, as set out in annex A, shall apply throughout the Community under the conditions laid down in the following articles.' Article 1, Council Regulation (EEC) No 3626/82 of 3 December 1982 on the implementation in the

The EU is internally bound by an international agreement it has not concluded through its inclusion in a piece of secondary legislation. In these cases, the binding force does not stem directly from the agreement, but from the regulation. However, it remains a matter of dispute whether agreements included through secondary legislation form an integral part of the EU order.[145]

The second context in which there is binding force to an agreement that the EU has not concluded but its Member States have, arises through factual substitution. The dynamic nature of the EU's competence determines that throughout the years it can supervene Member States' competence over agreements they signed. In these cases the EU replaces Member States in the management and implementation of the agreement.[146] This was the case in the GATT[147] and in the Nomenclature Convention.[148] In these cases, the CJEU found that even though the EU was not a party to the agreements they bound it as a result of the transfer of competence in those areas.

To sum up, the EU's treaty-making practice adds another layer of complexity to the understanding of when the EU is bound by an international agreement, and consequently can be responsible for its breach. First, there is no doubt that the EU is internationally bound by the agreements it has signed. Likewise, Member States are also internationally bound by the agreements they have entered into. Second, by virtue of article 216 (2) TFEU, EU Member States are internally bound by the agreements concluded by the EU. Similarly, in some specific cases, the EU is internally bound by Member States' international agreements.

Third, the precise extent to which they are bound by the agreements in mixed situations seems unclear. While there is no doubt that both of them are internationally bound by the whole agreement, unless it has been established otherwise, the relation between them within the agreement, although characterized by ambiguity, is moving towards a vertical relationship. The expansive jurisdiction of the CJEU in relation to mixed agreements regardless of the competence involved or whether

Community of the Convention on International Trade in Endangered Species of Wild Fauna and Flora [1982] OJ L 384, pp. 1–61.

145 Cremona, (n 68) 12. In favour of considering an integral part of the EU legal order: Case C-439/01 *Libor Cipra and Vlastimil Kvasnicka v Bezirkshauptmannschaft Mistelbach* [2003] ECR I-00745. Contra: Case C-308/06 *The Queen on the Application of Intertanko and Others v Secretary of State for Transport* para. 50.

146 Holdgard, (n 84) 195.

147 Case 22-24/72 *International Fruit Company* [1972] ECR 1219.

148 Case 38/75 *Douaneagent der NV Nederlandse Spoorwegen v Inspecteur der invoerrechten en accijnzen* [1975] ECR 1439.

it has been exercised shows the reach and powers of the compliance mechanism that the 'Europeanization' of international law entails. As a consequence of the extension of EU law's normative pull to international law, even within mixed agreements, the relations of responsibility in those situations will be more complex, since even though the Member States might still retain some competence as regards the agreement, they have nevertheless to comply with the agreement as it was an obligation vis-à-vis the EU.

1.4 The Implementation of EU Law and the International Responsibility of the EU

Having established when the EU and its Member States are bound by an agreement, it is necessary to examine how the EU implements its law. The necessity for this analysis stems from the fact that only by understanding how EU law is implemented will it be possible to comprehend how the rules of attribution should work when confronted by the EU and/or its Member States' breach of an international agreement.

Prior to this analysis, some light must be shed on why it is necessary to examine the way the EU implements its law and not the implementation of international agreements binding upon it. First, the 'Europeanization' of an international agreement entails the expansion of EU constitutional principles to that agreement. Therefore, in principle, there should be no difference in the way the EU implements its own law and its international agreements. Furthermore, when speaking about the international responsibility of the EU, the breach of an international agreement will usually stem from the conduct of an EU or Member State organ in compliance with some sort of EU or Member State regulation.[149]

Second, the shift of the analysis from the implementation of international agreements to the EU's multi-level system of implementation gives a clearer picture of how international responsibility works in relation to the EU. An examination of the implementation of international agreements in the EU would obviously focus on the nature of the obligations enshrined in them. Therefore, the discussion would move from how and when the EU and its Member States can breach an agreement to how a self-executing agreement is incorporated into the EU legal order.[150] Whereas the discussion about the direct effect of international agreements is quite an interesting one, in actual fact, the analysis of the implementation of

[149] Klabbers, (n 2) 279. [150] Mendez, (n 99) 16.

EU law provides a better understanding on how the architecture of the EU works, especially in relation to the attribution of conduct to the EU or to its Member States. In other words, while significantly relevant on its own, the discussion on the direct effect of international agreements does not necessarily shed light on the articulation of the international responsibility of the EU. Instead, to better understand how the EU would breach its international obligations, it is necessary to analyse how it acts, how its actions can eventually lead to a breach of international law, and whether that breach should be attributed to the EU.

1.4.1 Normative Control in the EU

1.4.1.1 Executive Federalism, Dédoublement Fonctiennel and EU Constitutional Principles

The EU's multi-level implementation system has its origins in the limited resources put at the disposal of IOs, and subsequently the EU, at their respective inceptions.[151] Nowadays, this fact has been implicitly constitutionalized in article 291 (1) TFEU that provides: 'Member States shall adopt all measures of national law necessary to implement legally binding Union acts'. This provision recognizes an inherent problem regarding the implementation of EU law. While Member States' administrations from an institutional perspective are not integrated into the EU's administrative machinery, they are nonetheless required to implement EU law.[152] Moreover, unlike national administrations, which can give instructions to a particular administrative organ to act in a certain sense, the EU can only address the Member States in their collective capacity.[153] By way of example, the EU cannot give instructions to the customs authorities in Naples on how to implement the Common Customs Code. It will have to direct the instructions to Italy. In other words, Member States' administrations are autonomous from the EU's, which operate as decentralized European administrations from a functional perspective.[154] This way of implementing law has been defined as executive federalism,[155] and it is

151 Klabbers, (n 2) 279. Cf. Moshe Hirsch, *The Responsibility of International Organizations towards Third Parties: Some Basic Principles* (Martinus Nijhoff 1995) 64.

152 Robert Schütze, *From Dual to Cooperative Federalism: The Changing Structure of European Law*, vol 391 (Oxford University Press 2009) 57.

153 Robert Schütze, 'From Rome to Lisbon: "Executive Federalism" in the (New) European Union' [2010] 47(5) Common Market Law Review 1385, 1420.

154 Schütze, (n 152) 57.

155 Pieter Jan Kuijper, 'International Responsibility for EU Mixed Agreements' in Christophe Hillion and Panos Koutrakos (eds), *Mixed Agreements Revisited: The EU and Its Member States in the World* (Hart 2010) 213. Cf. Frank Hoffmeister, 'Litigating against the European Union and Its Member States – Who Responds under the ILC's Draft Articles

the system that traditionally has followed federal states like Germany.[156] The EU has a very limited layer of federal bureaucracy, thus directly applicable legislation automatically becomes part of the law of the land of the Member States and is implemented and applied by Member States' authorities.[157]

The main consequence of the adoption of executive federalism within the EU means that Member States are put in a somewhat bipolar situation. From a Member States' perspective, their authorities have a dual role. On one hand, Member States' authorities implement Member States' own law. But on the other hand, they are EU organs or agents from a functional perspective. This *dédoublement fonctionnel*[158] draws a picture in which an act of an organ of an EU Member State could also be an act of the EU, while another act albeit adopted by the same organ would not. Consequently, one of the main issues with the application of the responsibility rules to the EU concerns the identification of the functions that the organ was carrying out when breaching the agreement.[159] In mixed situations this problem will be even more relevant since both the EU and its Member States are bound by the same international obligations.

Yet, the EU's executive federalism raises some questions concerning uniformity in the implementation of EU law. Twenty-eight different administrations are required to implement the same piece of legislation and there is, therefore, a risk of distortion in the implementation of EU law. It could be argued that any distortion in the implementation of EU law by a national administration should be taken as a sign that, in reality, there is no such a thing as a *dédoublement fonctionnel* of Member States' authorities. The lack of a uniform implementation could be interpreted as a lack of functional integration and consequently it would be difficult to argue that the attribution of the conduct of a Member State organ should be attributed to the EU and not to the Member State.[160] Therefore, the question of the uniform and effective implementation of EU law on one hand shows the degree to which Member States' authorities are functionally integrated in the EU's multi-level implementation system, and on the other makes the case for the attribution of conduct to the EU and not Member States.

To provide an example, a distortion in the application of the EU customs regulation in a national administration could be based on a national

on International Responsibility of International Organizations?' [2010] 21(3) European Journal of International Law 723, 741.

156 Robert Schütze, *European Union Law* (Cambridge University Press 2015) 327.

157 Kuijper, (n 155) 213.

158 Higgins, (n 17) 841.

159 Kuijper and Paasivirta, (n 103).

160 See infra Chapter 3.

regulation contradicting the EU norm being applied. A situation of this kind would cast some doubts over the precise nature of the role the national authority is performing. Given that customs is the EU's exclusive competence, is the national authority acting as an EU authority even though it is incorrectly implementing the EU's regulation?[161] Or, since it is implementing a national regulation, could the national authority be considered to be acting as a national administration, even though EU Member States no longer retain competence over customs regulation?

The EU's response to these questions can be found in its constitutional principles. By virtue of the principle of primacy, any departure from an EU norm not expressly authorized by the EU constitutes a breach of EU law. Primacy would ensure the uniformity of EU law throughout the Member States.[162] Therefore, to determine under which role the Member States' authority is performing, it is necessary to examine whether there is some kind of EU norm that obliges the authority to act in the way it did. The principle of primacy determines that whenever there is an EU norm, Member States must comply with EU law.

By contrast, the lack of institutional integration into the EU's implementing machinery can be seen as a danger to the principle of primacy as a tool for ensuring the uniform application of EU law since EU law's primacy needs an effective mechanism of enforcement to ensure its uniformity in a decentralized legal system. In other words, without effective enforcement of the primacy principle, it would be difficult to argue that Member States' authorities are acting as EU administrations rather than as Member States' administrations.

Furthermore, the principle of direct effect provides for an effective mechanism to ensure that the principle of primacy is enforced in the Member States.[163] The bottom-up approach of direct effect, added to the

161 Article 207 (ex article 133) TFEU.

162 In the Commission's words: '[the principle of Primacy] applies to all provisions contained in the [EU] Treaty and in acts of the [EU] institutions. It also applies against any provision of national law at any level, including member States' constitutions. This means that whenever a Court of a Member State encounters a conflict between a provision of [Union] law and a provision of its national law, it must set aside the provision of national law, and apply [Union] law only.' WTO, *European Communities – Selected Customs Matters: Report of the Panel* (16 June 2006) WT/DS315/R and WT/DS315/AB/R para 4.69.

163 Ibid para 4.70. The CJEU has recognized the direct effect of certain international agreements. Nonetheless, it is not the focus of this section to analyse how the rights of individuals are affected by the agreement entered by the EU. For an analysis of the issues raised by that question, see: Jean-Victor Louis, 'L'insertion des accords dans l'ordre juridique de la Communauté et des Etats membres' in Jean-Victor Louis and

top-down approach of primacy ensures the effective application of EU law in a way never seen before in an IO.[164] The scope for individuals to invoke the application of EU law against its national administrations in the Member States' courts would provide for another safeguard that would ensure the effective application of EU law.

1.4.1.2 Extending the EU Constitutional Principles outside the Realm of Executive Federalism: The Broad Understanding of Implementation of EU Law

Although the notion of executive federalism enshrined in article 291 TFEU might connote a strict vision of what constitutes implementation under EU law by which only acts of an applicatory nature would amount to implementation,[165] the CJEU has nonetheless adopted a broad concept of implementation as to include: Member States' organs acting as EU agents (executive federalism),[166] Member States' organs enacting and applying measures in accordance with EU law,[167] and whenever Member States' action are conceived as originating from the EU.[168]

The principles of primacy and, to a certain extent, direct effect, apply to all these implementing scenarios, regardless of the competence or the type of norm involved.[169] Likewise, these principles, strictly speaking, apply to situations falling outside the scope of the EU's executive federalism. Even in situations in which the EU is exercising its shared competence or the EU legal act is not directly applicable, like Framework Decisions, EU law takes precedence over Member States' law.

Marianne Dony (eds), *Commentaire J Megret Le Droit de la CE et de l'Union Européenne Relations Exterieures*, vol 12 (Université de Bruxelles 2005).

164 Nollkaemper, (n 92) 53. 165 Schütze, (n 153) 1385.

166 Daniel Sarmiento, 'Who's Afraid of the Charter? The Court of Justice, National Courts and the New Framework of Fundamental Rights Protection in Europe' (2013) 50(5) Common Market Law Review 1267, 1274.

167 Like transposing and complying with a directive, Emily Hancox, 'The Meaning of 'Implementing' EU Law under Article 51(1) of the Charter: Åkerberg Fransson' (2013) 50(5) Common Market Law Review 1411, 1418.

168 Case C-617/10 *Åkerberg Fransson* [nyr] ECR para. 18. However, Member States acting under the umbrella of the ESM Treaty would not amount to implementing EU law. Case C–370/12 *Pringle v Ireland* [nyr] ECR para. 179; Sarmiento, (n 166) 1273.

169 In Simmenthal, the CJEU argued that 'any recognition that national legislative measures which encroach upon the field within which the [Union] exercises its legislative power or which are otherwise incompatible with the provisions of [EU] law had any legal effect would amount to a corresponding denial of the effectiveness of obligations undertaken unconditionally and irrevocably by Member States pursuant to the Treaty and would thus imperil the very foundations of the [Union]', Case 106/77 *Amministrazione delle Finanze dello Stato v Simmenthal SpA* [1978] ECR 629 para. 18.

By way of example, in *Melloni* the Court of Justice understood that the principle of primacy extended to those areas in which Member States are not acting as EU organs, but instead are covered by principles like mutual trust and recognition.[170] The case concerned the issue of a European Arrest Warrant (EAW) by the Italian Judicial Authorities against an individual residing in Spain (Mr Melloni) and whether a Spanish national court could refuse to implement it due to the fact Mr Melloni had been judged *in absentia* in Italy and that would constitute a breach of his fundamental right to an effective judicial protection as recognized by the Spanish Constitutional Court.[171] Unlike in an executive federalism scenario where it is a European institution that adopts a legislative act that needs to be implemented by the Member States' authorities, the EAW had not been issued by any European institution but by an Italian judge. Nevertheless, the CJEU understood that inasmuch as the EAW against Mr Melloni had been adopted by virtue of a Framework Decision, allowing the Spanish Court to refuse its execution would constitute a breach of the principle of primacy.[172] *Melloni* shows how the reach of the principle of primacy extends beyond the realm of the EU's executive federalism and delves into the waters of the implementation of EU law broadly speaking, imposing the same kind of obligations and consequences on the Member States' authorities regardless of whether the act that needs to be implemented is an EU act *sensu stricto*.

In any case, it should be acknowledged that, especially when dealing with the implementation of EU law the uniform application of EU law might be a more difficult task to achieve.[173] Member States' administrations might all implement a particular EU law; however, the law they implement could be their own version of that EU law. For instance, procedural autonomy in addition to the degree of discretion that Member States' administrations enjoy when implementing directives, might cast some doubts on the uniformity of that implementation.

Besides the principle of direct effect, other principles ensure the effective application of EU law as a means of guaranteeing its primacy over Member States' rules. In this respect, the principle of loyalty envisaged

[170] Cf. Case C-399/11 *Stefano Melloni v Ministerio Fiscal* [nyr] ECR.

[171] Schütze, (n 156) 463. [172] Case C-399/11 *Stefano Melloni v Ministerio Fiscal* para. 60.

[173] Paul Craig and Gráinne De Búrca, *EU Law: Text, Cases and Materials* (3rd edn, Oxford University Press 2003) 202. Eleftheria Neframi, 'The Duty of Loyalty: Rethinking Its Scope through Its Application in the Field of EU External Relations' 47 Common Market Law Review 323, 328.

in article 4 (3) TEU plays a fundamental role.[174] By establishing an obligation by which Member States must take measures to ensure the implementation of EU law, the EU Treaties recognize the obligation of effective implementation.[175] This principle of effectiveness has been the basis of the development of other obligations aimed at ensuring EU law primacy. For instance, the principle of loyalty was interpreted by the CJEU in a manner that established the obligation of consistent interpretation.[176] This obligation entails the effective implementation of EU law, as a means of safeguarding EU law's primacy. It not only implies the possibility of invoking EU law in national courts by individuals (direct effect), but also imposes an obligation on all Member States' institutions to act in accordance with EU law.

Furthermore, apart from this positive obligation of acting in conformity with EU law, the principle of loyalty also envisages a negative obligation on Member States. The effective implementation of EU law provides the mechanism by which Member States must refrain from adopting any measure that might jeopardize the effectiveness of EU law, either internal or external.[177] On the external side, it is worth noting that the CJEU has taken the position that Member States cannot assume any international

174 Article 4 (3) TEU: 'Pursuant to the principle of sincere cooperation, the Union and the Member States shall, in full mutual respect, assist each other in carrying out tasks which flow from the Treaties. The Member States shall take any appropriate measure, general or particular, to ensure fulfilment of the obligations arising out of the Treaties or resulting from the acts of the institutions of the Union. The Member States shall facilitate the achievement of the Union's tasks and refrain from any measure which could jeopardise the attainment of the Union's objectives'; for a comprehensive analysis of the principle of loyalty in EU law see: Marcus Klamert, *The Principle of Loyalty in EU Law* (Oxford University Press 2013).

175 Neframi, (n 174) 330.

176 Case C-106/89 *Marleasing SA v La Comercial Internacional de Alimentacion SA* [1990] ECR I-4135 para. 8. In Marleasing, the Court understood that Member States, by virtue of the duty of cooperation, must 'take all appropriate measures, whether general or particular, to ensure the fulfillment of that obligation, is binding on all the authorities of Member States including, for matters within their jurisdiction, the courts. It follows that, in applying national law, whether the provisions in question were adopted before or after the directive, the national court called upon to interpret it is required to do so, as far as possible, in the light of the wording and the purpose of the directive in order to achieve the result pursued by the latter.' Cf. Neframi, (n 174) 330.

177 For an analysis of the implications of the duty of cooperation in EU external relations see: Christophe Hillion, 'Mixity and Coherence in EU External Relations: The Significance of the "Duty of Cooperation"' in Cristophe Hillion and Panos Koutrakos (eds), *Mixed Agreements Revisited* (Hart 2010); Stephen Hyett, 'The Duty of Cooperation: A Flexible Concept' in Allan Dashwood and Cristophe Hillion (eds), *The General Law of EC External Relations* (Sweet and Maxwell 2000).

obligation that can affect EU rules.[178] Therefore, the principle of loyalty understood as an *effet utile* rule recognizes that Member States must not only effectively implement EU law, but also, from the moment there is an EU rule on the issue, refrain from acting internationally.

Overall, the loyalty principle, inasmuch as it is a principle of a federal nature,[179] could be considered the general principle underpinning article 291 TFEU.[180] Whereas article 291 TFEU imposes an obligation on the Member States to adopt all measures necessary to implement EU law, article 4 (3) TEU also requires Member States to refrain from adopting any measure that might endanger the effectiveness of EU law. Primacy and loyalty combine to ensure that EU law is implemented uniformly and effectively in every one of the 28 Member States, regardless of the form that the act might adopt.

Indeed, in situations like the implementation of regulations, the nature of the act in combination with the primacy principle clearly confirms that Member States' administrations are functionally acting as EU administrations. Instead, in situations in which the degree of Member States' discretion is higher (i.e. directives) primacy might not be enough to permit the classification of the organs implementing the directive as EU organs in a functional sense. Notwithstanding, the obligations enshrined in article 4 (3) TEU, taken in tandem with the primacy, show that although Member States might not be functionally acting as EU organs, they are not acting independently either.[181] This situation could be characterized as the EU exercising some kind of normative control over its Member States. Even though normative control is not a concept alien to other IOs,[182] since, as mentioned before, IOs also are faced with the same issues regarding the implementation of their *acquis*, it is argued here that it is the control that these principles add to the implementation of EU law that would show that EU Member States do not have a lesser degree of discretion when implementing EU law as they would have when implementing a rule from any other IO.

Therefore, whenever there is an EU norm, Member States would be under the normative control of the EU. Moreover, any action from a

[178] Case C-45/07 *Commission v Greece (IMO)* [2009] ECR I-00701 para. 30. Cf. *Opinion 1/76 Re: Inland Waterways*; Case C-246/07 *Commission v Sweden (PFOS)* [2010] ECR I-3317.

[179] De Baere, (n 5) 253. Contra: Klamert, (n 174).

[180] Schütze, (n 153) 1398.

[181] Hoffmeister, (n 155) 741.

[182] For an argument in favour of applying this concept to the UN, see: Antonios Tzanakopoulos, *Disobeying the Security Council: Countermeasures against Wrongful Sanctions* (Oxford University Press 2011).

Member State which might impinge on the effectiveness and uniform application of an EU norm would constitute a breach of EU law subject to judicial control. Thus, it would be reasonable to argue that, in those situations, the conduct of a Member State when acting under the umbrella of EU law should be considered as conduct of the EU. The breach of an international obligation by a Member State when implementing EU law would derive from the fact that the EU norm is in breach of that international obligation. Alternatively, the breach of an international obligation by a Member State would amount to a breach of EU law inasmuch as international agreements binding on the EU form an integral part of the EU legal order by incorrectly implementing the EU norm.

1.4.1.3 The EU Institutional Structure as Another Defining Element of the Specificity of Normative Control in the EU

The institutional structure would constitute the final element underpinning the EU's specific kind of normative control. Besides the principles that restrict Member States when implementing EU law, the enforcement mechanism set up to deal with any possible breaches of EU law adds another layer of control over the Member States when the EU *acquis*.

As a starting point it should be mentioned that the Commission plays a rather central role in the control of EU and international law. While it might be commonplace, it should be remembered that the Commission is entrusted with the power to ensure the correct application of EU law, including how Member States' authorities implement it. The corollary of that power is the Commission's power to conduct investigations and eventually start infringement proceedings against those Member States who do not correctly implement EU law.[183]

Inasmuch as international agreements are binding on the EU as an integral part of the EU legal order, the Commission can bring infringement proceedings against EU Member States over their failure to correctly implement those agreements. The powers of the Commission in this regard encompass not only the control of Union agreements but also mixed agreements, and stem from the obligation EU Member States have vis-à-vis the EU when implementing a Union agreement. Moreover, this obligation is rooted in the fact that the EU has assumed responsibility for the due performance of the agreement.[184] To sum up, if a Member State

183 Article 258 (ex article 226) TFEU empowers it to bring a claim to the CJEU on those grounds.

184 Case 104/81 *Kupferberg* para. 13.

does not correctly implement an international obligation binding on the EU, the EU could be held internationally responsible for the breach of that international obligation.[185]

The scope of those powers is not restricted to issues of implementation of the agreement regardless of its mixed nature; it also extends to broader issues of compliance. By way of example, in the *Étang de Berre* case, the Commission bought an action against France over its failure to comply with the obligations in the Convention for the Protection of the Mediterranean Sea against Pollution (a mixed agreement). In particular, the Commission argued that France was not complying with the Convention in relation to discharges of fresh water and alluvia into the marine environment, a matter not covered by EU legislation. The fact that the Convention was a mixed agreement, and that the EU had not yet legislated on that area did not stop the Commission from opening an infringement proceeding. The CJEU sided with the Commission's view and understood that even when there is no EU legislation there is a Union interest in compliance by both the EU and its Member States with obligations enshrined in a mixed agreement.[186]

The existence of a Union interest in complying with international obligations enshrined in mixed agreements could be seen as another way of framing the obligation that the EU has assumed for the due performance of the agreement. This seems to be confirmed by other cases like *Commission v Ireland*, where the Commission opened an infringement procedure against Ireland due to its failure to accede the Berne Convention for the Protection of Literary and Artistic Works (Berne Convention). The EEA Agreement established that all its parties should adhere to the Convention before 1 January 1995, yet Ireland did not. Facts such as that the EU could not accede the Convention or that the subject matter of the Convention fell within shared competence did not affect the Court's view that there was a Union interest in Ireland becoming a party to this agreement.[187]

It is submitted that the Commission exercises a close control over Member States' authorities. To a certain extent that control resembles that exercised by a federal administration over its different states.[188] Therefore, insofar as the control over the implementation of EU law is exercised

185 Kuijper, (n 155) 216. 186 C-239/03 *Commission v France (Ètang de Berre)* para. 29.

187 C- 13/00 *Ireland v Commission (Berne Convention)* para. 14. Cf. Neframi, (n 126) 335.

188 Cf. Schütze, (n 112); Schütze, (n 152).

in this way, the actions of Member States' authorities when acting as EU organs should be attributed to the EU, regardless of the transparent veil of the EU or the fact that those organs carry out a dual role.

Finally, that the CJEU plays a fundamental role in the control of both EU and international law is commonplace now.[189] The expansive view of the Court's jurisdiction, as regards mixed agreements mentioned before,[190] as well as its role in dealing with preliminary references on the interpretation of international agreements, is fundamental in understanding the institutional foundations of the EU's normative control. The institutional side of the EU's normative control is nevertheless closely intertwined with the principles informing that control. More specifically, the vertical relationship established by virtue of these principles determines to a certain extent the jurisdiction of the Court.[191] For instance, in two Orders of the Court concerning the implementation of the Memoranda of Understanding (MoUs) concluded by the Commission, among other institutions and Portugal in the framework of the Eurozone crisis, the Court has highlighted that in certain situations in which the relation between the Commission and the Member States is of a more horizontal nature, it will lack jurisdiction.[192]

1.4.2 *Centralized Implementation*

Notwithstanding, the important role of EU Member States in the implementation of EU law, the picture of the implementing structure would be incomplete if the institutions of the EU were omitted. In over 50 years of life, the EU has continued to develop implementing machinery.[193] Like a federal state, the EU has a centralized administration that implements its own laws.

European institutions and organs also implement EU law, and in some cases they are no different from the classical public administration of

[189] For an extensive overview of the role of the CJEU in relation to international law see: Koutrakos, (n 1) 229; Eeckhout, (n 31) 267.

[190] See note 130. [191] Hancox, (n 167) 1418.

[192] Case C-128/12 *Sindicato dos Bancários do Norte and Others, Order of 7 March 2013* [nyr] ECR; Case C-264/12 *Sindicato Nacional dos Profissionais de Seguros e Afins, Order 26 June 2014* [nyr] ECR. Cf. Sarmiento, (n 166) 1273. To see how even in these situations a case for the responsibility of the EU might be made, but not in terms of normative control, see Chapter 7.

[193] This implementing machinery is not constrained to the traditional EU institutions. More and more, the EU is creating new implementing bodies (agencies) within its own administrative system.

Member States.[194] Traditionally the Commission has exercised this executive power,[195] Competition Law and Stated Aids Control being two significant areas in which the Commission implements EU law. For instance, the European Commission can impose fines on individuals in situations where they do not comply with the competition rules laid down in European legislation.[196] In such situations, there would be no doubt that responsibility would be derived from that conduct and it should thus be attributed to the EU. Consequently, the decision of the Commission to authorize the merger between two energy companies that would lead to an eventual breach of the competition rules envisaged in the Energy Charter Treaty (ECT) should be attributed to the EU.[197]

1.5 Conclusions

The rules on responsibility require two basic elements to be present for the responsibility of an international subject to arise. First, the subject must be bound by the obligation it allegedly breached and second, that breach must be attributable to it. This chapter has shown the ways in which the EU and its Member States enter into international agreements. It has been argued that the EU's treaty-making practice, as a consequence of its treaty-making powers, does not shed enough light on the understanding of the specific effects of international agreements on the EU, especially those of a mixed nature.

In addition, this chapter has shown how the EU's executive federalism blurs the issue of whether an act should be attributed to the EU or to its Member States. Although there are straightforward situations in which the attribution of conduct is clear, there are others in which a careful legal examination will be required. Thus the analysis of the control exercised over the Member States' organs when they implement EU law would play a basic role in understanding the international responsibility of the EU. The constitutional principles of the EU combined with the institutional architecture to ensure compliance with EU law create a sort of normative

194 Cf. Angel Manuel Moreno Molina, 'La Administración Pública de los Estados miembros como Administración comunitaria. Referencia a la sitación española' in Luciano Parejo Alfonso and others (eds), *Manual de Derecho Administrativo Comunitario* (Centro de Estudios Ramon Areces 2000).

195 Derrick Wyatt and Allan Dashwood, *European Union Law* (5th edn, Sweet and Maxwell 2006) 41.

196 Paul Craig, *EU Administrative Law* (Oxford University Press 2006) 888.

197 Article 6 ECT.

umbrella under which Member States no longer act in a completely independent manner but rather in compliance with an EU norm. Whereas, as is the case with other IOs, the EU needs its Member States to implement its laws, the mechanisms of control aimed at ensuring effective and uniform implementation resemble more closely the 'check and balances' of federal states than the mechanisms of other IOs. Therefore, in those situations of normative control, even though Member States are not EU organs in either an institutional sense or functional one, any act that those Member States carry out should be attributed to the EU.

In relation to the EU's international responsibility and the attribution of conduct to the EU, it is necessary to have in mind, first, that the EU implements part of its *acquis* in a centralized manner. It has a bureaucracy that can breach an international obligation binding on the EU. Hence, the conduct of the organs of the EU's administration should be attributed to the EU. Second, the EU also implements its law in a decentralized fashion. The breach of international obligations binding on the EU committed by Member States' administrations while implementing EU law should be attributed to the EU either because the Member States' organs were functionally acting as EU organs (e.g. implementation of the Common Custom Code) or because the basic principles of EU law establish that when implementing or complying with EU law, Member States are no longer subjects which act independently. Consequently, a breach committed under the EU's normative control either stems from the fact that a particular piece of EU law might violate an obligation binding on the EU, or due to the fact that a Member State is not only breaching international law but also EU law.

2 Codifying of the Responsibility of International Organizations (I)

The Impact of ARIO's Rules of Attribution on the EU

2.1 Introduction

Undoubtedly, the discussion on the EU's international responsibility must be put in the wider context of the proliferation of multilateral agreements and the IOs' rise in international law. By way of example, most existing multilateral agreements have been negotiated and concluded under the auspices of an IO.[1] Similarly, apart from being institutionalized structures in which States cooperate,[2] IOs have the capacity to adopt legal acts and also conclude international agreements with other international subjects.[3]

However, this proliferation of IOs seems to entail a high political price.[4] The creation of IOs has led to a situation where they exist as legal subjects, but lack accountability and responsibility;[5] this, in turn, leads to an increase in normative and jurisdictional conflicts and the fragmentation of the international legal order.[6] Moreover, the evolution of the role that these subjects develop in the international arena has not been accompanied by an evolution of the mechanisms required to hold them internationally responsible.

1 José E. Alvarez, *International Organizations as Law-makers* (Oxford University Press 2005) 273; Catherine Brölmann, *The Institutional Veil in Public International Law: International Organisations and the Law of Treaties* (Hart 2007) 102.

2 Brölmann, (n 1) 27.

3 Jan Klabbers, *An Introduction to International Institutional Law* (Cambridge University Press 2009) 178.

4 Richard Collins and Nigel D. White, 'Moving beyond the Autonomy-Accountability Dichotomy: Reflections on Institutional Independence in the International Legal Order' [2010] 7(1) International Organizations Law Review 1, 2; Klabbers, (n 3) 310.

5 Jan Klabbers, 'The Transformation of International Organizations Law' [2015] 26(1) European Journal of International Law 9, 82.

6 Collins and White, (n 4) 2.

Rather than providing reparations, the discussions on the responsibility of IOs are more concerned with the allocation of powers between the State and the IO.[7] As a consequence, most of the issues regarding IOs' responsibility (or lack of it) will revolve around the issue of the attribution of a particular conduct, either to the IO or to its Member States. As happens with many of the issues concerning IOs, the regulation of their responsibility under international law shows the existing tension between their autonomous character and their functional nature.[8] Thus, the basic issues regarding the responsibility of IOs will touch upon the role of its Member States in relation to the commission of the internationally wrongful act and more specifically, to what extent the IO veil covers the actions of its Member States. Logically, all these issues have been the focus of the discussions about the ARIO.[9]

[7] André Nollkaemper, 'Constitutionalization and the Unity of the Law of International Responsibility' [2009] 16(2) Indiana Journal of Global Studies 535, 538.

[8] Catherine Brölmann, 'International Organizations and Treaties' in Jan Klabbers (ed), *Research Handbook on International Organizations: Contractual Freedom and Institutional Constraint* (Edward Elgar 2011) 2; Cf. Collins and White, (n 4); Jan Klabbers, 'The Emergence of Functionalism in International Institutional Law: Colonial Inspirations' [2014] 25(3) European Journal of International Law 645.

[9] See: Pieter Jan Kuijper and Esa Paasivirta, 'Further Exploring International Responsibility: The European Community and the ILC's Project on Responsibility of International Organizations' [2004] 1 International Organizations Law Review 111; Esa Paasivirta and Pieter-Jan Kuijper, 'Does One Size Fit All? The European Community and the Responsibility of International Organizations' [2005] XXXVI(I) Netherlands Yearbook of International Law 169; Pieter Jan Kuijper, 'Amsterdam Center for International Law. Introduction to the Symposium on Responsibility of International Organizations and of (Member) States. Attributed or Direct Responsibility or Both?' [2010] 7(1) International Organizations Law Review 9; Jean D'Aspremont, 'Abuse of the Legal Personality of International Organizations and the Responsibility of Member States' [2007] 4 International Organizations Law Review 91; Jean D'Aspremont, 'The Articles on the Responsibility of International Organizations: Magnifying the Fissures in the Law of International Responsibility' [2012] 9 International Organizations Law Review 15; Niels Blokker, 'Abuse of the Members: Questions Concerning Draft Article 16 of the Draft Articles on Responsibility of International Organizations' [2010] 7(1) International Organizations Law Review 35; Niels Blokker, 'Preparing Articles on Responsibility of International Organizations: Does the International Law Commission Take International Organizations Seriously?' in Jan Klabbers and Asa Wallendahl (eds), Research Handbook on the Law of International Organizations (Edward Elgar 2011); August Reinisch, 'Aid or Assistance and Direction and Control between States and International Organizations in the Commission of Internationally Wrongful Acts' [2010] 7(1) International Organizations Law Review 63; José E. Alvarez, 'Revisiting the ILC's Draft Rules on International Organization Responsibility' [2011] 105 Proceedings of the Annual Meeting (American Society of International Law) 344; Daphna Shraga, 'The ILC Draft Articles on Responsibility of International Organizations: The Interplay between the Practice and the Rule' [2011] 105 Proceedings of the Annual Meeting (American

It is against this background that not only the EU's international responsibility is analysed, but also the codification process carried out by the ILC on the responsibility of IOs. This chapter examines how the rules of attribution enshrined in the ARIO apply to the EU and its Member States. Even though the EU appears to be an IO like no other,[10] most of the problems revolving around the EU's international responsibility are dealt with in one way or another in the provisions of the ARIO. In particular, this chapter shows that the ARIO's approach to the attribution of conduct to the EU and its Member States when implementing EU law is not in complete harmony with the EU's autonomous nature. While the ARIO makes an effort to take into account the special features of the EU as an international actor, it fails to fully take into account the role of EU Member States when implementing EU law.

This chapter first lays down some key concepts that set the scene for the discussion on how the rules of attribution laid down in the ARIO apply to the EU. The methodological approach carried out by the ILC when codifying the diverse international practice concerning the responsibility of IOs, as well as the basic elements of that same responsibility, are examined. Second, the chapter analyses how the different rules of attribution envisaged in ARIO apply to the EU, and evaluates the extent to which they could apply to attribute responsibility to the EU for actions committed under its normative control.

2.2 The ARIO in the Context of the Codification of International Responsibility by the ILC

Article 57 of the Articles on State Responsibility (ASR)[11] opened the door for the ILC to codify the responsibility of IOs. Resolution 56/82 of the UN General Assembly recommended that the ILC examined the question. As a direct consequence of that mandate, Mr Giorgio Gaja was appointed as

Society of International Law) 351; Maurizzio Ragazzi, 'The ILC Draft Articles and International Financial Institutions: Select Considerations' [2011] 105 Proceedings of the Annual Meeting (American Society of International Law) 353; C. F. Amerasinghe, 'Comments on the ILC's Draft Articles on the Responsibility of International Organizations' [2012] 9 International Organizations Law Review 29; Pierre Klein, 'Les Articles sur la Responsibilité des Organisations Internationales: Quel Bilan tirer des travux de la CDI?' [2012] LVIII Annuaire Française de Droit International 1.

10 See previous chapter.

11 International Law Commission, 'Articles on the Responsibility of States for Internationally Wrongful Acts', in Report of the International Law Commission on the Work of its 53rd Session, UN Doc A/56/10 Chap. IV (2001) GAOR 56th Session Supp 10.

Special Rapporteur (SR) and a Working Group was established.[12] The SR issued eight reports with proposals of provisions to regulate the issue.[13] These reports were debated within the ILC, and most of the articles were provisionally adopted, some of them with modifications. Finally, in 2011, the ILC adopted the ARIO on second reading.[14]

This section examines both the personal and substantive scope of the ARIO's codification project as a way to contextualize the subsequent debate on how the ARIO applies to the EU. The first section examines the methodological approach used by the ILC in relation to the ARIO's personal scope. The second section focuses on how the ILC approached the issue of the articulation of that responsibility.

2.2.1 *Personal Scope: Approaching the Issue of the Heterogeneity of IOs' Nature*

Any attempt at codifying IO practice first encounters a methodological issue: the heterogeneity of IOs. ILC member Mr Wood clearly explains it when he asserts that this category of international persons – IOs – is infinitely varied in their functions and powers, in their status, rights and obligations, and in their relationships with members and others.[15] Do all IOs have to be treated equally in relation to responsibility? To what extent must the EU and the Universal Post Union be subject to the same rules on responsibility?

[12] ILC, 'First Report on Responsibility of International Organizations, by Mr Giorgio Gaja, Special Rapporteur' (26 March 2003) UN Doc A/CN.4/532, para. 1.

[13] ILC, 'Eighth Report on Responsibility of International Organizations, by Giorgio Gaja, Special Rapporteur' (14 March 2011) UN Doc A/CN.4/640; ILC, 'Seventh Report on Responsibility of International Organizations, by Giorgio Gaja, Special Rapporteur' (27 March 2009) UN Doc A/CN.4/610); ILC, 'Sixth Report on Responsibility of International Organizations, by Giorgio Gaja, Special Rapporteur' (1 April 2008) UN Doc A/CN.4/597; ILC, 'Fifth Report on Responsibility of International Organizations, by Giorgio Gaja, Special Rapporteur' (2 May 2007) UN Doc A/CN.4/583; ILC, 'Fourth Report on Responsibility of International Organizations, by Giorgio Gaja, Special Rapporteur' (28 February, 12 April and 20 April 2006) UN Doc A/CN.4/564, Add.1 and Add.2; ILC, 'Third Report on Responsibility of International Organizations, by Giorgio Gaja, Special Rapporteur' (13 May 2005) UN Doc A/CN.4/553; ILC, 'Second Report on Responsibility of International Organizations, by Giorgio Gaja, Special Rapporteur' (2 April 2004) UN Doc A/CN.4/541. Gaja, First Report on Responsibility of International Organizations (n 12).

[14] International Law Commission, 'Articles on the Responsibility of International Organisations' in Report on the Work of its 63rd Session, UN Doc A/66/10 Chap V (2011) GAOR 66th Session Supp 10.

[15] ILC, 'Sixth Committee Summary Record of the 15th Meeting, Held at Headquarters, New York' (28 October 2003) UN Doc A/C.6/58/SR.15, para. 8.

Obviously, while these questions are not new and are present in any debate regarding the codification of IO practice,[16] the ILC has traditionally avoided them. For instance, the 1989 Vienna Convention on the Law of the Treaties between States and International Organizations or between International Organizations (1989 VCLT) rejected any possible differentiation in treatment between IOs, based on their heterogeneous nature, and followed a unitary approach.[17] Though, as was mentioned in the commentary to article 2 1989 VCLT, the nature of the Convention limited the scope *ratio personae* to those IOs which had treaty-making powers attributed to them.[18]

With regard to the ARIO, the SR, in the same vein as the previous comment about the 1989 VCLT definition, understood that the mere fact of having international legal personality was not condition enough to be held responsible. Some special features were needed. In his own words:

> For an organization to be held as potentially responsible it should not only have legal personality and thus some obligations of its own under international law. What is required is also that in the exercise of the relevant functions the organization may be considered as a separate entity from its members and that thus the exercise of these functions may be attributed to the organization itself.[19]

Finally, he proposed a definition of IO that underlined the necessity of having an international nature (i.e. having States among its members) and carrying out state-like functions as the main elements of an IO:[20]

> For the purposes of the present draft articles, the term 'international organization' refers to an organization which includes States among its members insofar it exercises in its own capacity certain governmental functions.[21]

16 In reality they are present in any discussion about how to study and analyse IOs. Cf. Henry G. Schermers and Niels M. Blokker, *International Institutional Law: Unity within Diversity* (5th edn, Martinus Nijhoff 2003) 15. In relation to the study of IOs as a single field in international law see: Niels Blokker, 'The Floor Is to the Authors: Perspectives on the Law of International Organizations as a Separate Field of Study' [2008] 5(1) International Organizations Law Review 141.

17 Article 2.1 i) 1989 VCLT.

18 Commentary 23, article 2 1989 VCLT. For an in-depth analysis of the methodological discussions held in the ILC during the drafting of this Convention, see: Brölmann, (n 1) 182.

19 Gaja, *First Report on Responsibility of International Organizations* (n 12) 15.

20 Adela Rey Aneiros, *Una Aproximación a la Responsabilidad Internacional de las Organizaciones Internacionales* (Tirant Lo Blanch 2006) 37.

21 Article 2 Use of terms. Gaja, *First Report on Responsibility of International Organizations* (n 12) para. 18.

The definition of the SR stressed the special features of the IO. The mere existence of an IO does not make it *per se* internationally responsible: the IO must have some kind of public function to bear responsibility under international law. However, the use of a term like 'governmental functions' seemed slightly confusing.[22] First, it was uncertain what exactly constitutes a governmental function: state-like functions? Government functions in the strict sense (executive powers, for example)? Common administrative functions (the normal tasks that any secretariat would carry out: public contracts, human resources)? Second, it was unclear whether an IO can only bear responsibility from the acts derived from those governmental functions or not. While it is true that the reference to 'governmental functions' restricted ARIO's scope *ratio personae*, its use seemed to establish an analogy with States which most international doctrine deemed inappropriate.[23]

The ILC preferred not to follow the SR's definition. Instead, it preferred to go for a more general and less functional definition of an IO. The text of article 2 of the ARIO, approved by the ILC, reads as follows:

> 'International organization' means an organization established by a treaty or other instrument governed by international law and possessing its own international legal personality. International organizations may include as members, in addition to States, other entities.[24]

Moreover, the ILC followed its unitary approach towards IOs. But, unlike the SR's definition that went beyond the link between international legal personality and responsibility, the ILC stressed that link through the inclusion three elements in its definition. The first element refers to the necessity for the IO to be created by an instrument of international law. The ILC does not share the SR's less formal definition of an IO. While SR Gaja claimed that the legal nature of the constituent instrument was not relevant to the organization's responsibility, the inclusion of this formal requisite, the ILC argued, reflected *prevailing practice*.[25] However, it remained silent on the reasons for not including any residual practice

22 Laura Huici Sancho, *El hecho internacionalmente ilícito de las Organizaciones internacionales* (Bosch 2007) 36.

23 In general, see: Alvarez, (n 1) 71. Specifically criticizing the SR's definition: José Manuel Cortés Martín, *Las Organizaciones Internacionales: Codificación y Desarrollo Progresivo de su Responsabilidad Internacional* (Instituto Andaluz de Administración Pública 2008) 73; Rey Aneiros, (n 20) 37.

24 ILC, 'Report of the International Law Commission on the Work of Its 61st Session' (4 May–5 June and 6 July–7 August 2009) UN Doc A/64/10.

25 Gaja, *First Report on Responsibility of International Organizations* (n 12) para. 8.

such as organizations created by municipal law, which, according to the SR, 'assume the existence of an implied agreement under international law, one would be justified in assimilating the resulting organizations to those established by treaty'.[26]

The second element of the ILC's definition concerns the necessary international legal personality of the organization. The ILC understands that an IO is responsible to the extent that it has its own international legal personality. However, when establishing whether an explicit recognition of legal personality in the constituent instrument is needed, the ILC seems to take a factual approach towards international legal personality. In this regard, it argues that: 'the acquisition of legal personality under international law does not depend on the inclusion in the constituent instrument of a provision such as article 104 of the United Nations Charter'.[27] Later it makes reference to ICJ case law to support its reasoning.[28] Thus, some authors have interpreted this comment to mean that international legal personality is a characteristic inherent to an IO.[29]

Finally, the third element: the necessity of having a State as a member is just a rewording of part of the SR's initial definition. However, given that IOs are international legal subjects and more specifically have treaty-making power, a hypothetical scenario, in which two or more IOs could conclude a treaty creating a third one, could not be excluded. Therefore, following the definition given in article 2 ARIO as it stands today, this new third IO, created in a treaty granting it international legal personality, would not be subject to the ARIO insofar as it would not have a State among its members. This example shows how the traditional functional vision of the ILC on IOs' subjectivity prevails over any other consideration regarding their international nature. In this regard, the ILC continues to follow Reuter's functionalist approach towards IOs by which '[i]nternational organizations are neither sovereign nor equal; all their powers are strictly at the service of their Member States'.[30] This wil become especially evident in relation to the rules on responsibility contained in ARIO's Part V.

[26] Ibid. [27] Ibid. [28] Ibid. paras 42–43.

[29] Cortés Martín, (n 23) 79. Cf. Antoni Pigrau Solé, 'La Responsabilidad Internacional de la Comunidad Europea' in Fernando M. Mariño Menéndez (ed), *Acción exterior de la Unión Europea y comunidad internacional* (Boletín Oficial del Estado 1998) 173.

[30] ILC, 'Sixth report on the question of treaties concluded between States and international organizations or between two or more international organizations by Mr Paul Reuter, Special Rapporteur' (11 March 1977) UN Doc A/CN.4/298 (1977) II(1) Yearbook of the International Law Commission 119, 120.

2.2.2 The Object of the Responsibility: The Internationally Wrongful Act as the Core of the Responsibility under International Law

International responsibility arises as consequence of the commission of an internationally wrongful act.[31] Consequently, to understand when an international subject must be held responsible, it is necessary to delineate the basic elements of an internationally wrongful act. In this regard, article 2 ASR and article 4 ARIO identify two basic elements required for the responsibility to arise: 1) the breach of an international obligation; and 2) the attribution of that breach to an international subject.

2.2.2.1 The Breach of an International Obligation

International responsibility arises only in the event of a breach of an international obligation. Therefore, article 12 ASR and article 10 ARIO enshrine a broad definition of the breach. article 12 ASR considers that there is a breach of an international obligation when 'an act of that State is not in conformity with what is required of it by that obligation, regardless of its origin or character'. Moreover, the ILC's commentary describes this lack of conformity as flexible enough to cover the many different ways in which an obligation can be expressed, as well as the various forms that a breach may take.[32]

In addition, article 12 ASR[33] and article 10 ARIO establish that the origin of the international obligation does not alter the conclusion that responsibility will be entailed if it is breached.[34] The system of responsibility does not distinguish between an obligation enshrined in an international agreement, customary international law or any other source of international obligations. The only limit to the existence of the breach

31 Article 1 of the Articles on State Responsibility (ASR) reads as follows: 'Every internationally wrongful act of a State entails the international responsibility of that State.' ILC, 'Responsibility of States for Internationally Wrongful Acts'. Nevertheless, it must be underlined that there are other situations that could give rise to international liability but where the wrongful act is missing. This international liability for injurious consequences arising out of acts not prohibited by international law presents other features and questions which exceed the scope of the present study. See: Pierre Marie Dupuy, 'The International Law of State Responsibility: Revolution or Evolution?' [1989] 11 Michigan Journal of International Law 105, 112.

32 ILC, 'Report of the International Law Commission on the Work of Its 53rd Session' (23 April–1 June and 2 July–10 August 2001) UN Doc A/56/10 (2001) II(2) Yearbook of the International Law Commission 1, 55 para. 2.

33 Andrea Gattini, 'Breach of International Obligations' in André Nollkaemper and Ilias Plakokefalos (eds), *Principles of Shared Responsibility in International Law: An Appraisal of the Art* (Cambridge University Press 2014) 51.

34 ILC, *Report on the Work of Its 53rd Session* 55 para. 4.

is established in article 13 ASR. According to this provision, States can only breach international obligations that are binding upon them. Moreover, the breach can be committed by an act or an omission.[35] In other words, the broad conceptualization of the existence of a breach allows for not only action but also the lack of it not in conformity with a binding international obligation to give rise to responsibility.

In relation to the international responsibility of IOs, and in particular of the EU, their specific features should not in principle affect how a breach of an international obligation is established.[36] Inasmuch as they do not act in conformity with an international obligation binding upon them they would be breaching an international obligation.

2.2.2.2 Attribution of Conduct

Logically, someone must have committed a breach of an international obligation for the internationally wrongful act to exist. Even though international subjects do not act directly, the rules of attribution create a legal fiction by which the act of a physical or legal person should be considered as if the international subject had performed it.[37] Furthermore, the system of international responsibility sets up rules of attribution of an objective nature, i.e. they do not require any special intention in the commission of the breach for it to be attributed.[38] In other words, the objective nature of international responsibility relies on establishing a link between the breach of an international obligation and an international legal subject regardless of the original intention of the subject.[39] In this regard, the rules of attribution establish different ways to attribute conduct to an international legal person, ranging from the establishment of institutional links, to factual links or through the acknowledgement of the act as its own.[40]

Depending on the kind of link that one applies, the attribution of conduct could vary. This becomes especially relevant when dealing with the responsibility of the EU, and of other IOs as well. Inasmuch as the

[35] Article 2 ASR and article 4 ARIO. [36] Gattini, (n 33) 51.

[37] James Crawford, *State Responsibility: The General Part* (Cambridge University Press 2013) 114; Brigitte Stern, 'The Elements of an Internationally Wrongful Act' in James Crawford, Alain Pellet and Simon Olleson (eds), *The Law of International Responsibility* (Oxford University Press 2010) 202.

[38] Crawford, (n 37) 60. [39] ILC, *Report on the Work of Its 53rd Session* 36 para. 10.

[40] Francesco Messineo, 'Attribution of Conduct' in André Nollkaemper and Ilias Plakokefalos (eds), *Principles of Shared Responsibility in International Law: An Appraisal of the State of the Art* (Cambridge University Press 2014) 65.

EU acts through its Member States, the application of a factual link to a specific breach could in theory lead to the attribution of the conduct to the EU, whereas the application of an institutional link could hypothetically lead to the attribution of conduct to a Member State. Consequently, the examination of the rules of attribution as enshrined in the ARIO play a central role in shedding light on how the EU bears responsibility under international law and the extent to which it can also encompass the actions of its Member States when implementing EU law.

Having established that a breach of an internationally wrongful act has taken place and that it is attributable to an IO, that IO has an obligation to stop that breach and provide reparation where there was damage.[41] In addition, injured subjects could adopt countermeasures against the IO that has breached the international obligation to induce them to comply once again with that obligation.[42]

2.3 The Attribution of Conduct through the Establishment of an Institutional Link

2.3.1 A Preliminary Step: The Apportionment of Obligations and the Relationship with State Rules on Attribution

Before moving onto the examination of the specific rules of attribution envisaged in the ARIO, a preliminary issue needs to be discussed: is it possible to bear responsibility without attribution of conduct? The ILC seems to favour that possibility in relation to certain specific scenarios. Even though article 4 ARIO establishes the attribution as a necessary element for the responsibility to arise,[43] the ILC stressed that: 'article [4] is without prejudice to the existence of cases in which an organization's international responsibility may be established for conduct of a State or of another organization'.[44] Thus, the ILC recognizes that the responsibility of the IO or its Member States may stem from rules other than the rules of attribution. For instance, given that the ASR accepts the responsibility of a State in connection with the act of another State,[45] it seems logical that an IO could also incur joint responsibility in analogous situations.

41 Articles 30–31 ASR. 42 Article 49 ASR. 43 Vid supra. p. 1.

44 ILC, 'Report of the International Law Commission on the Work of Its 55th Session' (5 May–6 June and 7 July–8 August 2003) UN Doc A/58/10 (2003) GAOR 58th Session Supp No 10, para. 45.

45 Gaja, *Second Report on Responsibility of International Organizations* (n 13) para. 6.

Consequently, the ARIO includes a series of rules, which, while not being rules of attribution, also entail the responsibility of the IO or a State since they took part in the commission of the wrongful act.[46] In these situations, both the IO and the State could bear joint responsibility.[47]

In addition, the SR discusses the possibility of joint, or joint and several responsibilities of an IO and its Member States as a consequence of a single wrongful act committed by the IO or a Member State regardless of who performed the wrongful conduct. In other words, the SR analyses whether being bound by the same international obligations makes an IO and its Member States *per se* jointly responsible without the need to attribute the wrongful act to either one.

EU mixed agreements are put forward as the main and only example.[48] The SR's analysis starts with the traditional distinction used when examining the issue of responsibility within these agreements: in mixed agreements with declarations of competence the responsibility will be apportioned accordingly, and in mixed agreements without declarations of competence, joint responsibility would apply.[49] The SR considers that insofar as there is no instrument in the agreement apportioning the respective obligations of the EU and its Member States (like a declaration of competence),[50] both the EU and its Member States are bound by the whole agreement. Therefore, he argues, the responsibility would be joint towards third parties to the agreement,[51] regardless what is provided for in the rules of attribution. According to this view, since both the EU and its Member States are parties to the same agreement, the breach of a provision of that agreement by either one of them would automatically entail the responsibility of both the EU and its Member States.

[46] See next chapter. [47] See article 19 ARIO. [48] See previous chapter.

[49] See Marise Cremona, 'External Relations of the EU and the Member States: Competence, Mixed Agreements, International Responsibility, and Effects of International Law' (2006) EUI Law Working Paper 2006/22, 19, http://ssrn.com/abstract=963316; Cf. Marise Cremona, 'Who Can Make Treaties? The European Union' in Duncan B. Hollis (ed), *Oxford Guide to Treaties* (Oxford University Press 2012); Kuijper and Paasivirta, (n 9); Piet Eeckhout, *External Relations of the EU and the Member States Competence, Mixed Agreements, International Responsibility, and Effects of International Law* (2006); Giorgio Gaja, 'Some Reflections on the European Community's International Responsibility' in Henry G. Schermers, Ton Heukels and Philip Mead (eds), *Non-Contractual Liability of the European Communities* (Martinus Nijhoff 1988); Eleftheria Neframi, 'International Responsibility of the European Community and of Member States under Mixed Agreements' in Enzo Cannizzaro (ed), *The European Union as an Actor in International Relations* (Kluwer Law International 2002).

[50] See Chapter 4.

[51] Gaja, *Second Report on Responsibility of International Organizations* (n 13) para. 5.

The SR partly bases his argument on the joint responsibility of the EU and its Member States under mixed agreements in an obiter dictum from the CJEU. In the Court's words:

> In the absence of derogations expressly laid down by the Convention, the [Union] and its Member States as partners of the ACP States [States of Africa, the Caribbean and the Pacific] are jointly liable to those latter States for the fulfilment of every obligation from the commitments undertaken.[52]

He assumes that by virtue of this example, 'the attribution of conduct to the [EU] or a Member State does not appear to be relevant when deciding who is responsible'.[53] It must be highlighted that the Court's statement has never been put into practice. Even more, due to the specific nature of the old Lomé Convention this paragraph must necessarily be differentiated and qualified. Although multilateral in form, the Lomé Convention was substantively bilateral in nature.[54] The bilateral nature of the cooperation established in the agreement shifted relations between the EU, its Member States and the other parties to the agreement.[55] The relations established in these kinds of international agreements are reciprocal between blocks: the EU and its Member States assume a series of obligations vis-à-vis the ACP countries and *vice versa*.[56] The Lomé Convention did not establish any obligation between the EU and its Member States or between the EU Member States. Therefore, the Court's obiter dictum, by establishing the joint liability of the EU and its Member States, was acknowledging the inherent bilateral nature of the Lomé Convention in general terms.

In addition, as shown in the previous chapter, the responsibility of the EU is likely to arise in most cases as a consequence of the actual implementation of a piece of EU law by either the EU or a Member State. It is submitted that the rules of attribution would apply inasmuch as there is

52 Case C-316/91 *Parliament v Council* [1994] ECR 661 para. 296.

53 Gaja, *Second Report on Responsibility of International Organizations* (n 13) para. 5.

54 'The Convention was concluded, according to its preamble and Article 1, by the Community and its Member States of the one part and the ACP States of the other part. It established an essentially bilateral ACP-EEC cooperation,' C-316/91 *Parliament v Council* para. 29.

55 Ibid; cf. Pieter Jan Kuijper, 'International Responsibility for EU Mixed Agreements' in Christophe Hillion and Panos Koutrakos (eds), *Mixed Agreements Revisited: The EU and Its Member States in the World* (Hart 2010) 210.

56 Pieter Jan Kuijper and Esa Paasivirta, 'EU International Responsibility and Its Attribution: From the Inside Looking Out' in Panos Koutrakos and Malcolm D. Evans (eds), *The International Responsibility of the European Union: European and International Perspectives* (Hart 2013) 64; C-316/91 *Parliament v Council* para. 33.

an act that breaches an international obligation binding on both the EU and its Member States. To ascertain otherwise would diminish the international legal personality of the EU, and, to some extent, its autonomous character.[57] For instance, holding the EU and its Member States jointly responsible for an act committed by the European Commission, based solely on the fact that both the EU and its Member States are bound by the same agreement, entails accepting that the EU is not a different legal person from its Member States. In this scenario, Member States would be responsible for any act of the EU regardless of their involvement, and *vice versa*. Moreover, this hypothesis of joint responsibility remains a highly theoretical issue with no actual practice and the SR implicitly acknowledges it.[58] International practice seems to support the idea that the application of attribution rules rather than the apportionment of the obligations contained in an international agreement is the defining factor to establish responsibility.

Unfortunately, the ILC does not shed any light on the consequences of the lack of apportionment of obligations in terms of responsibility.[59] Perhaps it does not consider relevant to focus on this issue where there is almost no practice to codify, and that in principle it should not impact the way the attribution of responsibility is carried out.[60] In those cases where no express apportionment of the obligations of an agreement has been carried out, both the EU and its Member States are bound by the agreement as whole. Yet, being bound by the same obligations does not automatically entail the joint responsibility of the EU and its Member States.[61] Instead, the responsibility should be established by the application of clear rules of attribution, regardless of whether the EU and its Member States are bound by the same obligations.

In any case, the joint responsibility of an IO and its Member States on the basis of the lack of apportionment of obligations can be seen as an attractive outcome that could solve any responsibility gap. It is easier and more convenient to disregard any careful analysis of the attribution

[57] Kuijper and Paasivirta, (n 9) 127; Eeckhout 20.

[58] Gaja, *Second Report on Responsibility of International Organizations* (n 13) para. 5.

[59] ILC, 'Report of the International Law Commission on the Work of its 56th Session' (3 May–4 June and 5 July–6 August 2004) UN Doc A/59/10 (2004) GAOR 59th Session Supp 10, 100.

[60] Cf. Piet Eeckhout, 'The EU and Its Member States in the WTO – Issues of Responsibility' in Lorand Bartels and Federico Ortino (eds), *Regional Trade Agreements and the WTO Legal System* (Oxford University Press 2006) 459.

[61] Martin Björklund, 'Responsibility in the EC for Mixed Agreements' [2001] 70 Nordic Journal of International Law 373, 388.

of conduct and establish a rule of joint responsibility based on an *iure et de iure* presumption. Moreover, a general rule based on the joint responsibility of an IO and its Member States when both are bound by the same international obligations regardless of who has actually breached the obligation would diminish the IO's autonomous international legal personality.[62] Join responsibility does not take into account factors such as whether the IO has an institutional structure that is independent on its Member States, or whether the breach was committed by an organ which has no relationship whatsoever with the IO Member States. Member States would continue to be responsible for the actions of another international subject regardless of their actual involvement in the wrongful act.

Furthermore, a theory of joint responsibility based on the lack of apportionment of international obligations between the IO and its Member States would also mean that the IO would be responsible for any action of its Member States regardless of its participation in them. While the inherent logic of joint responsibility stems from the necessity of holding someone responsible, it can nevertheless be seen as an implicit denial of the effectiveness of the rules of attribution and of the rules of international responsibility as whole. The different scenarios in which shared responsibility would be the preferable outcome should be regulated on the basis of an actual analytical examination of the role that the IO and its Member States played when breaching an international obligation. For those reasons, it should be welcomed that the ILC decided that the lack of apportionment of international obligations will not play a role in how responsibility is attributed.

2.3.2 The Requirement of a Formal Organic Tie to Attribute Conduct to an IO

As with State responsibility, attribution plays a fundamental role in establishing the international responsibility of an IO.[63] Moreover, the analytical exercise that the attribution of conduct entails becomes even more

[62] Cf. Kuijper and Paasivirta, (n 9) 127; Eeckhout, (n 49) 20; Frank Hoffmeister, 'Litigating against the European Union and Its Member States – Who Responds under the ILC's Draft Articles on International Responsibility of International Organizations?' [2010] 21(3) European Journal of International Law 723.

[63] Kuijper and Paasivirta, (n 56); Pierre Klein, 'The Attribution of Acts to International Organizations' in James Crawford, Alain Pellet and Simon Olleson (eds), *The Law of International Responsbility* (Oxford University Press 2010); Luigi Condorelli and Claus Kress, 'The Rules of Attribution: General Considerations' in James Crawford and others (eds), *The Law of International Responsibility* (Oxford University Press 2010) 221; Crawford, (n 37) 113.

relevant when confronted with IOs with multi-layered systems of implementation, such as the EU. Insofar as EU Member States implement EU law as if they were organs of the EU, the attribution of an internationally wrongful act to the EU or to one of its Member States can negatively impact the EU's constitutional architecture.[64] Consequently, the analysis of the general rule of attribution enshrined in article 6 ARIO can set the tone as to how ARIO takes the EU into account.

Logically, the starting point of the analysis is article 6 ARIO. This provision, which is tailored upon article 4 ASR, reads as follows:

1. The conduct of an organ or agent of an IOs in the performance of functions of that organ or agent shall be considered an act of that organization under international law, whatever position the organ or agent holds in respect of the organization.
2. The rules of the organization apply in the determination of the functions of its organs and agents.

The general rule of attribution envisaged in this provision is the basic recognition of the functional personality of an IO. To pursue the objectives for which they were brought into existence, IOs are created with their own organs.[65] Logically, these organs will be composed of agents which will perform the duties attributed to that organ. Thus, insofar as an agent or an organ of an IO commits a wrongful act, the IO will be responsible.

Article 6 ARIO attributes the conduct of the organ or the agent to an IO through the establishment of a formal organic tie.[66] Yet, it does not give a clear definition of what would amount to an organic tie between an IO and one of its agents or organs the sense of this provision. There are two possible readings in this regard, which are especially relevant as regards the EU's normative control over its Member States. On one hand, it could be understood that article 6 ARIO is wide enough to cover the relationship between the EU and the organs of its Member States. Member States' organs may be regarded as agents of the EU.[67] This reading would entail that inasmuch as EU Member States' organs and agents are

[64] Kuijper and Paasivirta, (n 56) 69.
[65] For an analysis of the variety of organs, see, among many others: Ignaz Seidl-Hohenveldern, 'Les organes des organisations internationales' in René-Jean Dupuy (ed), *Manuel sur les organisations internationales* (Martinus Nijhoff 1988) 81.
[66] Klein, (n 64) 298.
[67] Stefan Talmon, 'Responsibility of International Organizations: Does the European Community Require Special Treatment?' in Maurizio Ragazzi (ed), *International Responsibility Today: Essays in Memory of Oscar Schachter* (Martinus Nijhoff 2005) 412.

functionally acting as organs of the EU, their conduct should be attributed to the EU.[68] Consequently, any internationally wrongful act committed by an EU Member State under the normative control of the EU would be considered an act of the EU by virtue of article 6 ARIO.

This reading would be further supported by reference to the rules of the organization envisaged in the second paragraph of article 6 ARIO.[69] As Ahlborn notes, 'the rules of the organization may, for example, have a role to play in the decision whether an organ of a Member State, or other entity or person, has acted as an organ under the normative control of the organization pursuant to Article 6'.[70] Therefore, since the EU constituent rules provide that EU Member States' organs when implementing EU law are functionally EU organs, the EU should bear responsibility for the actions of those EU Member States' organs.[71]

Alternatively, there is a more restrictive reading of what would amount to a formal organic tie in the sense of article 6 ARIO. According to this reading, the formal organic tie would result from legal instruments specific to the activities of the organization like personnel regulations.[72]

Besides the function which the organ or agent performs, that organ or agent must be somehow integrated within the organic structure of the IO.[73] When implementing an obligation coming from an IO, State authorities do not act as organs of the IO; they continue to be State organs and agents. As a result of this approach, EU Member States' organs could not be considered EU organs, since they are not formally integrated within the IO structure.[74] Only the actions of the EU bodies, offices and agencies would be covered by this provision.[75] Thus, if a certain decision of the Commission in the field of competition law were to be considered in breach of an international obligation binding on the EU, it would be attributed to the EU. Likewise, the actions of EU Delegations in third countries would be attributable to the EU.[76]

68 Hoffmeister, (n 63) 746.

69 Article 2 of the ARIO envisages, within that category, 'the constituent instruments, decisions, resolutions and other acts of the organization adopted in accordance with those instruments, and established practice of the organization'.

70 Christiane Ahlborn, 'The Rules of International Organizations and the Law of International Responsibility' [2011] 8(2) International Organizations Law Review 397, 481.

71 Kuijper and Paasivirta, (n 9) 116.

72 Klein, (n 64) 298.

73 José Manuel Cortés Martín, 'European Exceptionalism in International Law? The European Union and the System of International Responsibility' in Maurizio Ragazzi (ed), *Responsibility of International Organizations: Essays in Memory of Sir Ian Brownlie* (Martinus Nijhoff 2013) 195.

74 See Chapter 1. Klein, (n 64); Kuijper and Paasivirta, (n 9); Paasivirta and Kuijper, (n 9).

75 Kuijper and Paasivirta, (n 56) 51.

76 Ibid.

The SR supports this narrow reading of article 6 ARIO that does not consider EU Member States' organs as EU organs when they are acting under the EU's normative control. According to Gaja, international practice would confirm his position. The SR puts forward the *Bosphorus* case as an example of how international practice does not support a wide reading of the concept of 'organ' in terms of the attribution of conduct.[77] In this case, the ECtHR dealt with the implementation of an EU sanctions regulation by Ireland. The Strasbourg Court found that 'a Contracting Party is responsible under article 1 of the [ECHR] for all acts and omissions of its organs regardless of whether the act or omission in question was a consequence of domestic law or of the necessity to comply with international legal obligations'.[78] Nevertheless, this paragraph of the ECtHR ruling should be put in context. On one hand, the ECtHR is dealing with a special situation by which a State has transferred sovereign power to an international (supranational) organization but that organization cannot itself be held responsible under the ECHR for decisions of its organs as long as it is not a party to the ECHR.[79] The attribution of the specific conduct to Ireland seems to stem from the lack of accession of the EU to the ECHR. If the EU were to accede to the ECHR, a similar conduct would be attributed to the EU.[80]

The position adopted by the SR and implicitly endorsed by the ILC, closes the door for the establishment of the responsibility of the EU on the basis of normative control by virtue of article 6 ARIO.[81] As Kuijper and Paasivirta rightly argue, the requirement of a formal organic tie

> does not capture the core features of the EU action, since the Member States are seen as remaining sovereign and not constituting organs of the organisation in a formal sense. Consequently, the Member States would always be responsible, as

77 *Bosphorus Hava Yollari Turizm Ve Ticaret Anonim Şirketi v Ireland* [2006] 42 EHRR 1.

78 Ibid. 79 Ibid.

80 See article 3 (2) of the Draft Accession Agreement: 'The European Union may become a co-respondent to the proceedings in respect of an alleged violation notified by the Court if it appears that such allegation calls into question the compatibility with the Convention rights at issue of a provision of European Union law, including decisions taken under the TEU and under the TFEU, notably where that violation could have been avoided only by disregarding an obligation under European Union law.'

81 Commentary 6 to article 6 ARIO provides that 'an organ or agent of an international organization may be an organ or agent who has been seconded by a State or another international organization. The extent to which the conduct of the seconded organ or agent has to be attributed to the receiving organization is discussed in the commentary on article 7.' This means that the definitive criterion for the attribution of a conduct of a State organ to an IO is effective control, and not a reading of the definition of organ or agent in light of the relevant rules of the organization. Klein, (n 64) 299.

the immediate actors, should acts be attributed on purely organic lines. The fact that normative decisions are taken at the EU level (Council, Parliament) and on the basis of a proposal by an independent institution (Commission) is basically ignored.[82]

In short, even though unfortunately article 6 ARIO does not deal with EU normative control scenarios, it does not mean that article 6 ARIO could not apply to the EU. As mentioned earlier, the EU has its own organs and agents that could eventually breach an international obligations binding on the EU. In these scenarios, article 6 ARIO would apply and the conduct would be attributed to the EU, which would thus be responsible.

2.3.3 Attribution of Ultra Vires Conducts and the Institutional Link

IOs only act to the extent that they have powers conferred to them. Therefore, what would happen in a situation where an IO organ acts outside its functions as enshrined in the rules of the organization? Article 8 ARIO, called *Excess of authority or contravention of instructions*, aims to cover this type of situation:

> The conduct of an organ, an official or another person entrusted with part of the organization's functions shall be considered an act of the organization under international law if the organ, official or person acts in that capacity, even though the conduct exceeds authority or contravenes instructions.

Article 8 ARIO is the logical companion to the general rule of attribution of article 6 ARIO.[83] The purpose of article 8 ARIO is to bridge the gap created by the intersection between formal organic links as a means of attributing conduct to the IO and the functional nature of the IO. In other words, in the same manner that article 6 ARIO applies to the wrongful acts committed by IOs agents within the limits of their functions as enshrined in the rules of the organization, article 8 ARIO attributes to an IO the acts of its agents, when they exceed either their functions or the powers conferred upon the IO.

Even though the rules of the organization are not mentioned in the article, they will play an important role in the application of the provision. To know whether the organ acted ultra vires when it committed the internationally wrongful act, the rules of the organization should be examined. The rules would allow an international judge to consider on what grounds the wrongful act should be attributed to the IO: article 6 ARIO or article 8 ARIO? Even though in practice the consequences will be

82 Kuijper and Paasivirta, (n 56) 54.

83 ILC, *Report on the Work of Its 56th Session* 116.

identical, the election of one over the other should be based on an actual examination of the rules of the organization.

However, the rules of the organization will be irrelevant in attempting to determine whether the act gives rise to responsibility. In other words, the internal validity of the internationally wrongful act is irrelevant.[84] For instance, the fact that a breach of a provision of a mixed agreement committed by the Commission through exceeding its competences also constitutes a breach of EU law is irrelevant in terms of the international responsibility of the EU. The Commission's internally invalid conduct will be attributed to the EU externally.

The ILC in its commentary reflects upon the distinction between the internal and the international validity of the act:

> Article [8] only concerns attribution of conduct and does not prejudice the question whether an ultra vires act is valid or not under the rules of the organization. Even if the act was considered to be invalid, it may entail the responsibility of the organization. The need to protect third parties requires attribution not to be limited to acts that are regarded as valid.[85]

Thus, article 8 ARIO, by complementing article 6, resolves the struggle between the IO's incomplete international legal personality and the necessity of someone being held responsible. In the same manner as articles 27 and 46 1989 VCLT, articles 6 and 8 ARIO set aside any question concerning the attributed powers in favour of third parties.

2.4 Factual Attribution: Facing the Limited Resources of IOs

In the previous chapter it was discussed how the limited resources the EU had at its disposal are the main reason for the EU's multi-level implementation system. IOs likewise, have limited resources and often do not have enough personnel to carry out their tasks.[86] As a consequence, an IO Member State's organ will have a dual nature, either being an organ of the State or of the IO. For example, a Dutch soldier participating in a UN peacekeeping operation is at the same time both an agent of the Netherlands, since he or she is formally integrated into the structure of the Dutch administration, and an agent of a UN organ, since functionally he or she is carrying out a task entrusted to the UN. Similarly, an Italian customs official, though formally tied to the Italian executive, functionally acts as an organ of the EU when applying the EU common customs tariff.

[84] Huici Sancho, (n 22) 111. [85] ILC, *Report on the Work of Its 56th session* 117.

[86] Moshe Hirsch, *The Responsibility of International Organizations towards Third Parties: Some Basic Principles* (Martinus Nijhoff 1995) 64; Crawford, (n 37) 189.

Thus, there might be situations in which the conduct of a State organ would give rise to the responsibility of an IO; article 7 ARIO aims to cover this kind of situation. The provision that is entitled 'Conduct of organs or agents placed at the disposal of an international organization by a State or another international organization' provides as follows:

> The conduct of an organ of a State or an organ or agent of an international organization that is placed at the disposal of another international organization shall be considered under international law an act of the latter organization if the organization exercises effective control over that conduct.

In contrast to article 6 ARIO, which attributes conduct to an IO through a formal organic link, article 7 ARIO establishes the link between the IO and the organs placed at its disposal through the notion of effective control. In international practice, the notion of a control link has traditionally had some priority over any other types of link, clearly explaining the significant role that it has played in the inception of the ARIO.[87] Given the necessity of effective control to attribute the conduct of a State to an IO, what is typically understood as effective control should be analysed, and which type of situations it covers.

The ILC understands that the effectiveness of the control exercised would have to be examined through a 'factual criterion'.[88] In other words, the examination should be done on a case-by-case basis. Nevertheless, the ILC gives some guidelines on how to assess the effectiveness of the control. The control is effective when it is exclusive and derives from a direct command.[89]

Furthermore, in relation to the kind of situations that this provision covers, the SR, following the international practice regarding the effective control of State organs placed at the disposal of an IO, narrowed the scope of application of this provision. Article 7 ARIO, as he argues, 'was tailored for military operations'.[90] The vast bulk of examples put forward concern the area of peacekeeping operations,[91] and most of the scholarly texts written on the issue clearly follow that link.[92]

Hence, would it be possible to argue that this provision could apply outside the field of peacekeeping? In principle, it could not be excluded that there might be other situations, outside that area of international

87 Hirsch, (n 87) 62. 88 ILC, *Report on the Work of Its 56th Session* 114.
89 Ibid. 90 Gaja, *Seventh Report on Responsibility of International Organizations* (n 13) 9.
91 Gaja, *Second Report on Responsibility of International Organizations* (n 13) 14.
92 Hirsch, (n 87) 66; Pierre Klein, *La responsabilité des organisations internationales dans les ordres juridiques internes et en droit de gens* (Bruylant 1998) 387; cf. Marten Zwanenburg, *Accountability of Peace Support Operations* (Martinus Nijhoff 2005) 363.

law, where an IO might exercise effective control over the State organs placed at its disposal. Could it be understood that, inasmuch as a State organ is implementing a rule or regulation, it is under the control of the IO? Furthermore, would that control be effective in the sense of article 7 ARIO?

Some scholars have answered these questions in the affirmative when discussing the EU's international responsibility. For instance, Steinberger argues that the EU exercises some degree of effective control over Member States' organs by virtue of the judicial control exercised by the CJEU.[93] This interpretation of article 7 ARIO would foster a unitary view of the EU multi-level implementation system when dealing with its international responsibility. Yet, Kuijper and Paasivirta recognize that even though the idea of Member State organs being 'placed at the disposal of' the EU grates at the ears of the average EU lawyer,[94] in international law 'the actual degree of control of the [Union] institutions over Member State organs is generally considered too weak'.[95]

Likewise, some international scholars contend that the control exercised by the EU through its norms and legal rules cannot be considered effective, in the sense of article 7 ARIO. In particular, they argue that this normative or legal control cannot lead to the attribution of conduct to the EU, or any other IO. While Hirsch argues that legal control may lead to the responsibility of the IO to the extent that the Member State 'had no discretion but to comply with the organization's measure',[96] he signals that this control is not factual or operational, so article 7 ARIO could not apply to situations of normative control.[97] Thus, when examining the EU's responsibility as a consequence of its normative control over Member States' implementing bodies, the actual margin of discretion of the latter should be examined. Hence, that analysis would be done on a case-by-case basis, because, as Jacqué points out: '*face à une norme communautaire, l'Etat Membre dispose d'une marge d'appreciation variable*'.[98]

Furthermore, Klein specifically examines the EU case. When looking at the actual degree of control it exercises when a Member States' organ

[93] Eva Steinberger, 'The WTO Treaty as a Mixed Agreement: Problems with EC's and the EC Member States' Membership of the WTO' [2006] 17(4) European Journal of International Law 837, 851.

[94] Kuijper and Paasivirta, (n 9) 127. [95] Ibid.

[96] Hirsch, (n 87) 87. [97] See Chapter 3.

[98] Jean Paul Jacqué, 'Communauté européenne et Convention européenne des droits de l'homme' in Louis-Edmond Pettiti, Emmanuel Decaux and Pierre-Henri Imbet (eds), *La Convention européenne des droits de l'homme Commentaire article par article* (Economica 1999) 92.

implements the *acquis communautaire*, he follows the view of Jacqué in acknowledging that the margin of appreciation might differ from case to case. However, Klein understands that in the majority of the cases, Member States' organs enjoy a certain discretion, so: *'l'organisation n'exerce en effet qu'une autorité très limitée sur ses membre en pareilles circonstances, et son contrôle sur ces derniers n'est pas établi à suffisance'*.[99]

To sum up, the special rule of attribution envisaged in article 7 ARIO aims to reflect a specific set of relations pertaining to responsibility. Nevertheless, the provision is drafted in a broad way, opening the possibility not only for its application to new fields where a similar degree of effective control may develop, but also, as has been seen in the *Behrami and Saramati* case,[100] opening the door to a complete misreading of the rationale underpinning the provision.[101] Even though this provision may not be overly relevant to the specific object of this study, its potential application to the EU cannot be discounted. More specifically, article 7 ARIO could easily be applied to internationally wrongful acts committed by Member State agents placed at the disposal of the EU. Currently this practice is gaining more relevance within the framework of ESDP, mainly because of the peacekeeping missions being deployed under that umbrella.[102] Therefore, it cannot be excluded that eventually situations concerning the behaviour of EU troops will eventually be scrutinized in the light of article 7 ARIO.[103]

2.5 Attribution of a Conduct to an IO due to the Acknowledgement of That Conduct as Its Own

Traditionally the rules of attribution function on the basis of objective elements. There is an organic link, a control link or a territorial link.[104] All these links between the subject committing the internationally wrongful act and the subject being held responsible are outside any subjective

99 Klein, (n 93) 385.

100 *Behrami and Behrami v France, Saramati v France, Germany and Norway* [2007] 45 EHRR SE10.

101 Marko Milanović and Tatjana Papić, 'As Bad as It Gets: The European Court of Human Rights' Behrami and Saramati Decision and General International Law' [2009] 58(2) International and Comparative Law Quarterly 267; Gaja, *Seventh Report on Responsibility of International Organizations* (n 13).

102 Milanović and Papić, (n 102) 295.

103 Frederik Naert, 'The International Responsibility of the Union in the Context of Its CSDP Operations ' in Malcolm D. Evans and Panos Koutrakos (eds), *The International Responsibility of the European Union European and International Perspectives* (Hart 2013).

104 Hirsch, (n 87) 62.

consideration: if the act was committed by an agent under the IO's control, the IO in question is responsible, regardless of any consideration concerning the real will of the IO or the agent.

Article 9 ARIO is not founded on any of those objective criteria. Moreover, it is not drafted on the basis of any objective element that allows the conduct to be attributed to the IO. Instead, article 9 ARIO is based on the subjective will of an IO to be held responsible, regardless of whether the previous rules would attribute the wrongful act to it. The provision, called 'Conduct acknowledged and adopted by an international organization as its own' provides that:

> Conduct which is not attributable to an international organization under the preceding draft articles shall nevertheless be considered an act of that international organization under international law if and to the extent that the organization acknowledges and adopts the conduct in question as its own.

While the ASR also reflect this situation in its article 11,[105] some concerns should nonetheless be raised in relation to the cases put forward by the SR, and reproduced by the ILC in its commentary.[106] First, the existing practice regarding attribution through acknowledgement of the conduct by IOs is doubtful. The SR identified the European Commission's oral pleading before a WTO panel in the framework of the Local Area Network (*LAN*) *dispute* involved an acknowledgement of the responsibility by the EU.[107] The European Commission declared that the EU was 'ready to assume the entire international responsibility for all measures in the area of tariff concessions, whether the measure complained about has been taken at the [EU] level or at the level of Member States'.[108]

However, the SR should have also made clear that neither the panel nor the Appellate Body explicitly accepted the acknowledgement of the conduct as the rule for attributing the act to the EU.[109] Furthermore,

105 ILC, *Report on the Work of Its 56th Session* 122.

106 Gaja, *Second Report on Responsibility of International Organizations* (n 13)27.

107 WTO, *European Communities – Customs Classification of Certain Computer Equipment – Panel Report* (22 June 1998) WT/DS62/R, WT/Ds67/R and WT/DS68/R, as modified by Appellate Body Report WT/DS62/Ab/R, WT/DS67/Ab/R and WT/DS68./Ab/R. See Chapter 5. Cf. Andrés Delgado Casteleiro and Joris Larik, 'The "Odd Couple": The Responsibility of the EU at the WTO' in Panos Koutrakos and Malcolm D. Evans (eds), *The International Responsbility of the European Union: European and International Perspectives* (Hart 2013) 233. See Chapter 6.

108 WTO, *European Communities – Customs Classification of Certain Computer Equipment* (Oral pleading of the European Commission to the Panel) (12 June 1997) para. 6. Also can be found in: Gaja, *Second Report on Responsibility of International Organizations* (n 13) 27.

109 Gaja, *Second Report on Responsibility of International Organizations* (n 13) 27.

in the other example put forward by the SR, the International Criminal Tribunal for the former Yugoslavia did not take the view that the IO had acknowledged the conduct in question.[110]

Second, even though this provision can be seen as a possible solution concerning the lack of a rule of attribution for acts committed by Member States when implementing IO obligations, it should not be viewed as a satisfactory solution.[111] On one hand, leaving the attribution of responsibility to the will of an IO diminishes the legal character of the rules of attribution. The acknowledgement of the act by an IO as its own might be seen as a compromise solution, in which legal reasoning has played no role. On the other hand, the ILC does not clarify what should be understood by acknowledgement or acceptance. Should an IO declaration to that effect, concerning a particular case where one of its Member States is involved, be understood as a general declaration of acknowledgement of conduct as its own which would apply to any equivalent case? If that is the case, what are the specific effects of that acknowledgement? To what extent would the IO be bound by it? Moreover, is this attribution exclusive? Could the Member State also be held responsible? And furthermore, do the third parties involved in the responsibility relation have a say in this acknowledgement process? If it is being understood that an IO's will might apply to establish the attribution of a wrongful act to it, third parties must also play a role in deciding whether the conduct should be attributed to the IO.

2.6 Conclusions

The rules of attribution as laid down in articles 6 to 8 ARIO provide a wide range of options for attributing an internationally wrongful act to an IO. The ARIO tries to cover as many situations as possible to provide reparations for internationally wrongful acts attributable to IOS.

Nonetheless, the rules of attribution of the ARIO have not been exempt from a degree of criticism. The ILC not only remains silent on the issue of the apportionment of international obligations between IOs and its Member States, but also adopts a functionalist approach to the issue of the attribution of acts of the IOs' Member States to the IO when Member States implement IO norms. The ILC, perhaps due to its codification function, follows the traditional line of international law. In this regard, the codification of the normative control as an attribution criterion would

110 Ibid 28. 111 Cortés Martín, (n 23) 279.

have been particularly welcomed. As has been shown, the EU's multi-level implementation system is built upon the basic foundation of the '*dédoublement fonctionnel*' of its Member States' organs, and the attribution of those acts to the EU would consequently entail the EU's exclusive responsibility over those issues. Whereas this outcome would have conferred a higher degree of autonomy to the international legal personality of all IOs, it is clear that the ILC has decided that in those situations, the wrongful act would not be attributed to the EU. While in relation to mixed agreements the wrongful act would generally be attributed to the Member State when implementing EU law, in relation to Union agreements it would be difficult to argue that it should be the EU Member State bearing responsibility. Following the ARIO, the EU's conduct could not be attributed to it either organically or functionally, unless it would acknowledge it as its own. Since the EU Member States are not internationally bound by Union agreements, and the conduct cannot be attributed to the EU, a more than possible responsibility gap would arise.

3 Codifying of the Responsibility of International Organizations (II)

The Impact of ARIO's Rules of Responsibility on the EU

3.1 Introduction

As can be seen from the previous chapter, the responsibility relations between IOs and Member States not only pose a challenge to the conceptualization of IOs as international subjects, but also to its Member States. The shift towards global governance entails an entangled web of institutions, mechanisms, relationships and processes among States, IOs as wells as other actors[1] that shows how States are no longer the only subjects in the international arena. The interdependence between the different international actors at the root of the current debates on international law and global governance increases the number of situations where questions of joint or shared responsibility between IOs and States might arise.[2] Moreover, the ARIO's recognition that under certain circumstances a conduct carried out by a State organ or agent might not entail the responsibility of that State, but to the responsibility of an IO instead challenges the State-centred conception of international law. States are no longer the only subjects that can be internationally responsible. IOs, like the EU, can also be held responsible, and in some situations for actions carried out by State organs or agents.

These discussions on the shifting nature of international law and global governance are to a certain extent reflected in the debates concerning the shared/joint responsibility of IOs and/or States under international law.

1 Bart Van Vooren, Steven Blockmans and Jan Wouters, 'The Legal Dimension of Global Governance: What Role for the European Union? An Introduction' in Bart Van Vooren, Steven Blockmans and Jan Wouters (eds), *The EU's Role in Global Governance: The Legal Dimension* (Oxford University Press 2013) 3.

2 André Nollkaemper, 'Introduction' in André Nollkaemper and Ilias Plakokefalos (eds), *Principles of Shared Responsibility in International Law: An Appraisal of the State of the Art* (Cambridge University Press 2014) 4.

The ARIO devotes its Chapter IV of Part One and its Part Five in its entirety to these issues. On one hand, Chapter IV of Part I ARIO establishes the rules regarding the responsibility of the IO for the acts of a State or another IO. On the other, Part Five tries to answer the classical issue of States' responsibility for acts attributable to an IO.

While some of the issues will be common to both chapters and could apply equally to other IOs, the special nature of the relationship between the EU and their Member States will raise different types of questions in each of them. In particular, issues surrounding the responsibility of the EU for the actions of a State will focus on the degree of control that the EU has over its Member States and whether a rule of responsibility and not a rule of attribution is the correct approach to tackle the issue. In contrast, the responsibility of a State for the actions of the EU will inevitably lead to discussions on the secondary and subsidiary nature of the responsibility of the Member States for the conduct of an IO, and the extent to which these could apply to the EU.

This chapter is divided into four sections. The first section deals with the articulation of shared responsibility within the rules of the ARIO. The second part focuses on the responsibility of the EU for acts attributed to a State and whether the rules enshrined in the ARIO could apply to situations of normative control. The third section examines the issue of the responsibility of States for acts attributed to the EU, and the issue of the piercing of the IO's veil as envisaged in the ARIO. The fourth section analyses whether the *lex specialis* provision of article 64 ARIO could better accommodate the EU's responsibility for those actions committed under its normative control.

3.2 The Relation between the Rules of Attribution and the Rules of Responsibility: When Is Responsibility Shared?

Initially, it may appear that the fact that the ARIO declares that an IO or a State is responsible for a conduct that is not attributable them under articles 6 – 9 ARIO might exclude the responsibility of the subject to whom the act is attributable. For instance, it could be argued that by virtue of the application of a provision of Chapter IV of Part I ARIO, the responsibility of a State would be excluded as matter of fact in favour of the responsibility of the IO. Such a view would allow for the EU to be solely responsible for the breach of an international obligation committed by one of its Member States during the implementation of a piece of EU law. Even though the conduct is attributable to one or more Member States under the ASR, the application of a provision of Chapter IV of Part I ARIO would exclude the attribution of the conduct to the Member States.

However, articles 19 and 63 ARIO exclude that possibility. Both provisions envisage that the rules of responsibility are 'without prejudice to the international responsibility of the State or international organization which commits the act in question'.[3] In other words, these chapters do not have exclusive effects *per se*. On one hand, the State which breached the international obligation would be responsible due to the rules of attribution. On the other, the IO (in the aforementioned example, the EU) would be responsible if the rules of responsibility say so. Thus, in a situation like that mentioned previously, by virtue of these provisions, the responsibility would be shared if both the EU and the Member State were to be bound by the same international obligations, like in a mixed agreement scenario. By contrast, in situations where the EU is the only party to the international agreement besides the third party, the EU would be solely responsible for actions attributable to its Member States. Conversely, by virtue of the Part Five, the IO would be responsible as long as the conduct may be attributable to it, and the State would be responsible to the extent that the rule of responsibility would provide for it.

The ILC has thus taken an intermediate position between those who argue for the sole responsibility of IOs (e.g. the EU, through the European Commission)[4] and those who claim that the transparent nature of IOs call for the responsibility of its Member States in every situation.[5] By virtue of the rules of responsibility that are examined later, each different situation that gives rise to responsibility will vary depending on the manner in which an internationally wrongful act was committed. While in principle it should be welcomed that the ILC has accepted that under certain circumstances the responsibility might be shared between an IO and a State as it would be between multiple States under the ASR,[6] as it is shown in what follows, the general scope of articles 19 and 63 ARIO is

[3] This is the exact wording of article 16. Article 30 reproduces it but omits the reference to the IOs since the chapter relates to the responsibility of States.

[4] See: ILC, 'Responsibility of International Organizations: Comments and Observations Received from International Organizations' (14 February 2011) UN Doc A/CN.4/637.

[5] Ian Brownlie, 'The Responsibility of States for the Acts of International Organizations' in Maurizio Ragazzi (ed), *International Responsibility Today: Essays in Memory of Oscar Schachter* (Martinus Nijhoff 2005).

[6] On the issue of joint responsibility and the ASR, see: Helmut Philipp Aust, *Complicity and the Law of State Responsibility* (Cambridge University Press 2011).

not exempt from raising application issues, especially when dealing with the joint responsibility of an IO and one of its Member States.

3.3 Responsibility of the IO in Connection with an Act of a State

The notion of responsibility of an international subject as a consequence of an act committed by another international subject is not new. The ASR already foresaw that possibility in its articles 16 to 19. Those provisions reflected the fact that 'often the internationally wrongful act results from the collaboration of several States rather than of one State acting alone'.[7] This fact, as SR Gaja acknowledged in his third report, is also extendable to IOs.[8] However, due to the special relationship established between the IO and its Member States, there might be situations where the rules regulating the responsibility of an IO in connection with an act of a State will not provide the most adequate solution. In that event another rule would be necessary to address that special relationship. Section 3.3.1 focuses on the first group of rules of responsibility of IO in connection with acts committed by another international subject, whereas Section 3.3.2 focuses on the second set of rules.

3.3.1 Responsibility of an IO for the Conduct of a State Irrespective of Whether the Latter Is a Member of the Former

Articles 14, 15 and 16 ARIO enshrine situations in which an IO participates in the commission of an internationally wrongful act by another subject irrespective of whether that subject is a member to the IO in question.[9] While article 14 ARIO, which sets the responsibility of an IO when it aids or assists in the commission of an internationally wrongful act, does not directly concerns situations of normative control, articles 15 and 16

[7] Comment 2 to Chapter IV, International Law Commission, 'Articles on the Responsibility of States for Internationally Wrongful Acts' in Report of the International Law Commission on the Work of its 53rd Session, UN Doc A/56/10 Chap. IV (2001) GAOR 56th Session Supp 10.

[8] ILC, 'Third Report on Responsibility of International Organizations, by Giorgio Gaja, Special Rapporteur' (13 May 2005) UN Doc A/CN.4/553 para. 10.

[9] ILC, 'Report of the International Law Commission on the Work of Its 61st Session' (4 May–5 June and 6 July–7 August 2009) UN Doc A/64/10. For a general overview of the issues of joint responsibility in international law, see: *Aust*, (n 6); Olivier Corten, 'La "complicité" dans le Droit de la responsabilité internationale: un concept inutile?' [2011] LVII Annuaire Française de Droit International 57.

ARIO, on account of the notions used to attribute responsibility, are more interesting for the scope of this study.[10]

3.3.1.1 Coercion and Normative Control

The purpose of article 16 ARIO is the regulation of the coercion that an IO might exercise over a State or another IO, to force them to commit an internationally wrongful act. The concept of coercion should be understood in such a way that the coerced subject has 'no effective choice but to comply with the will of the IO'.[11] In this regard, it should be pointed out that the lack of effective choice precludes the wrongfulness of the act for the coerced subject.[12] Therefore, article 16 ARIO shifts the responsibility of the act from the subject which actually committed it, to the IO that coerced the subject into the violation. Logically the responsibility would be attributed exclusively to the IO.

Moving to the question of the responsibility of an IO for acts of Member States when they are implementing the IO's *acquis*, could it be argued that the obligation on the Member States to implement an IO norm that is an internationally wrongful act is equivalent to coercion of the Member State to commit the violation? A positive answer to this question would not be consistent with the previous articles, in particular the general rule of attribution. Since, according to the ILC, normative control does not amount to de facto or effective control, it would not be logical to consider it coercion, which implies an even stronger level of control than that actually exercised.[13] Furthermore, article 16 ARIO does not require the act, if committed by the IO, to be an internationally wrongful act.[14]

10 In principle, the analogous wording of this provision with article 16 ASR determines that the concept of aid and assistance will work in a similar vein. Moreover, the concepts of aid and assistance do not require any situation of control or analogous concept. Thus, the IO would be in an equal-to-equal relation with the State or IO to which it is providing aid or assistance. ILC, 'Report of the International Law Commission on the Work of Its 57th Session' (2 May–3 June and 11 July–5 August 2005) UN Doc A/60/10 (2005) GAOR 60th Session Supp 10, 96. However, there are cases in which situations of aid and assistance concerning the EU and its Member States might arise: see Chapter 6.

11 Ibid.

12 Article 16 ARIO establishes: 'The act would, but for the coercion, be an internationally wrongful act of the coerced State or international organization.' *Mutatis mutandi*, in comment 4 to article 18 of the Articles on State Responsibility, the ILC notes that 'the equation of coercion with *force majeure* means that in most cases where article 18 is applicable, the responsibility of the coerced State will be precluded *vis-à-vis* the injured third State.'

13 Cf. James Crawford, *State Responsibility: The General Part* (Cambridge University Press 2013) 419.

14 ILC, *Report on the Work of Its 57th Session* 100.

3.3.1.2 Direction and Control

Nor does article 15 ARIO require the act, if committed by the IO, to be an internationally wrongful act. The latter provision, concerns the direction and control exercised over the commission of an internationally wrongful act, provides that:

> An international organization which directs and controls a State or another international organization in the commission of an internationally wrongful act by the State or the latter organization is internationally responsible for that act if:
>
> (a) That organization does so with knowledge of the circumstances of the internationally wrongful act; and
> (b) The act would be internationally wrongful if committed by that organization.

In the same way as article 16 ARIO revolves around the notion of coercion, article 15 ARIO focuses on the concept of 'direction and control'.[15] While the concept of coercion denotes a higher degree of control over a State or an IO than the concept of 'direction and control', that does not mean that all degrees of normative control could trigger the application of this provision. More specifically, even though the SR Gaja did not seem keen on widening the concept of control 'as to encompass normative control',[16] the ILC nevertheless understood that

> the adoption of a binding decision on the part of an international organization could constitute, under certain circumstances, a form of direction or control in the commission of an internationally wrongful act. The assumption is that the State or international organization which is the addressee of the decision is not given discretion to carry out conduct that, while complying with the decision, would not constitute an internationally wrongful act.[17]

15 For a critique of the ILC's concept of 'direction and control', see: August Reinisch, 'Aid or Assistance and Direction and Control between States and International Organizations in the Commission of Internationally Wrongful Acts' 7 International Organizations Law Review 63, 73.

16 It is worth mentioning that the SR's reasoning on the issue of the normative control as control in the sense of article 14 ARIO is not as straightforward as it might have been expected. As it has been mentioned earlier, the SR denied the possibility of considering the normative control as factual control. Notwithstanding, in his third report he seemed to be open for that possibility in certain situations. In particular he mentions 'cases in which the organization's power to bind member States through its decisions is accompanied by elements that ensure enforcement of those decisions, so that normative control would correspond in substance to factual control', Gaja, *Third Report on Responsibility of International Organizations* (n 8) 15.

17 See commentary 4 to article 15 ARIO. ILC, *Report on the Work of Its 57th Session* 98.

Hence, this provision could be relevant when speaking about the EU, its Member States, the implementation of EU law and the violation of an international obligation. Article 15 ARIO requires that the conduct attributable to the Member State should have, as a consequence, an internationally wrongful act, and that it should be a violation of an international obligation binding on both parties. In a mixed agreement scenario in which an EU Member State breaches an obligation enshrined in that agreement due to the implementation of a binding EU decision, the EU would be responsible by virtue of this provision. By contrast, in relation to a Union agreement, since the Member States would not be internally bound by the agreement, they could not commit the international wrongful act.[18] Consequently, by extension, the EU could not be responsible by virtue of article 15 ARIO. Thus, the EU, and any IO analogous to it, could be held responsible as a result of the normative control it exercises over its Member States only insofar as the Member States were also bound by international obligations being breached.

In addition, not every normative control situation would fall under this provision. The ILC requires that the Member State would have no discretion when acting.[19] The binding force of the instrument used to direct and control should be taken as the principal guideline that asserts Member States' lack of discretion. Thus, this provision could be considered to cover any responsibility deriving from a EU binding act insofar as it complies with the requisites enshrined within it. However, it should also be mentioned that the ILC in its commentary to article 17 ASR established a high threshold of direction and control to be met for the provision to apply:[20]

> The term 'controls' refers to cases of domination over the commission of wrongful conduct and not simply the exercise of oversight, still less mere influence or concern. Similarly, the word 'directs' does not encompass mere incitement or suggestion but rather connotes actual direction of an operative kind.[21]

Both the notions of 'oversight' and 'actual direction of an operative kind' seem to remit us to the concept of effective control which would not normally cover scenarios of normative control,[22] not even the EU's normative control. Therefore, the notion of binding force used by the ILC

[18] See article 2 ASR and article 4 ARIO.

[19] See commentary 4 to article 15 ARIO; ILC, *Report on the Work of Its 57th Session* 98.

[20] Reinisch, (n 15); Crawford, (n 13) 414.

[21] Commentary 7 to article 17 ARIO.

[22] See Chapter 2.

would amount to a sort of effective control,[23] which would not normally encompass the degree of oversight that normative control entails.

Once the responsibility of the IO has been established, the extent to which the Member State should also be responsible for that act must be established. While article 18 ARIO excludes the possibility of the IO bearing sole responsibility as a general rule, it has also been shown how article 15 ARIO expressly recognizes the sole responsibility of the IO when exercising coercion. Therefore, while in principle the notion of 'direct and control' would not exclude the joint responsibility of the IO and the State,[24] under certain circumstances, it could nonetheless be argued that since the notion of control and the lack of discretion give no scope for manoeuvre to the member of the IO, this could eventually create a situation of *force majeure*, precluding the wrongfulness of the Member State.[25] Yet, this second possibility would be very difficult to sustain, since article 16 ARIO explicitly precludes the wrongfulness of the coerced subject,[26] and the defence of superior orders does not exist in international law.[27]

3.3.2 The Responsibility of an IO for Its Decisions and Authorizations

The use of binding force as the criterion with which to establish the 'notion of direction and control' in situations of an IO's normative control over its Member States adds internal consistency to this section of the ARIO given the wording of article 17 (1) ARIO:

> An international organization incurs international responsibility if it circumvents one of its international obligations by adopting a decision binding member States or international organizations to commit an act that would be internationally wrongful if committed by the former organization.

Whereas the ILC points out that there is partial overlap between this provision and articles 15 and 16 ARIO,[28] that overlap gives it the appearance of a complementary provision which aims to regulate a similar situation

[23] Reinisch identifies an overlap between articles 7 and 15 ARIO: 'Given that the difference between such "effective control" leading to the attribution of another subject's acts and the high requirements for 'direction and control' over another subject's acts may be insignificant the future will have to show whether the distinction is workable in practice.' Reinisch, (n 15) 77.

[24] By virtue of article 19 ARIO.

[25] Crawford, (n 13) 417; José Manuel Cortés Martín, 'European Exceptionalism in International Law? The European Union and the System of International Responsibility' in Maurizio Ragazzi (ed), *Responsibility of International Organizations: Essays in Memory of Sir Ian Brownlie* (Martinus Nijhoff 2013) 194.

[26] See note 12. [27] Commentary 10 to article 17 ASR.

[28] Commentary 15 to article 17 ARIO.

but, due to the specific subjective circumstances, the situation covered by article 17 ARIO would not fall within the scope of article 15 and 16 ARIO. Thus, the provisions would apply on an alternative basis.[29] Unlike articles 15 and 16 ARIO in which the influence of the IO over its members forces the latter to commit an internationally wrongful act, article 17 (1) ARIO does not require a breach by an IO Member State of an international obligation with which it has agreed to comply. Instead, it requires that by virtue of a binding decision on a Member State, which obliges it to perform an act, the IO would avoid the responsibility that it would have incurred if it had performed that act itself.

The provision establishes two requisites for it to apply. First, the adoption of a binding decision by an IO would lead some or all of its members to commit an act that would be internationally wrongful if committed by the IO. Second, by doing so, it would circumvent one of its international obligations The second requisite could be seen as redundant, since the circumvention is already implicitly mentioned in the first requirement.[30] However, the ILC embeds in the concept of circumvention some intention on the part of the IOs to take advantage of the separate legal personality of its members to avoid compliance with an international obligation. According to the ILC, the evidence of such an intention will depend on the circumstances.[31] This reintroduction of a subjective element in the determination of responsibility that the law of responsibility had tried to move away from[32] will be difficult if not almost impossible to prove.[33]

[29] Commentary 5 to article 16 ARIO. ILC, *Report on the Work of Its 57th Session* 105. The ILC has interpreted article 16 (3) of the ARIO, which provides as follows: 'Paragraphs 1 and 2 apply whether or not the act in question is internationally wrongful for the member State or international organization to which the decision, authorization or recommendation is directed.'

[30] Niels Blokker, 'Abuse of the Members: Questions Concerning Draft Article 16 of the Draft Articles on Responsibility of International Organizations' [2010] 7(1) International Organizations Law Review 35, 42: 'To "circumvent" seems to mean: to "get round", to intentionally bypass and thereby escape a violation of an obligation. However, the first requirement already covers the idea that an organization is responsible for its decisions requiring members to do things that would be wrongful if carried out by the organization. Therefore: what does this add to the first requirement?'

[31] Commentary 4 to article 17 ARIO.

[32] Jean D'Aspremont, 'The Articles on the Responsibility of International Organizations: Magnifying the Fissures in the Law of International Responsibility' [2012] 9(1) International Organizations Law Review 15, 25.

[33] Nataša Nedeski and André Nollkaemper, 'Responsibility of International Organizations in Connection with Acts of States' [2012] 9(1) International Organizations Law Review 33, 48; Blokker, (n 30) 43.

Moving to the potential application of this provision to the EU, article 17 (1) ARIO has particular relevance to the EU's normative control, and more precisely to the scope for compliance with the international obligations that it has assumed, but its members have not. The obvious example would concern the implementation of a Union agreement by a Member State. As has been explained previously, the rules of attribution do not recognize the '*dédoublement fonctionnel*' of EU Member States' organs.[34] In addition, the EU can sign agreements that internationally would not bind its Member States. Therefore, the EU could issue a binding norm on its Member States that would violate an obligation of a Union agreement, and by virtue of the rules on attribution of the ARIO, it would not be responsible for that breach; nor would the Member States since they are not parties to the Union agreement.

Yet, the application of this provision to the EU's normative control would be limited due to the requirement of a subjective element introduced with the concept of circumvention. Consequently, given that some kind of *dolus* is required, it will be very difficult to prove the intent of the EU to violate an international obligation by way of its normative control. In short, it is difficult to foresee a scenario in which the EU knowingly makes use of the normative control it has over its members to avoid compliance with its international obligations and that it can be proved.[35]

Furthermore, article 17 ARIO does not finish in its first paragraph. Paragraph 2 provides that

> an international organization incurs international responsibility if it circumvents one of its international obligations by authorizing Member States or international organizations to commit an act that would be internationally wrongful if committed by the former organization and the act in question is committed because of that authorization.

The wording of this provision identifies another situation in which, although there is no binding decision, the responsibility is nonetheless attributed to the IO. In principle, the responsibility of an IO because of its authorization of a conduct should not be problematic since there is a decision by the IO that backs the conduct. For instance, in relation to the EU, it would be logical to hold the EU responsible for the breach of one of its international obligations, if that breach were a consequence

[34] See Chapter 2. [35] Cf. Blokker, (n 30) 43.

of State aid that was authorized by the European Commission. Ultimately, such authorization is another form of normative control insofar as it would have not been performed if the conduct had not been authorized.[36]

Finally, since article 17 ARIO does not require the member that committed the violation of the international obligation to be bound by it, the logical consequence should be the sole responsibility of the IO that circumvented one of its international obligations through its Member States.[37] Yet, this does not mean that the provision would not apply if the Member State were also bound by the international obligation. In those situations, following article 19 ARIO, the IO and the Member States that implemented the decision would be jointly responsible. While, in principle, article 17 ARIO provides a rule that would apply to breaches committed by EU Member States acting under the EU's normative control, the conceptual difference between the rules of attribution and the rules of responsibility shows that these rules do not take into account the special features of the EU's normative control.[38] The ancillary nature of the rules of responsibility[39] shows that the ARIO does not consider that IOs, and the EU among them, should bear responsibility for the wrongful acts committed under its normative control.

On the contrary, the rules of responsibility show that only inasmuch as an internationally wrongful act can be attributed to a State, the responsibility of the IO would be a secondary issue. Against this background, the responsibility of the EU will most likely always be linked to the prior establishment of the responsibility of its Member States. Even though this outcome is fully consistent with the rationale underpinning these provisions, one cannot but wonder if certain situations should have taken much more into account the special nature of the bond between an IO, like the EU, and the Member States' organs that implement its *acquis*. More specifically, this should have been the case with article 17 ARIO which touches upon the basic elements of the nature of the relationship established between the IO and its Member States.

[36] See Chapter 7 for an example of such a situation.

[37] Article 9 of the ARIO and article 13 of the Articles on State Responsibility.

[38] Frank Hoffmeister, 'Litigating against the European Union and Its Member States – Who Responds under the ILC's Draft Articles on International Responsibility of International Organizations?' [2010] 21(3) European Journal of International Law 723, 727; Cortés Martín, (n 25) 194.

[39] Crawford, (n 13) 395.

3.4 State Responsibility in Connection with an Act of an IO

As in the previous section, in Part V of the ARIO, there are two different sets of norms. On one hand, the ILC regulates those situations in which a State can exercise some kind of control over an IO's commission of an internationally wrongful act regardless of whether it is a member of an IO. On the other, Part Five establishes Member States' responsibility for the instrumental use of an IO.

3.4.1 Framing the Question of the Responsibility of a State for the Acts of an IO

Before we enter into the analysis of how these provisions could impact on the EU's external activities, it is necessary to establish the state of the law and the art in relation to the State responsibility for IO actions. The provisions enshrined in Part V ARIO could be seen as the ILC's response to the debates on the secondary responsibility of the Member States of an IO for the acts of the latter.

Obviously, responsibility carries with it an obligation of reparation, which in many occasions will entail economic compensation of some sort. Therefore, it could be expected that both the IO and its Member States will try to avoid being held liable by each trying to hide behind the other. Since in certain situations IOs might not bound by the same international obligations as their Member States,[40] the possibility of an avoidance of responsibility by an IO or by its Member States through the use of the argument that the conduct should be attributed to the other, raises the spectre of all parties avoiding responsibility and no reparation at all.[41] The apparent dichotomy between autonomy of an IO and its lack of responsibility[42] is best shown by the fact that members of an IO might hide behind the IO personality to dodge their international obligations. The possibility of such a situation, along with other scenarios in which IOs have not lived up to their obligations, has raised the issue of the secondary responsibility of IOs' Member States for those breaches committed by an IO.

[40] This is, for instance, the case in relation to most international human rights treaties.

[41] Jan Klabbers, 'The Transformation of International Organizations Law' [2015] 26(1) European Journal of International Law 9, 82.

[42] Richard Collins and Nigel D. White, 'Moving beyond the Autonomy-Accountability Dichotomy: Reflections on Institutional Independence in the International Legal Order' [2010] 7(1) International Organizations Law Review 1.

3.4.1.1 The Race to the Bottom in International Responsibility

In theory, inasmuch as an IO is a different legal subject with its own functions and responsibilities, in a case brought against an IO member for the conduct of an IO, the members would typically argue that the distinct legal personality of the IO in question precludes the responsibility of the IO member. For instance, in the *Legality of Use of Force* case, the Netherlands argued that the alleged violation of the Genocide Convention could not be attributable to it, but to NATO.[43] In the same vein, the French government argued in the *Bankovic* case that the ECtHR lacked jurisdiction *ratio personae* insofar as 'the bombardment was not imputable to the respondent States but to NATO, an organisation with an international legal personality separate from that of the respondent States'.[44] Likewise, in *Berhami and Saramati*, the French government argued on the basis of the separate legal personality of the IO: 'The French contingent was placed at the disposal of KFOR which, from a security point of view, exercised effective control in Kosovo'.[45]

In a different scenario, the EU institutions have also retorted to a similar argumentation when pleading in the CJEU and the GC (at that time the CFI). In fact, cases such as *Kadi*[46] or *Yusuf*[47] show how the EU used, inter alia, the fact that it is implementing an international obligation stemming from another IO as an argument to justify human rights violations.[48]

43 *Legality of Use of Force (Serbia and Montenegro v Netherlands)* (Preliminary Objections of the Kingdom of the Netherlands) [2000] ICJ Written Proceedings para. 7.2.2.

44 *Banković et al. v Belgium, the Czech Republic, Denmark, France, Germany, Greece, Hungary, Iceland, Italy, Luxembourg, the Netherlands, Norway, Poland, Portugal, Spain, Turkey and the United Kingdom* (2002) 41 ILM 517, para. 32.

45 *Behrami and Behrami v France, Saramati v France, Germany and Norway* [2007] 45 EHRR SE10, para. 27.

46 Case C- 402/05 P and C-415/05 P *Yassin Abdullah Kadi, Al Barakaat International Foundation v Council of the European Union and Commission of the European Communities* [2008] ECR I-6351.

47 Case T-306/01 *Yusuf and Al Barakaat International Foundation v Council and Commission* [2005] ECR I-3533 para. 206.

48 Case C- 402/05 P and C-415/05 P *Yassin Abdullah Kadi, Al Barakaat International Foundation v Council of the European Union and Commission of the European Communities* para. 262. Although *Kadi* concerned the internal lawfulness of regulation implementing a UN Security Council Resolution, the arguments of the binding force of the UN obligations clearly resemble the arguments of the separate legal person of the IO. For instance, the Council put forward in *Kadi* the argument that 'so far as concerns the internal lawfulness of the contested regulation, the latter, inasmuch as it puts into effect resolutions adopted by the Security Council pursuant to Chapter VII of the Charter of the United Nations, in principle escapes all review by the Community judicature, even concerning observance of fundamental rights, and so for that reason enjoys immunity from jurisdiction.'

3.4.1.2 Responses to the Race to the Bottom: Secondary Responsibility and the Piercing of the IO's Veil

The previous cases show the tension that exists between different views on the autonomy of IOs. On one hand, insofar as IOs are just a manifestation of States' will to cooperate to achieve certain objectives, Member States should be responsible for the acts of the IO, a view that could be described as functionalist.[49] Therefore, if an IO breaches an international obligation (regardless of whether it is bound by it), its Member States should bear the responsibility.

This functionalist view is best exemplified by Brownlie, who argued in favour of Member States' responsibility for the acts of an IO. He considered that, in reference to the separate legal personality of an IO from its Member States,

> it cannot be reasonable to create a licence to harm the interests of third States by creating an international organization. There is surely a presumption, based upon public interest and ordinary logic, that, if the organization is not empowered to make reparation to third States, the Member States are under such a duty.[50]

Even though he overlooked, and to a certain extent neglected other rationales that inform the responsibility of IOs, such as the question of the allocation of powers and the international subjectivity of the organizations, Brownlie stresses in his argumentation the ultimate rationale that stems from the basic aim of State responsibility: providing reparations to the injured party.[51] Alvarez would also favour this functionalist approach to Member States' responsibility on the basis of policy reasons so States would 'devise internal mechanisms' to prevent their IOs from breaching international law and when breaches did occur provide

[49] Catherine Brölmann, 'International Organizations and Treaties' in Jan Klabbers (ed), *Research Handbook on International Organizations: Contractual Freedom and Institutional Constraint* (Edward Elgar 2011) 286; cf. Jan Klabbers, 'Contending Approaches to International Organizations: Between Functionalism and Constitutionalism' in Jan Klabbers and Asa Wallendahl (eds), *Research Handbook on the Law of International Organizations* (Edward Elgar 2011).

[50] Brownlie, (n 5) 359; cf. Sienho Yee, 'The Responsibility of State Members of an International Organization for Its Conduct as a Result of Membership or Their Normal Conduct Associated with Membership' in Maurizio Ragazzi (ed), *International Responsibility Today: Essays in Memory of Oscar Schachter* (Martinus Nijhoff 2005) 325; Moshe Hirsch, *The Responsibility of International Organizations towards Third Parties: Some Basic Principles* (Martinus Nijhoff 1995) 136.

[51] André Nollkaemper, 'Constitutionalization and the Unity of the Law of International Responsibility' [2009] 16(2) Indiana Journal of Global Studies 535, 536.

remedies.[52] However, while the policy considerations that support Alvarez's reasoning are valid, and signal an important issue in relation to IOs, i.e. their lack of accountability, the consideration of the piercing of the veil as a principle of general application, seems doubtful. Otherwise put, it would seem that the piercing of the veil and the complete disregard of the legal personality of an IO is a disproportionate stick to use to achieve better accountability within the IO.[53]

In a similar functionalist vein, although based on a completely different argument, D'Aspremont also favours the piercing of the institutional veil in those cases in which Member States abuse the IO's international legal personality through the exercise of excessive control over the decision-making process of the organization.[54] However, this excessive control, he argues, could hardly take place within the EU or the UN, but in an IO where there is no balance of power between the Member States.[55]

On the other hand, another set of views that could be described as constitutionalist[56] would argue that the separate legal personality of an IO would safeguard its Member States from any responsibility as a consequence of an act of the former. Since the moment Member States create a new IO with a different legal personality and a constituent instrument, they can only be responsible if the constituent agreement said so, and to the extent of the limits imposed by it.[57]

This was the position the *Institut de Droit International* took in its 1995 Resolution on the responsibility of Member States for the acts of an IO (the 1995 Resolution).[58] The 1995 Resolution was the consequence of an increased concern over the issue as it arose in the practice at the beginning

52 José E. Alvarez, 'Revisiting the ILC's Draft Rules on International Organization Responsibility' [2011] 105 Proceedings of the Annual Meeting (American Society of International Law) 344.

53 José Manuel Cortés Martín, 'The Responsibility of Members due to Wrongful Acts of International Organizations' [2013] 12(4) Chinese Journal of International Law 679, 681; José Antonio Pastor Ridruejo, 'La interrelación de los sistemas de protección de los derechos fundamentales' in Enrique Álvarez Conde and Vicente Garrido Mayol (eds), *Comentarios a la Constitución Europea*, vol 2 (Tirant Lo Blanch 2005) 1666.

54 Jean D'Aspremont, 'Abuse of the Legal Personality of International Organizations and the Responsibility of Member States' [2007] 4 International Organizations Law Review 91, 91.

55 Ibid. 56 Klabbers, (n 49) 13.

57 Chittaranjan Felix Amerasinghe, 'Liability to Third Parties of Member States of International Organizations: Practice, Principle and Judicial Precedent' [1991] 85 American Journal of International Law 259, 181.

58 IDI, 'The Legal Consequences for Member States of the Non-fulfilment by International Organizations of Their Obligations toward Third Parties' (Session of Lisbon, 1995).

of the 1990s.[59] However, an analysis of the practice at that time showed that there was no general rule supporting either Member States' responsibility, 'due solely to their membership' or their concurrent or subsidiary responsibility.[60]

The 1995 Resolution constitutes the perfect example of the constitutional approach towards IOs' legal personality and responsibility. No policy consideration, or legal rules, argues the *Institut de Droit International*, can undermine the veil of the IO. Moreover, there is only one exception that reinforces the constitutional approach of the 1995 Resolution. Article 6 of the 1995 Resolution provides that the rules of the IO determine 'the question of the liability of the members of an international organization for its obligations'.[61] In other words, Member States' responsibility as a consequence of their membership to an IO is only acceptable if the constituent Treaty creating it says so. Applied to the EU, this would mean that insofar as the EU Treaties are silent as regards its Member States' responsibility for the actions of the EU, it must be assumed, following this approach, that as a matter of principle, EU Member States cannot be held responsible as a consequence of their EU membership.

The support for a subsidiary liability has remained limited within international law because a regime of indirect responsibility takes for granted that an IO is by principle unable to meet its obligations.[62] Furthermore, it also assumes that Member States create IOs to avoid complying with their international obligations, and that it is for the IO and its Member States to prove otherwise.

The effectiveness of a legal system very much depends on the effectiveness of its responsibility rules, inasmuch as they are the mechanism that ensures effective compliance. The current practice regarding the

59 Cortés Martín, (n 53) 694. 60 IDI, (n 58).

61 Rosalyn Higgins, 'The Responsibility of States Members for the Defaults of International Organizations: Continuing the Dialogue' in Rosalyn Higgins (ed), *Themes and Theories: Selected Essays, Speeches, and Writings in International Law*, vol 2 (Oxford University Press 2009) 920. Moreover, the Internal Law Association confirmed in its *2004 Report on Accountability of International Organizations* that 'in the absence of a clause in the constitutive instrument, which excludes or limits the responsibility, it cannot be presumed that members are to be held accountable, unless there are evidences demonstrating that States or the international organization, by means of its acceptance, [gave reasons to assume otherwise].' ILA, 'Accountability of International Organizations' (Berlin Conference, May 2004).

62 Jan Klabbers, *An Introduction to International Institutional Law* (Cambridge University Press 2009) 288.

responsibility of IOs points to a struggle within international law. On one hand, the effectiveness of the responsibility rules is undermined by structural deficiencies: IOs are not parties to many international agreements to which their Member States are, opening possible responsibility gaps. But, on the other hand, there are no clear rules that address this situation. In this regard, the ILC's task of codifying and developing the rules regarding the responsibility of IOs should a priori be welcomed as not only a good initiative, but also a necessary one.

3.4.2 The Participation in the Decision-Making Process of an IO as Aid, Assistance, Control or coercion

Articles 58, 59 and 60 ARIO establish the States' responsibility for the same acts as 14, 15 and 16 ARIO but shift the position between the State and the IO. Due to their general phrasing, these provisions cover both situations where the State is member to the IO performing the internationally wrongful act, and where the State is not a member of the IO performing the internationally wrongful act. Thus, in those situations where the State is not a member of the IO committing the breach of an international obligation, the same arguments, doubts and concerns expressed in their mirror provisions of Chapter IV of Part Two will apply here.[63]

Yet, the relationship established between a State and IO as a consequence of the former being a member of the latter might alter the scope of the provisions. Due not only to the transparent nature of IOs, but also to the internal role that States play in the organs of an IO,[64] a Member State could be held responsible according to these provisions for the mere fact of being a member of the IO which has committed the internationally wrongful act.[65]

The ILC rightly does not accept that possibility. It considers that, when commenting on article 58 ARIO, 'a State does not *per se* incur international responsibility for aiding or assisting an international organization of which it is a member when it acts in accordance with the rules of the organization'.[66] Nevertheless, it does not rule out the possibility of holding Member States responsible for their participation in the

63 ILC, *Report on the Work of Its 61st Session* 160.

64 Henry G. Schermers and Niels M. Blokker, *International Institutional Law: Unity within Diversity* (4th edn, Martinus Nijhoff 2003) 51.

65 Yee, (n 50) 442; contra. Cortés Martín, (n 53) 688.

66 Yee, (n 50) 442; commentary 5 to article 58 ARIO.

decision-making of an IO. The ILC, as well as the SR,[67] contend that there are borderline cases, in which the coercion, the direction and control or the aid and assistance could be attributed to the Member State through their participation in the decision-making process of the organization.[68] In those cases, they argue 'the factual context such as the size of the membership and the nature of the involvement will probably be decisive'.[69]

While the size of the membership might not pose any more problems than the determination of how many members of an IO are necessary for one of them to coerce, or control, that IO, the 'nature of the involvement' raises more questions because of the concept's inherent indeterminacy. In relation to this issue, the *Institut de Droit International* proposed that one of the criteria to take into account when attempting to determine the liability of the member of an IO for the acts of the latter should be acquiescence.[70] Thus, it could be understood that a member is involved in the commission of wrongful act inasmuch as it agrees with it since nothing better shows acquiescence than a vote in favour of the adoption of the IO act which resulted in the breach of an international obligation. Could this logic be extended to argue that a Member State that votes for the adoption of an act that is internationally wrong is assisting, directing or even coercing the IO into its performance?

This issue has been the subject of an ongoing debate among international law scholars. According to Klein, Member States that voted for the adoption of an internationally wrongful act should be held responsible since they are collaborating in the violation of an international obligation.[71] Sarooshi also puts forward the idea that insofar as the act is committed the members are responsible since they did not stop the IO before it violated an international obligation.[72] These authors argue that

[67] ILC, 'Fourth Report on Responsibility of International Organizations, by Giorgio Gaja, Special Rapporteur' (28 February, 12 April and 20 April 2006) UN Doc A/CN.4/564, Add.1 and Add.2, para. 62.

[68] Commentary 4 to article 58 ARIO.

[69] ILC, *Report on the Work of Its 61st Session* para. 160.

[70] See article 5; IDI (n 58) 3. Against; Brownlie, (n 5) 355.

[71] Pierre Klein, *La responsabilité des organisations internationales dans les ordres juridiques internes et en droit de gens* (Bruylant 1998) 469. 'Le vote de chacun des membres, dans le mesure où il permet l'adoption par l'organisation d'une décision – par hypothèse – contraire aux obligations internationales de cette dernière apparaît en effet comme un acte par lequel un Etat apporte son assistance à l'organisation international dont il est membre pour la perpétration d'un fait internationalement illicite par celle-ci.'

[72] Dan Sarooshi, *International Organizations and Their Exercise of Sovereign Powers* (Oxford University Press 2005) 64; cf. Amerasinghe makes an *a contrario* reading of the idea of secondary responsibility of Member States of an IO: 'resting the outcome of the issue of

the transparent veil that covers IOs means that the mere act of voting constitutes a form of control or assistance in the commission of a wrongful act.

By contrast, some authors have argued that supporting the view that the Member States' vote constitutes assistance in the sense of article 58 ARIO denies the autonomous character of IOs, and more specifically its separate international legal personality.[73] This would not only undermine the autonomy of IOs by assuming that the Member States' *longa manus* controls every act of the IO,[74] but it also would contradict the characterization of IOs as international legal subjects. For instance, Jacqué has approached this issue from the perspective of the attribution of conduct. He states that, regardless of the manner in which its Member States have voted, the act of the IO is always attributable to it. He bases this argument on the idea that while a majority voting system accounts for a higher degree of autonomy for an IO, the voting within an IO is not an expression of the members' will but a procedure that cannot modify the nature of the act being adopted.[75]

Whereas the vote could be used to ascertain the acquiescence of the members of an IO, and subsequently to determine the nature of their involvement in the commission of an wrongful act, it should be interpreted in a restrictive manner, not only because of the consequences that it might entail for the legal personality of IOs, but more so because the scant case law which does exist on the issue of members' secondary responsibility appears to be contradictory.[76] Moreover, this case law on Member States' responsibility for an act of an IO does not focus on whether Member States' responsibility stems from the way they voted within the IO's organs, but rather focuses on the secondary responsibility of the Member States as a result of their membership.[77] Consequently, it would be

concurrent or secondary liability on the theory that state members are responsible for the decisions of the organization in one way or another may not only involve a fictitious assumption of participation in decision making, but also raise the question why the minority that is against a certain decision should be held in the same way as the majority,' Amerasinghe, (n 57) 274.

73 José Manuel Cortés Martín, *Las Organizaciones Internacionales: Codificación y Desarrollo Progresivo de su Responsabilidad Internacional* (Instituto Andaluz de Administración Pública 2008) 301.

74 Rolando Quadri, 'Cours général de droit international public' [1964] 113 Recueil de Cours de la Académie du Droit International 237, 477.

75 Jean Paul Jacqué, *Elements pour un théorie de l'acte juridique en droit international public* (L.G.D.J. 1972) 362. Cf René-Jean Dupuy, 'Le droit des relations entre les organisations internationales' [1960] 100 Recueil de Cours de la Académie du Droit International 544.

76 Cortés Martín, (n 73) 303.

77 Cortés Martín, (n 53).

almost impossible to establish that insofar as an EU Member State voted within the Council in favour of certain action which resulted in breach of an international obligation, that Member State has some responsibility under article 58 ARIO.

3.4.3 *Responsibility in Case of Provision of Competence to an IO*

Member States' responsibility for the acts of an IO does not stop at the possibility of considering Member States' actions within the IO as a way of controlling, aiding or coercing the IO. The ILC codifies another two situations in which a State could be responsible for the actions of an IO: articles 61 and 62 ARIO.

Likewise, article 17 ARIO aimed to regulate the circumvention of international law through the IO's normative control over its Member States, article 61 ARIO, called '*Circumvention of international obligations of a State member of an international organization*' aims to establish the responsibility of the member of an IO when they used the latter to circumvent their international obligations. This has been one of the most debated provisions of the ARIO and has suffered plenty of modifications throughout the codification process.[78] As it stands today, article 61 ARIO reads as follows:

> 1. A State member of an IO incurs international responsibility if, by taking advantage of the fact that the organization has competence in relation to the subject matter of one of the State's international obligations, it circumvents that obligation by causing the organization to commit an act that, if committed by the State, would have constituted a breach of the obligation.
> 2. Paragraph 1 applies whether or not the act in question is internationally wrongful for the IO.

Two main comments can be made to the final version of this provision: a first comment on the use of the concept of circumvention, and a second related to the on the legal policy considerations underpinning this provision.

Starting with the notion of circumvention, article 61 ARIO is a reflection of article 17 ARIO due partially to the use of the term 'circumvention' in both of the provisions. When speaking about article 17 ARIO, the introduction of that term was highly problematic since it reintroduces a subjective

[78] For an overview of the different modifications and the reactions to each version see: Odette Murray, 'Piercing the Corporate Veil: The Responsibility of Member States of an International Organization' [2011] 8(2) International Organizations Law Review 291.

element from which rules on international responsibility had departed. Yet, this does not mean that even a notion of circumvention based on objective factors would be a better solution concerning not only article 17 ARIO but also, especially, article 61 ARIO. More specifically, a notion of circumvention devoid of intent would broaden the scope of application of the latter provision. For instance, the lack of any specific intent to circumvent an international obligation by providing competence to an IO could lead to a situation in which, as a general rule, a member could be held responsible simply for the fact of being a member of an IO which was correctly exercising its competences, and had no special interest in breaching the international obligation which bound its member.[79] Therefore, Member States' responsibility by virtue of article 61 ARIO necessarily involves some level of intent to circumvent an international obligation that binds the State.

The question then will be to determine to what extent the commission of an act was an *unwitting result* of the State's behaviour within the IO.[80] While there is no doubt that this provision will cover any situation relating to the 'abuse of rights' or bad faith of a Member State,[81] any other situation to which this provision may apply in principle should take into account the participation of the member violating its international obligation. Even though the issues concerning how circumvention would be proved would still persist, this interpretation of the term 'circumvention' would reduce the scope of application of article 61 ARIO. Only the clearest examples of an instrumental use of an IO to breach international law would be covered by this provision.[82] The examples put forward by the SR seem to point into this direction, like the *ad hoc* creation of a shell IO to breach the obligations contained in article 61 ARIO.[83]

In relation to the second criticism concerning the legal policy considerations, there is an underlying '*solange*' rationale enshrined in the provision, and the explicit reference to the *Bosphorus* case[84] made in the commentary seems reinforce this view.[85] In *Bosphorus*, the ECtHR analysed the extent to which a EU Member State could be held responsible for a violation of

[79] Commentary 2 to article 61 ARIO.

[80] Esa Paasivirta, 'Responsibility of a Member State of an International Organization: Where Will It End? Comments on Article 60 of the ILC Draft on the Responsibility of International Organizations' [2010] 7(1) International Organizations Law Review 49, 59.

[81] ILC, *Report on the Work of Its 61st Session* 163.

[82] Paasivirta, (n 82) 53.

[83] Gaja, *Fourth Report on Responsibility of International Organizations* (n 67) Add. 1 para. 68.

[84] ECtHR, *Bosphorus Hava Yollari Turizm Ve Ticaret Anonim Şirketi v Ireland* [2006] 42 EHRR 1.

[85] Commentaries 3–5 to article 61 ARIO.

the ECHR committed under the EU's normative control. Given the fact that the EU is not a party to the ECHR, the ECtHR understood that, as long as the EU provided protection equivalent to that of the ECHR, Member States would not be responsible for the acts of the EU. However, instead of following the ECtHR, by establishing a two-step analysis of the responsibility of the EU's Member States for acts of the EU through the *iuris tantum* presumption of equivalent protection,[86] the ILC directly assumed that, if there is a breach of an international obligation, responsibility has to be attributed. The article responds to the idea that there are situations where the institutional veil of the IO is an excuse for Member States to avoid the obligations that they assumed in international agreements to which the IO is not a party. However, by omitting the first part of the '*solange*' test, i.e. whether the IO provides equivalent protection to that provided under the international regime the IO has breached, the provision adopts an extreme functionalist view of the IO.

Furthermore, factual scenarios in which this debate has arisen are rather exceptional. The only practice regarding this issue can be found in ECtHR case law. The Strasbourg Court has followed an unequivocal line of reasoning in its judgment on the responsibility of IOs (which always deny the possibility of piercing the institutional veil and subsequently the application of this provision). For instance, in *Bosphorus*, it used the '*solange*' doctrine so as to understand that as long as the EU provides equivalent protection to that of the ECHR, its Member States are not responsible for the EU's acts under the ECHR. In *Senator Lines*,[87] it denied the claim based on procedural issues. The Court understood that companies, such as Senator Lines, are not entitled to bring cases to the ECtHR. In *Berhami* and *Saramti*,[88] it denied the claim based on the lack of jurisdiction *ratio personae*. Since a subject – the UN – which is not a party to the ECHR, committed the violations, the Court could not exercise jurisdiction. Finally, in *Bankovic*,[89] it denied the claim based on a lack of jurisdiction *ratio loci*. In this case, Bankovic and others brought a claim against the NATO Member States that were parties to the ECHR over the bombing of Serbia by NATO

86 *Bosphorus Hava Yollari Turizm Ve Ticaret Anonim Şirketi v Ireland. Judgment of 30 June* para. 156.

87 ECtHR, *Senator Lines GmbH v Austria, Belgium, Denmark, Finland, France, Germany, Greece, Ireland, Italy, Luxembourg, the Netherlands, Portugal, Spain, Sweden and the United Kingdom* [2004] 39 EHRR SE3.

88 *Behrami and Behrami v France, Saramati v France, Germany and Norway.*

89 *Bankovic et al v Belgium, the Czech Republic, Denmark, France, Germany, Greece, Hungary, Iceland, Italy, Luxembourg, the Netherlands, Norway, Poland, Portugal, Spain, Turkey and the United Kingdom* [2002] 41 ILM 517.

forces. The ECtHR interpreted its jurisdiction by applying strict territorial limits. Insofar as Serbia was not a party of the ECHR, any violation committed there, irrespective of whether it had been committed by an ECHR Member, was out of the court's territorial jurisdiction. Article 61 ARIO tries to codify an aspiration of the international legal system since, in the previously mentioned case law, the ECtHR has never held a Member State responsible for the acts of an IO.[90]

Against this background, only the CJEU has incidentally mentioned the possibility of Member States' responsibility for acts of an IO in the *Eurocontrol* case.[91] In this preliminary ruling, the CJEU had to determine whether Eurocontrol, an IO in charge of establishing and collecting charges levied on users of air navigation services, constituted an undertaking in the sense of EU's competition rules. When assessing to what extent Eurocontrol was exercising public authority, the CJEU made the following statement:

> Eurocontrol acts in that capacity on behalf of the Contracting States without really having any influence over the amount of the route charges. Responsibility for the fact, relied upon by SAT before the national court, that the amounts of the charges vary in time or with respect to the areas overflown, cannot be attributed to Eurocontrol, which merely establishes and applies a common formula in the circumstances set above, but to the Contracting States which set the amount of the rates per unit.[92]

Thus, the CJEU seems to be denying Eurocontrol's autonomous nature, since it establishes that, when collecting the levies, it is acting on behalf of its contracting parties.[93] By contrast, it could nonetheless be argued that the Court's interpretation of Eurocontrol's powers show that Eurocontrol does not exercise any kind of normative control over its contracting parties. In fact, as it is envisaged in its constituent instrument, it does not have the competence to fix route charges in its specified functions. Each Eurocontrol member individually establishes its own rates for the use of its airspace. Then a single charge, making up the sum of the charges, is calculated and collected by Eurocontrol for each flight. The charged are collected on behalf of the Contracting States to whom they are paid.[94] Therefore, the CJEU is not piercing the veil of Eurocontrol with that statement. More specifically, it is acknowledging the functional nature

[90] Cf. Cedric Ryngaert, 'Oscillating between Embracing and Avoiding Bosphorus: The European Court of Human Rights on Member State Responsibility for Acts of International Organizations and the Case of the EU' [2014] 39 European Law Review 176.

[91] Case C-364/92 *SAT Fluggesellschaft mbH v Eurocontrol* [1994] ECR I-43.

[92] Ibid.

[93] Cortés Martín, (n 73) 309.

[94] C-364/92 *SAT Fluggesellschaft mbH v Eurocontrol* 23.

of Eurocontrol by way of establishing that the power to fix charges still rests within its contracting parties' powers and not Eurocontrol. In other words, Eurocontrol could not be responsible because the powers to establish route charges have not been transferred to it. Therefore, the conduct of fixing the charges to be levied on users of air navigation services could not be attributed to Eurocontrol, but to the contracting parties who had fixed those charges and retained that competence.

In relation to the potential application of this provision to the EU, it is worth noting that its application to mixed or Union agreements would not be possible, in view of the fact that the EU would be bound by the international obligation which in principle it would be violating. Hence, it could only be applied to situations where the EU cannot become a member of the agreement either because it has no external competence on the issue, or due to the fact that that the agreement is only open to States. The EU is in this complicated situation not only in relation to the ECHR but also in relation to other international agreements or organizations, like the International Civil Aviation Organization (ICAO), for instance. Therefore, given a situation in which the EU exercises its conferred powers in an issue in which the ICAO has also competence, an EU Member State could be in a situation in which both IOs would issue contradicting norms in the field of civil aviation. Members of both organizations would have to decide to apply one over the other, for instance the EU norm over the ICAO one. Thus they would be violating their commitments under the ICAO. In this situation, where there are two conflicting norms and a breach of one of them as a consequence of an obligation laid down in the other, article 60 could apply. Therefore, by virtue of this provision, the EU's international personality should be completely disregarded and the EU's Member States should be held responsible for an act of the EU that contradicts the ICAO.[95]

Moving to article 62 ARIO, this provision envisages another scenario in which a State could be held responsible for an act of an IO. Article 62, entitled 'Responsibility of a State member of an international organization for an internationally wrongful act of that organization' reads as follows:

[95] This situation took place in the Hushkits dispute within the ICAO. – 'Admissibility of US–EU "Hushkits" Dispute before the ICAO' [2001] 95(2) American Journal of International Law 410. Cf. Allan Rosas, 'International Dispute Settlement: EU Practices and Procedures' [2003] 46 German Yearbook of International Law 284, 312. Nevertheless the contrary situation cannot be excluded either. For instance, in the *Intertanko* case, the CJEU was asked if it was possible to interpret EU law in the light of the Marpol Convention, an agreement to which the EU is not a party. Case C- 308/06 *The Queen on the application of Intertanko and Others v Secretary of State for Transport* [2008] ECR I-4057.

1. A State member of an international organization is responsible for an internationally wrongful act of that organization if:
   (a) it has accepted responsibility for that act towards the injured party; or
   (b) it has led the injured party to rely on its responsibility.
2. Any international responsibility of a State under paragraph 1 is presumed to be subsidiary.

This provision raises two main comments: one regarding the necessity of this provision, and the other relating to the consequence of its application.

First, this article could be seen as redundant. Article 62 ARIO establishes the responsibility of a Member State of an IO insofar as the Member State accepts that responsibility, in the same way as article 11 ASR regulates the attribution of conduct to a State if it acknowledges the conduct as its own. While it should be acknowledged that the rules that attribute conduct and the rules that attribute responsibility constitute two different conceptual paths, any acceptance of responsibility of a State for an act of an IO could also be covered by that provision. Yet, since article 57 ASR appears to rule out that possibility, it could be argued that the scope of the will of a State to acknowledge a conduct as it own does not, regardless of the open wording of article 11 ASR, cover that conduct of IOs.

Furthermore, article 62 ARIO makes reference to the acceptance of responsibility. This concept cannot be found in any other provision of the ARIO, and to some extent it appears to be linked with the idea of acknowledgement. However, insofar as it speaks of responsibility, and not of attribution of conduct, the article seems to be aimed at situations in which a State does not want to acknowledge an act as its own but nevertheless wants to be held responsible when responsibility arises for the organization. This differentiation could be interpreted as being not only artificial, but also as highlighting the lacuna left by article 11 ASR, insofar as the acknowledgement of conduct is not the same as the acknowledgement of responsibility.

In relation to the shape that the acceptance can take, the ILC comments that the acceptance 'may be expressly stated or implied and may occur either before or after the time'.[96] Nevertheless, no practical examples exist in which a Member State has accepted responsibility, either explicitly or implicitly, for an IO act.[97]

96 Commentary 6 to article 62 ARIO.

97 Commentary 7 to article 62 ARIO only makes reference to the opinion of Lord Ralph Gibson in the Court of Appeals case concerning the International Tin Council which referred to acceptance of responsibility in the constituent document. *Maclaine Watson &*

The second comment to be made on article 62 ARIO concerns the subsidiary nature of its responsibility. The ILC does not explain on what grounds they decided the acceptance of responsibility of a Member State is subsidiary to the responsibility of the IO:

> Acceptance of responsibility by a State could relate either to subsidiary or to joint and several responsibility. The same applies to responsibility based on reliance. As a general rule, one could only state a rebuttable presumption. Also in view of the limited nature of the cases in which responsibility arises according to the present article, it is reasonable to presume that, when Member States accept responsibility, only subsidiary responsibility, which has a supplementary character, is intended.[98]

This reference to subsidiary responsibility shows how the whole article is not in principle aimed at regulating the responsibility of a State for the acts of an IO when it commits an internationally wrongful act, but rather at regulating the subsidiary liability of Member States for any breach committed by the IO when the IO is not exercising public authority functions. This provision specifically aims to regulate the issue of private responsibility. This can be easily derived from the cases used here as examples, since both of them relate to the breach of contracts with private individuals by the IO, not international obligations. The *International Tin Council* litigation addressed the liability of the members of that IO towards individuals with whom the Tin Council had concluded contracts.[99] Thus, this provision seems more applicable to possible IO breaches of municipal law breaches in its host State and its possible immunities, than to violations of international obligations.[100]

Part V of the ARIO regulating the responsibility of a State for the acts of an IO is a clear example of the kind of fundamental issues that the ILC has faced during the codification of the responsibility of IO: the lack of practice. There are not enough cases in which an international tribunal has held a Member State responsible for an act of an IO. Moreover, when

Co. Ltd v International Tin Council [1989] 3 All ER 523 172. This obiter dictum allows the SR to reflect upon the issue of implied and express acceptance, but no practice is put forward. ILC, *Report on the work of its sixty-first session* 169.

98 ILC, *Report on the work of its sixty-first session* 171; Commentary 13 to article 62 ARIO.

99 Romana Sadurska and C. M. Chinkin, 'The Collapse of the International Tin Council: A Case of State Responsibility?' [1990] 30 Virginia Journal of International Law 845; Amerasinghe, (n 57).

100 E.g. Italian Court of Cassation in its judgment No. 149, *Istituto Universitario Europeo v Piette*, 18 March 1999, *Giustizia civile*, vol 49 (1999) I-1309.

faced with this situation, the international tribunal avoids looking inside an IO to hold its member responsible. Therefore, international practice reflects the view that the international legal personality of an IO must prevail over other policy considerations.

Whereas the ILC cannot avoid answering these questions that have so long been discussed in international doctrine but so long avoided in international practice, its effort should be welcomed. In this regard, while the first three provisions might succeed in this effort, due to its broad wording, article 61 ARIO could pose more problems than it would solve.[101]

3.5 *Lex Specialis* Rule and the EU's Normative Control

In article 64 ARIO, entitled '*Lex Specialis*', the ILC envisages the possibility of special rules covering the same areas as the ARIO.[102] The provision accepts the possibility of understanding the 'rules of the organization applicable to the relations between the international organization and its member' as *lex specialis*, by which an IO could put aside the application of the ARIO.[103] First, the ARIO expressly mentions the possibility for more specialized rules of attribution to exist besides those it has codified.[104] More specifically, the ILC signals that a special rule of attribution might exist in relation to the EU, and 'other potentially similar organizations'.[105] Second, according to the ILC, by virtue of this special rule of attribution, the breaches committed by Member States of the EU when implementing EU law should be attributed to the EU.

It could be argued that the ILC is recognizing that a special rule of attribution based on normative control might exist in relation to the EU.[106]

101 Cf José Antonio Pastor Ridruejo, (n 53) 1655–1667.

102 Article 64 ARIO: 'These articles do not apply where and to the extent that the conditions for the existence of an internationally wrongful act or the content or implementation of the international responsibility of an international organization, or a State in connection with the conduct of an international organization, are governed by special rules of international law. Such special rules of international law may be contained in the rules of the organization applicable to the relations between an international organization and its members.'

103 Pieter Jan Kuijper, 'International Responsibility for EU Mixed Agreements' in Christophe Hillion and Panos Koutrakos (eds), *Mixed Agreements Revisited: The EU and Its Member States in the World* (Hart 2010) 222.

104 ILC, *Report on the Work of Its 61st Session* 173; Commentary 1 to article 64 ARIO.

105 Ibid; Commentary 2 to article 64 ARIO.

106 Hoffmeister, (n 38) 728; contra Cortés Martín, (n 25) 128; Christiane Ahlborn, 'The Rules of International Organizations and the Law of International Responsibility' [2011] 8(2) International Organizations Law Review 397, 452.

The ILC seems to establish that normative control based on a functional attribution. The EU would be responsible by virtue of article 64 ARIO for the conduct of EU Member States' organs insofar as they are acting as EU organs. The ILC's reference to the *WTO Panel Report on EC – Trademarks*[107] points in that direction.

> [The Panel Report] accepted the European [Union] explanation of what amounts to its *sui generis* domestic constitutional arrangements that [Union] laws are generally not executed through authorities at [Union] level but rather through recourse to the authorities of its Member States which, in such a situation, 'act *de facto* as organs of the [Union], for which the [Union] would be responsible under WTO law and international law in general.[108]

Under this provision, the attribution of conduct based on the EU's normative control would not stem from the mere fact that it has normative control, but the intensity of that normative control.[109] Inasmuch as all IOs exercise some degree of normative control over their Member States when acting within their sphere of competence, it is the lack of freedom that the normative control imposes that would determine the application of this provision in detriment of article 17 ARIO.

Besides this example, the ILC seems reluctant to recognize any practice regarding the attribution of conduct based on the normative control that an IO might exercise over its Member States. The ILC comments in the subsequent examples that, regardless of the WTO practice, the ECtHR has remarked that in any event the commission of a wrongful act committed under the EU's normative control would continue to be attributed to the EU Member State that performed it.[110] Conversely, leaving aside the criticisms concerning the ILC's preference of the ECtHR over the WTO

[107] WTO, *European Communities – Protection of Trademarks and Geographical Indications for Agricultural Products and Foodstuffs, Panel Report* (20 April 2005) WT/DS174/R.

[108] Ibid. For an analysis of the WTO practice in relation to the EU's responsibility, see Chapter 5. Also, Andrés Delgado Casteleiro and Joris Larik, 'The "Odd Couple": The Responsibility of the EU at the WTO' in Panos Koutrakos and Malcolm D. Evans (eds), *The International Responsbility of the European Union European and International Perspectives* (Hart 2013).

[109] Ahlborn, (n 106); Antonios Tzanakopoulos, *Disobeying the Security Council. Countermeasures against Wrongful Sanctions* (Oxford University Press 2011) 40. To better understand the intensity of the EU's normative control, see Chapter 1.

[110] Commentaries 5 and 6 to article 64 ARIO; cf. Daniel Müller, 'Union Européenne et Responsabilité International' in Myriam Benlolo-Carabot, Ukas Candas and Eglantine Cujo (eds), *Union Européenne et Droit International En l'honneur de Patrick Dlaillier* (Pedone 2012) 355.

Dispute Settlement System,[111] it is worth mentioning that the operation of normative control can be detected in the case law of the ECtHR.[112] As Tzanakopoulos shows, the ECtHR's jurisprudence effectively acknowledges that the Member State is under the normative control of the EU, given that it has no discretion in the implementation of the EU's measure and 'because reviewing the implementing act would amount to review of the decision of the [EU], the ECtHR invents a different standard of review (a very lax one at that) to avoid ever having to go into the issue'.[113] Though not directly, the ECtHR embeds a certain notion of normative control in its analysis of the attribution of conduct to an EU Member State when it implements EU law. Consequently, contrary to what the ILC has argued, the ECtHR would not in any event attribute the conduct to a Member State without taking into account the context of normative control in which that conduct was carried out.

To conclude, by the establishment of this *lex specialis* rule, the ILC seems to be trying to appease the criticisms of the EU during the codification exercise. Nevertheless, it is unclear whether article 64 ARIO could create enough legal space as to allow the further development of a *lex specialis* rule concerning the responsibility of the EU.[114] In this regard, it is submitted that, so far, increasingly the international practice while recognizing that the EU's normative control entails the international responsibility of the EU, it is still fleshing out the details of how such a special rule would operate, as well as its scope of application.

3.6 Concluding Remarks

The ARIO provides a set of rules that could be applied to the EU. However, in some cases, the broad wording of the provisions may yield undesired results, such as article 61 ARIO. Furthermore, as has been seen in some recent cases, International Courts have had problems in correctly applying its provisions,[115] and are developing the rules of responsibility of IOs in a

[111] Pieter Jan Kuijper, 'Amsterdam Center for International Law. Introduction to the Symposium on Responsibility of International Organizations and of (Member) States. Attributed or Direct Responsibility or Both?' [2010] 7(1) International Organizations Law Review 9, 18; Hoffmeister, (n 38).

[112] Tzanakopoulos, (n 109) 42; Hoffmeister, (n 38) 734.

[113] Tzanakopoulos, (n 109) 43; cf. Kuijper, (n 103) 217.

[114] Kuijper, (n 103) 223.

[115] *Behrami and Behrami v France, Saramati v France, Germany and Norway*. Marko Milanović and Tatjana Papić, 'As Bad as It Gets: The European Court of Human Rights' *Behrami and Saramati* Decision and General International Law' [2009] 58(2) International and Comparative Law Quarterly 267.

direction which the SR and the ILC do completely not agree with.[116] This is perhaps one of the main shortcomings of the codification project. The different situations which give rise to responsibility, which the ARIO aims to regulate, combined with the heterogeneity of the subject to which it applies, can give rise to multiple and contrasting applications of the same rules.

In particular, the rules of responsibility of States for the acts of an IO can be problematic. On one hand, they are not based on a great deal of international practice,[117] and on the other, the consequences that these provisions entail may seem disproportionate to the initial wrongful acts. In this regard, while piercing the veil of the IO should be seen as the last resort,[118] it is not entirely clear whether the ARIO agrees with the exceptional circumstances in which the responsibility of Member States for acts of IOs should be recognized.

Furthermore, the ARIO tries to shed some light on some issues concerning the EU's responsibility in a mixed agreement situation. By virtue of these articles, the subject responsible for the commission of an internationally wrongful act can be identified regardless of the division of competences. By identifying the most common situations in which an IO can breach an international obligation, a third party to a mixed agreement could easily target the responsible subject on the EU side of the agreement. Furthermore, by establishing the possibility of holding both the EU and the Member State that committed the breach jointly responsible in cases of normative control (article 17 ARIO), the ARIO favours the possibility of bringing claims against the EU. However, from an EU perspective, joint responsibility as the consequence of an act performed by one of its Member States under its normative control could be seen as an odd outcome. To a certain extent, it implies a breach of the EU's international legal personality inasmuch as a Member State is functionally acting as an EU organ. Therefore, according to the ARIO, a violation of a mixed agreement committed by a Member State authority when implementing EU law, would invoke the joint responsibility of the Member

[116] See Commentary 10 to article 7 ARIO. The SR considers 'as a matter of policy, the approach taken by the European Court of Human Rights is unconvincing' and considers that '[w]ithout denying the importance of this jurisprudence, it would be difficult to accept, simply on the strength of the judgment in *Behrami and Saramati*, the criterion there applied as a potentially universal rule.' ILC, 'Seventh Report on Responsibility of International Organizations, by Giorgio Gaja, Special Rapporteur' (27 March 2009) UN Doc A/CN.4/610); Giorgio Gaja, *Seventh Report on Responsibility of International Organizations* (2009) para. 30.

[117] Alvarez (n 52). [118] Cf. Murray, (n 78).

State and the EU. Such a result is inconsistent with the idea of the IO as an international subject distinct from its Member States. Conversely, in relation to Union agreements, identical facts would lead to situations in which the State would not be responsible but nevertheless the EU would due to its normative control. In any case, the introduction of a subjective element through the concept of circumventions makes it more difficult (if not impossible) to establish responsibility by virtue of article 17 ARIO.

This chapter has shown how the ARIO, although providing a comprehensive set of rules concerning the responsibility of IOs, does not contain any rule that could easily apply to situations of normative control. While it leaves the door open for this rule to be established through the notion of *lex specialis*, the hypothetical application of these provisions could not only put EU Member States in a position in which they would have to choose between complying with the judgment of an international court or with EU law, but also undermine the separate legal international personality of the EU.

4 EU Declarations of Competence to Multilateral Agreements

A Useful Internal Reference Base?

4.1 Introduction

The joint participation of the EU and its Member States in an international agreement blurs the extent of the rights and obligations governed by the agreement.[1] The use of this mixed formula can create situations of uncertainty for third parties since it avoids the question of the division of competence between the EU and its Member States in matters governed by the mixed agreement.[2] The desire of third parties to a mixed agreement to know the scope of the competence and the responsibility of the EU and its Member States has been the driving force behind a specific treaty-making practice developed by the EU in the framework of multilateral agreements.[3] Within these multilateral conventions, third parties want to know beforehand who is voting (to avoid a double exercise of

[1] See Chapter 1. Cf. Ruling 1/78 *Re: Draft Convention of the International Atomic Energy Agency on the Physical Protection of Nuclear Materials, Facilities and Transport* [1978] ECR 2151, para. 35. Cf. C. D. Ehlermann, 'Mixed Agreements: A List of Problems' in D. O'Keeffe and H. G. Schermers (eds.) *Mixed Agreements* (Kluwer Law and Taxation 1983) 3–21.

[2] See: R. Schütze, 'Federalism and Foreign Affairs: Mixity as a (Inter)national Phenomenon' in C. Hillion and P. Koutrakos (eds), *Mixed Agreements in EU Law Revisited: The EU and Its Member States in the World* (Hart 2010) 81. Cf. J. Groux, *The European Communities in the International Order* (Commission of the European Communities 1985) 325; J. Roldán Barbero, 'La CEE y el Convenio sobre Derecho del Mar de 1982: consideraciones sobre la relación entre el Derecho de Comunitario y el Derecho Internacional' [1991] 18(2) *Revista de Instituciones Europeas* 551; J. Temple Lang, 'The Ozone Layer Convention: A New Solution to the Question of Community Participation in "Mixed" International Agreements' [1986] 23 CML Rev 157; J. Heliskoski, *Mixed Agreements as a Technique for Organizing the International Relations of the European Community and Its Member States* (Kluwer Law International 2001).

[3] F. Hoffmeister, 'Curse or Blessing? Mixed Agreements in the Recent Practice of the European Union and Its Member States' in C. Hillion and P. Koutrakos (eds), *Mixed Agreements in EU Law Revisited: The EU and Its Member States in the World* (Hart 2010) 259.

voting rights); who is implementing (to ensure compliance); and, more importantly; who is responsible for a breach of the agreement (even before an internationally wrongful act has been committed): the EU and/or its Member States?[4] In response to these concerns, the EU makes a declaration when concluding the mixed agreement delimiting the extent to which the international agreement falls within EU competence.[5] In other words, declarations of competence are an attempt to apportion responsibilities within a multilateral agreement based on who has competence (the EU and/or its Member States) over issues covered by specific provisions of the multilateral agreement.

These declarations of competence externalize an internal matter (i.e. the vertical division of competences).[6] Moreover, the vertical division of competences is one of the most complex and debated issues in EU external relations law, not only among scholars,[7] but also among the EU institutions.[8]

Initially, declarations of competence were supported by neither the Commission[9] nor the CJEU.[10] In their view, the distribution of competences should have remained an internal issue. However, in recent years both the Commission and the CJEU have gradually accepted the possibility of clarifying the internal division of competences to third parties to mixed agreements. The Commission has learned to recognize that third parties might require a declaration of competence from the EU

[4] P. J. Kuijper, *Of 'Mixity' and 'Double-Hatting': EU External Relations Law Explained* (Amsterdam University Press 2008) 12.

[5] A list of the declarations of competence made by the EU can be found at the European Commission Treaty Office Database: http://ec.europa.eu/world/agreements/view Collection.do.

[6] The vertical division of competences concerns the division of competences between the EU and its Member States. By contrast, the horizontal division of competences concerns the division of competence between the different EU institutions. E. Neframi, *L'action extérieure de l'Union européenne. Fondements, moyens, principes* (LGDJ 2010) 79.

[7] For a recent and complete overview see: P. Eeckhout, *EU External Relations Law* (Oxford 2011) 11–163; E. Neframi, (n 6), 21–75; M. Cremona, 'External Relations and External Competence of the European Union: The Emergence of an Integrated Policy' in Paul Craig and Gráinne de Burca (eds), *The Evolution of EU Law* (2nd edn, Oxford University Press 2010) 217–268.

[8] Some recent examples: Case C-246/07 *Commission v Sweden (PFOS)* [2010] ECR I-3317; Opinion 1/08 *GATS* [2009] ECR I-11129; Case C-45/07 *Commission vs. Greece (IMO)* [2009] ECR I-701; Opinion 1/03 *Competence of the Community to conclude the new Lugano Convention on jurisdiction and the recognition and enforcement of judgments in civil and commercial matters* [2006] ECR I-1145.

[9] I. Macleod, I. D. Hendry and S. Hyett, *The External Relations of the European Communities: A Manual of Law and Practice* (Clarendon 1996) 325.

[10] Ruling 1/78/EURATOM, *Nuclear Materials*, [1978] ECR 2151.

so it can conclude the agreement and it relies on them when pleading in Luxembourg.[11] Moreover, the CJEU has used them increasingly when interpreting mixed agreements,[12] and when dealing with complex external competence issues,[13] leading the Court to acknowledge that declarations of competence constitute 'a useful reference base'.[14]

Despite their gradual acceptance by the CJEU and the Commission, declarations of competence create uncertainty as regards their legal effects and effectiveness. This chapter examines these declarations from a practical perspective. The first section conceptualizes the declarations: first by establishing their basic features; second, by questioning which are their legal effects; and third, by identifying a list of problems attached to these instruments. The second section focuses on both internal and external practice regarding declarations of competence. The section puts forward some recent developments concerning the use of declarations of competence in the CJEU. The third section provides a set of conclusions assessing the overall effectiveness of the declarations balanced with the problems that they entail.

4.2 Declarations of Competence: An Attempt at Conceptualization

4.2.1 *Basic Features of Declarations of Competence*

4.2.1.1 Basic Content of the Participation Clauses Which Enshrine the Obligation of Making a Declaration of Competence

Declarations of competence are designed to comply with the conditions established in the participation clause of an international agreement to

[11] European Commission. Non-Paper, Disconnection Clauses (on file with the author). While disconnection clauses and declarations of competences are completely different instruments, they are part of the toolbox that the EU uses when dealing with the concerns of third parties. See: Jan Klabbers, *Treaty Conflict and the European Union* (Cambridge University Press 2009). Marise Cremona, 'Disconnection Clauses in EU Law and Practice' in Christophe Hillion and Panos Koutrakos (eds), *Mixed Agreement Revisited* (Hart 2010) 160–186. Jan Klabbers, 'Safeguarding the Organizational Acquis: The EU's External Practice' [2007] 4 (1) International Organizations Law Review 57. Loïc Azoulai, 'The Acquis of the European Union and International Organizations' [2005] 11 (2) European Law Journal 196.

[12] Case C-240/09 *Lesoochranárske zoskupenie VLK v Ministerstvo zivotného prostredia Slovenskej republiky (LZ)* [2011] ECR I-01255. Case C-459/03 *Commission vs. Ireland (MOX Plant)* [2006] ECR I-4635.

[13] E.g. Case C-246/07 *Commission v Sweden (PFOS)* [2010] ECR I-3317; Case C-29/99 *Commission v Council (Convention on Nuclear Safety)* [2002] ECR I-11221; Case C-94/03 *Commission v Council (Rotterdam Convention)* [2006] ECR I-1; Opinion 2/00 *Cartagena Protocol* [2001] ECR I-9713.

[14] Case C-459/03 *Commission vs. Ireland (MOX Plant)*, para. 109.

which the EU and its Member Sates intend to become parties. In other words, participation clauses are those provisions of an international agreement establishing the conditions under which an IO can participate in that international agreement.[15] They do this in two ways. First, the agreement can be opened to IOs without establishing any condition besides the signature and the ratification of the agreement. Second, the international agreement may establish some requisites for the accession of the IO. These requisites are typically due to the mixed nature of the agreement. For instance, the international agreement might require the IO to make a statement on the division of powers between the IO and its Member States (declaration of competence), or on the management of voting rights.[16] Participation clauses requiring a declaration of competence have most often been used in multilateral conventions which cover issues related to environmental law.[17]

The existence of a declaration of competence always responds to the exigency envisaged in an international agreement clarifying the distribution of competence between an IO and its Member States. There are no cases in which the EU (or any other IO) has made a declaration of competence without the agreement expressly requiring it to do so.

Although it is not explicitly recognized, participation clauses are designed with the EU and its Member States in mind. Since the United Nations Convention for the Law of the Seas (UNCLOS), international agreements have opted to refer to a particular category, such as Regional Economic Integration Organization (hereinafter REIO), instead of a general one, like IO, or the specific name of the organization.[18] These provisions

[15] J. J. Feenstra, 'A Survey of the Mixed Agreements and Their Participation Clauses' in D. O'Keeffe and H. G. Schermers (eds) *Mixed Agreements* (Kluwer Law and Taxation 1983) 207–248.

[16] See: IAEA Convention on Nuclear Safety (adopted 17 June 1994, entry into force 24 October 1996) 1963 UNTS 293, Art 30 (4) (iv).

[17] E.g. Basel Convention on the Control of Transboundary Movements of Hazardous Wastes and Their Disposal (adopted 22 March 1989, entry into force 5 May 1992) 1673 UNTS 126; Convention on the Protocol and Use of Transboundary Watercourses and International Lakes (adopted 17 June 1999, entered into force 4 August 2005) 2331 UNTS 202; Cartagena Protocol on Biosafety to the Convention on Biological Diversity (adopted 29 January 2000, entered into force 11 September 2003) 2226 UNTS 208; Convention on the Transboundary Effects of Industrial Accidents (adopted 17 March 1992, entered into force 19 April 2000) 2105 UNTS 457; United Nations Convention to Combat Desertification in Those Countries Experiencing Serious Drought and/or Desertification, Particularly in Africa (adopted 14 October 1994, entered 26 December 1996) 1954 UNTS 3; United Nations Framework Convention on Climate Change (adopted 9 May 1992, entered into force 21 March 1994) 1771 UNTS 107.

[18] Temple Lang, (n3), 157–176.

establish the general obligation of declaring the extent of the competence when both the REIO and at least one of its Member States are parties to the agreement. Some participation clauses also establish subsidiary mechanisms to ensure that the declaration made by the REIO answers the question of the division of competences in a quick and trustworthy way.[19] For instance, Annex IX of the UNCLOS establishes, in the first place, the obligation of making 'a declaration specifying the matters governed by this Convention in respect of which competence has been transferred to the organization by its Member States which are Parties to this Convention'.[20] In addition, UNCLOS envisages a mechanism to force compliance with the obligation of making a declaration of competence.[21] Article 6 of Annex IX establishes that if the REIO and its Member States fail to provide clarification on the division of competence on a certain issue they will be subject to joint and several liability.

The importance of a subsidiary mechanism such as this must not be overlooked, as it is a good way to encourage the REIO and its Member States to clearly establish the distribution of competences. Thus, if they do not comply with this provision, the uncertainty over responsibility for implementation leads to joint liability of the REIO and its Member States.[22]

4.2.1.2 Common Formal Structure of Declarations of Competence

Despite the freedom given by participation clauses to REIOs on how to report their competences on matters related to the international agreement, the EU has developed a standard practice. All declarations of competence have a similar basic structure. First, declarations often begin by signalling the existence of an EU competence on the issue. For example, the declaration made pursuant to the Convention on Biological Diversity reads: 'In accordance with the relevant provisions of the [TFEU], the [Union]

[19] P. J. Kuijper, 'International Responsibility for EU Mixed Agreements' in C. Hillion and P. Koutrakos (eds), *Mixed Agreements Revisited: The EU and Its Member States in the World* (Hart 2010) 225.

[20] Article 5 (1) Annex IX UNCLOS.

[21] P. J. Kuijper and E. Paasivirta, 'Further Exploring International Responsibility: The European Community and the ILC's Project on Responsibility of International Organizations' [2004] 1 International Organizations Law Review 111.

[22] On the issue of joint liability of the EU and its Member States in multilateral environmental agreements see: A. Nollkaemper, 'Joint Responsibility between the EU and Member States for Non-Performance of Obligations under Multilateral Environmental Agreements' in Elisa Morgera and Gracia Marín Durán (eds), *The EU and International Environmental Law* (Cambridge University Press 2012).

alongside its Member States has competence to take actions aiming at the protection of the environment'. In this first part the declaration does not evaluate the nature of the competence; it simply signals its existence.

Second, the declaration explains the aspects of the international agreement covered by EU competence. Depending on the declaration, this part will take a different shape. The declaration can determine the existence of EU competence by linking it to the existence of EU legislation on issues covered by the international agreement.[23] It can also acknowledge the existence of EU competence on general subject matters like environment protection or trade in goods.[24] Declarations can also establish the existence of EU competences by making reference to both general subjects and EU legislation.[25]

Finally, some declarations have a clause which signals the dynamic character of EU competence.[26] For instance, the declaration made to the UN Convention on the Rights of Persons with Disabilities mentions that 'the scope and the exercise of [Union] competence are by their nature, subject to continuous development'.[27]

4.2.2 Legal Effects of the Declarations of Competence

The legal consequences of a declaration of competence may be different in international law than in EU law. From an international point of view, the question of the legal effects of the declaration relates to the binding force of the statements made in the declarations towards third parties to the agreement. From an (internal) EU perspective, the question of legal effects relates to the internal value of the division of competence made

[23] E.g. Montreal Protocol on Substances That Deplete the Ozone Layer (adopted 16 September 1987, entered into force 1 January 1989) 1522 UNTS 3.

[24] E.g. Rotterdam Convention on the Prior Informed Consent Procedure for Certain Hazardous Chemicals and Pesticides in International Trade (adopted 10 September 1998, entered into force 24 February 2004) 2244 UNTS 337; Kyoto Protocol to the United Nations Framework Convention on Climate Change (adopted 11 December 1997, entered into force 16 February 2005) 2303 UNTS 162; Cartagena Protocol on Biosafety to the Convention on Biological Diversity (adopted 29 January 2000, entered into force 11 September 2003) 2226 UNTS 208.

[25] E.g. Convention on the Protection and Promotion of the Diversity of Cultural Expressions (adopted 20 October 2005, entered into force 18 March 2007) 2440 UNTS 311. Council Decision (EU) 2006/719/EC of 5 October 2006 on the accession of the Community to the Hague Conference on Private International Law [2006] OJ L 297/001.

[26] Cf. Declaration by the European Community in accordance with article 34(3) of the Cartagena protocol, note 20.

[27] Declaration concerning the competence of the European Community with regard to matters governed by the United Nations Convention on the Rights of Persons with Disabilities [2010] OJ L 23/55.

in the declaration. In other words, internally the main question would be to what extent can the statement made in a declaration in relation to a competence affect the development of that specific competence?

At an international level, it is possible to consider declarations of competence as one of these instruments made by one party related to the conclusion of the agreement and accepted by the other parties in the sense of article 31 (2) of the Vienna Convention on the Law of the Treaties.[28] This would give them an interpretative value. In the event of a conflict related to the competence, the declarations would serve as an interpretative tool.[29] They are *an authoritative statement* on the scope of the parties' commitment under the agreements.[30]

At the internal level, the issue of the legal effects of declarations of competence is relevant to the extent that the declarations could be used to expand the scope of EU competence on a specific issue mentioned in a declaration.[31] It is not clear whether the classification of a competence made in a declaration as exclusive could determine its exclusiveness internally.[32] Strictly speaking, declarations of competence cannot create new spheres of EU powers.[33] Moreover, the Court could use them as evidence that a competence has been exercised in a specific case.[34] Consequently, the possibility that declarations have some internal effects when used as interpretative tools by the CJEU cannot be excluded.[35]

Therefore, since the Court could refer to the declaration to interpret the agreement in respect to which it was made,[36] could a declaration of competence be challenged in the CJEU? Such a scenario could arise as a consequence of the different views of the competence to be included in a specific declaration. This was the case with the Convention on Nuclear Safety (the Convention).[37] The Council made a declaration to this Convention (concluded by virtue of the EURATOM Treaty) which the Commission considered as incomplete since it did not include all the competences which fell within the scope of the Convention.

28 Macleod, Hendry and Hyett, (n 7), 324. 29 See Chapter 5.

30 P. Okawa, 'The European Community and International Environmental Agreements' [1995] 15 Yearbook of European Law 169, 176.

31 N. A. Neuwahl, *Mixed Agreements: Analysis of the Phenomenon and Their Legal Significance* (EUI 1988) 89.

32 I. Macleod, I. D. Hendry and S. Hyett, (n 9), 325. 33 Ibid.

34 Case C-459/03 *Commission vs. Ireland (MOX Plant)* para. 105.

35 F. Hoffmeister, (n 4), 249–268.

36 P. Koutrakos, 'The Intepretation of Mixed Agreements' in C. Hillion and P. Koutrakos (eds), *Mixed Agreements in EU Law Revisited: The EU and Its Member States in the World* (Hart 2010) 128–129.

37 Case C-29/99 *Commission v Council (Convention on Nuclear Safety)* [2002] ECR I-11221.

The Court considered that declarations of competence have legal effects which flow from their inclusion in the decision that concludes an international agreement.[38] More specifically, the CJEU considered that, by not drafting the declaration as complete as possible, the Council breached its duty of cooperation towards the Commission.[39] An incomplete declaration of competence not only runs against the interests of the other contracting parties of the Convention on Nuclear Safety,[40] but also against the Union inasmuch as it does not enable it to comply fully with international law.[41]

The CJEU considered that declarations of competence have the same legal effects as the concluding decisions to which they are attached and can therefore be challenged. Declarations of competence do not have independent legal effects but rather form part of the concluding decision. Furthermore, by virtue of the duty of cooperation, EU institutions have a Union obligation to make the most complete declaration of competence possible. However, the completeness of declarations of competences is not an easy obligation to comply with, as will be shown in the next section.

4.2.3 Main Problems Associated with Declarations of Competence

There are two important points concerning declarations of competence that need to be analysed: the way in which declarations establish EU competence in relation to a multilateral agreement; and the question of managing a dynamic system of competence with an instrument like a declaration attached to an international agreement. As was already mentioned, declarations of competence deal with the vertical division of powers within the European Union. They attempt to clarify whether a certain competence lies at EU level or at Member State level. However, competences do not always lie either at EU level or at Member State level. The competence picture is much more complex.

First, the treaties enshrine different types of competences.[42] Yet, there are situations in which it is not clear which kind of competence the EU has exercised and their precise scope, for example due to the use of multiple legal bases when adopting the piece of legislation.[43] Moreover, different competences can cover the same subject in international agreements. In *Opinion 1/94*, the Court recognized that the competence used to conclude an agreement might be different than the competence needed to

[38] Ibid, para. 40. [39] Ibid, para. 69. [40] Ibid, para. 70. [41] Ibid, para. 71.

[42] Article 2 TFEU. See Chapter 1.

[43] Cf. Case C-94/03 *Commission v Council (Rotterdam Convention)* [2006] ECR I-1; P. Koutrakos, 'Legal Basis and Delimitation of Competence in the EU' in M. Cremona and B. De Witte (eds), *EU Foreign Relations Law* (Hart 2008) 171–198.

implement it.[44] For instance, the WTO Agriculture Agreement was concluded by virtue of the EU's exclusive competence on CCP. By contrast, its implementation has been done through internal measures adopted under a shared competence (agriculture).[45] Therefore, the fact that the EU might have exclusive competence to conclude an agreement does not prevent the fact that the implementation might be done through shared competence, or *vice versa*.

Second, the dynamic nature of EU competence adds another layer of complexity. Regardless of the catalogue of competences in the Lisbon Treaty,[46] EU competence is subject to continuous change and evolution.[47] The ERTA principle is the perfect example of the evolutionary nature of EU competence. This principle recognizes the existence of EU powers not explicitly conferred by the Treaties,[48] and establishes that the competence of the Union to conclude international agreements may arise not only from an express conferment by the Treaty, but may also flow implicitly from other provisions of the Treaty and from measures adopted within the framework of those provisions by EU institutions.[49] This doctrine is now codified in article 216 TFEU, which allows the EU to conclude international agreements where the conclusion of that 'agreement is necessary to achieve, within the framework of the Union's policies, one of the objectives referred to in the Treaties, or is provided for in a legally binding Union act or is likely to affect common rules or alter their scope'. Therefore, even though the Treaties do not expressly provide for the possibility of the EU to act in a certain field, the EU nevertheless might act if, for instance, it is necessary to achieve an EU objective. Moreover, the conditions under which this implied power becomes exclusive have also evolved through the case law of the CJEU.[50] In a nutshell, the system of division of competences is not only subject to constant change by virtue of the notion of implied powers, but also impacted by the conditions under which these implied powers arise and the exact scope of the competence.

[44] Opinion 1/94 *Competence of the Community to conclude international agreements concerning services and the protection of intellectual property* [1994] ECR I-5267.

[45] Opinion 1/94, *Competence of the Community to conclude international agreements concerning services and the protection of intellectual property* para. 29.

[46] Articles 3–6 TFEU. [47] See Chapter 1.

[48] See: Case 22/70 *Commission v Council (ERTA)* [1971] ECR I-263, para. 16; cf. Cremona, (n 7) 217–268; C. Hillion, 'ERTA, ECHR and Open Skies: Laying the Grounds of the EU System of External Relations' in M. Maduro and L. Azoulai, *The Past and Future of EU Law: The Classics of EU Law Revisited on the 50th Anniversary of the Rome Treaty* (Hart 2010) 224–233.

[49] Opinion 1/03, para. 114. [50] See Chapter 1.

4.2.3.1 How Declarations of Competence Clarify the Vertical Division of Powers in the EU

Therefore, how do declarations of competence explain the vertical division of competence? In practice, declarations of competence to mixed agreements usually appear in two scenarios: first, agreements that contain elements falling under both EU exclusive competence and shared competence; and, second, agreements that only fall under a shared competence. Examples of the former would be the UNCLOS, the Rotterdam Convention,[51] the UNESCO Cultural Diversity Convention,[52] or the Codex Alimentarius.[53] The concluding decision of all these mixed agreements includes an article of exclusive competence and at least one article of shared competence. In all these agreements the pertinence of a statement on the division of competences can be understood to the extent that there are two different types of competence covering the whole agreement.

Examples of the latter relate mainly to environmental issues[54] that are a shared competence.[55] From this point of view, it would not be useful to make a declaration stating the division of competences, since the EU and its Member States have shared competence over the subject matter of the agreement.

For instance, the declaration of competence made to the Aarhus Convention[56] starts by acknowledging the external competence of the EU to enter into environmental agreements. Then the declaration quotes the four objectives laid down in article 191 (1) TFEU. However, to what extent does listing the EU objectives in the environmental field help third parties understand whether a particular provision of the Aarhus Convention is to be implemented by the EU or its Member States? First, the environment is

51 Rotterdam Convention.

52 Convention on the Protection and Promotion of the Diversity of Cultural Expressions.

53 Council Decision (EU) 2003/822/EC of 17 November 2003 on the accession of the European Community to the Codex Alimentarius Commission [2003] OJ L 309/14–21.

54 Stockholm Convention on Persistent Organic Pollutants (adopted 22 May 2001, entered into force 17 May 2004) 2256 UNTS 119; Cartagena Protocol, note 24; Kyoto Protocol, note 24; Convention on the Transboundary Effects of Industrial Accidents, note 15; United Nations Convention to Combat Desertification, note 18; Convention on the Protection and Use of Transboundary Watercourses and International Lakes, note 18; United Nations Framework Convention on Climate Change, note 18; Convention on Biological Diversity, OJ 1993 L 309/0003–0020; Basel Convention, note 18.

55 L. Krämer, *EC Environmental Law* (5th edn, Sweet and Maxwell 2003) 95.

56 Council Decision (EU) 2005/370/EC of 17 February 2005 on the conclusion, on behalf of the European Community, of the Convention on access to information, public participation in decision-making and access to justice in environmental matters [2005] OJ L 124, 3.

a shared competence, and, by virtue of article 2 (2) TFEU, 'Member States shall exercise their competence to the extent that the Union has not exercised its competence'. The objectives envisaged in article 191 TFEU are not to be interpreted in a pre-emptive way.[57] In other words, the mention of an objective envisaged in the TFEU does not mean that the EU has sole competence over it. Second, this declaration fails to clarify the division of competence to the extent that it does not even state the nature of the competence. The only indication that third parties receive as to the matters for which the EU is responsible is through a clause which explains the doctrine of pre-emption: 'The European [Union] is responsible for the performance of those obligations resulting from the Convention which are covered by [Union] law in force.'[58]

Furthermore, in some declarations, the EU establishes its competence through reference to pieces of legislation and policy documents, such as Commission Communications. In the declaration to the UN Convention to Combat Desertification, apart from a list of EU legislation, one of the general instruments mentioned is a Communication on development co-operation.[59] It suffices to say that Commission Communications do not have any legal nature whatsoever. In the Climate Change Convention, the EU included in the list environmental programmes.[60] This reference to policy documents as a way to establish the division of competences may mislead third parties on where the competence stands on a particular issue.

4.2.3.2 Managing a Dynamic System of Competences with a Static Instrument

Apart from explaining the vertical division of competences within the EU, declarations of competence also try to clarify how EU competences evolve. The EU's system of competence is still open to new developments. The ERTA principle is a paradigmatic example of the dynamic character of EU competence.[61]

57 Krämer, (n 55) 8.

58 This clause is also envisaged, inter alia, in the Declarations to the Stockholm Convention, the Cartagena Protocol and the Rotterdam Convention.

59 Communication from the Commission to the Council and to the European Parliament concerning development cooperation policy in run-up to 2000, SEC (92) 915 final.

60 Council Decision 89/625/EEC of 20 November 1989 on two specific research and development programmes in the field of the environment – STEP and EPOCH [1989] OJ L 359.

61 See supra. Section 4.2.3.

The final clause of some declarations of competence acknowledges the continuous development to which EU competence is subject. Yet, the declaration does not help third parties to the agreement. The participation clause, apart from demanding a declaration stating the division of competences between the EU and its Member States, imposes an obligation to make substantial changes known.[62] Taking that into account, such final clauses could be seen as a way of avoiding the obligation of updating the declarations.

The dynamic character of EU competence imposes on the EU the obligation of keeping declarations up to date. This obligation might be seen as a fairly straightforward task. However, declarations have never been updated.[63] This becomes especially problematic in those declarations which establish EU competence through a list of EU legislation. For example, in the Convention on Climate Change, from a total of 11 norms, only one remains in force,[64] while in the UN Convention to Combat Desertification none of the legal norms cited is in force, with only the political documents remaining 'in force'.[65] This lack of updates creates uncertainty on the existence of EU competence to the extent that a specific norm cited may not still be in force. Furthermore, the lack of updates for the declarations also means that new legislation is not included in the declarations. Therefore, declarations of competence which make reference to legislation not only misinform third parties, but are also incomplete.

Overall, these problems show the extent to which declarations of competence fail to clarify the division of competence for the benefit of third

62 See: Article 44.1 UN Convention on the Rights of Persons with Disabilities.

63 The only exception being the declaration to the Rotterdam Convention which was amended as a result of the judgment of the CJEU in Case C-94/03 *Commission v Council (Rotterdam Convention)*, J Heliskoski, 'EU Declarations of Competence and International Responsibility' in M. D. Evans and P. Koutrakos (eds), *The International Responsibility of the European Union International and European Perspectives* (Hart 2013) 206.

64 Council Directive 92/6/EEC of 10 February 1992 on the installation and use of speed limitation devices for certain categories of motor vehicles in the Community [1992] OJ L 57/27–28.

65 Resolution of the Council and the Representatives of the Governments of the Member States, meeting within the Council of 1 February 1993 on a Community programme of policy and action in relation to the environment and sustainable development [1993] OJ C 138/1. Communication from the Commission to the Council and to the European Parliament concerning development cooperation policy in the run-up to 2000, SEC(92) 915 final. Commission communication in accordance with Council Regulation (EEC) No 1973/92 of 21 May 1992 establishing a financial instrument for the environment (LIFE), relating to priority actions to be implemented in 1995 [1994] OJ C 139/3.

parties to multilateral (mixed) agreements. In addition, they fail to provide a complete answer to the question of EU competences on the matters governed by the agreement. These declarations externalize not only the internal division of competences, but also the problems and questions attached to the vertical division of powers in the EU.

4.3 Declarations of Competence in the CJEU

By analysing existing internal practice on the issue, it will be possible to test the relevance and usefulness of the declarations as a way of helping third parties understand EU internal division of competences concerning a multilateral agreement. This section examines the most recent practice concerning the declarations. Interestingly, although declarations of competence are designed to be applied externally[66] they are also increasingly being applied internally.[67] More and more the CJEU uses these instruments to deal with internal discussions on the vertical division of powers within mixed agreements. Thus, there is the possibility of diverging (and conflicting) interpretations internally and externally. Moreover, this divergence could negatively affect the EU as an international actor. Third parties to a mixed agreement and international courts interpreting those agreements could read the declaration in a completely different way than the reading given by the CJEU. On one hand, an international court could acknowledge Member States' external competence (and responsibility) on a certain issue of a mixed agreement; while, on the other hand, the CJEU could recognizes the EU's external competence (and responsibility) on the same issue. Furthermore, these conflicting readings of a declaration of competence could not only endanger EU compliance with its obligations under a mixed agreement, but also Member States' compliance with EU law.

In recent years, declarations of competence have increasingly been invoked in front of the CJEU. Initially, the Court embraced them as a useful reference base. Yet, the Court's use of declarations is not as consistent as might be expected. In this regard, two cases show how declarations of competence have played an important role in the internal discussion about the vertical division of competence while, at the same time, illustrate the different approaches that the Court has taken to deal with declarations of competence.

[66] See Chapter 5. [67] See notes 10 and 11.

4.3.1 *A Useful Reference Base: The* MOX Plant *Case*

In the *MOX Plant* case, the Court used the declaration of competence made pursuant to UNCLOS to establish its jurisdiction. Moreover, this case constitutes an interesting example since it shows how the declaration of competence on UNCLOS was used in the framework of a case before the CJEU, while it was not mentioned in the international legal proceedings which gave rise to the action at the CJEU.[68]

In this case, Ireland brought an action under UNCLOS against the UK concerning the operation of a MOX plant in Sellafield. As mentioned earlier, UNCLOS is a mixed agreements with an attached declaration of competence. As a consequence of this action, the Commission brought an infringement action against Ireland. It was the Commission's understanding that by instituting dispute settlement proceedings against the UK under the UNCLOS concerning the MOX plant, Ireland had failed to fulfil its obligations under articles 344 (ex article 292) TFEU (the CJEU's exclusive jurisdiction) and 4 (3) (ex article 10 TEC) TEU (the duty of sincere cooperation).[69]

According to settled case law, the CJEU's jurisdiction over mixed agreements extends not only to those provisions of the agreement falling within the EU's exclusive competence but also to those which are covered by a shared competence.[70] Therefore, it seems logical for both parties to rely on the declaration of competence in order to make their point on the existence, or lack, of an EU competence.[71] Likewise, AG Maduro referred to the declaration to establish the jurisdiction of the Court, while pointing out its 'lack of clarity and elegance'.[72]

Logically, since both parties and the Advocate General had used the declaration of competence to shed some light on the issue of the exclusive jurisdiction of the Court, so did the CJEU. According to it, the declaration confirmed that a transfer of shared competence, 'in particular in regard to the prevention of marine pollution, took place within the framework of

68 See Chapter 5. 69 Case C-459/ 03 *Commission vs. Ireland (MOX Plant)*, para. 1.

70 Case C-431/05 *Merck Genéricos Produtos Farmacêuticos* [2007] ECR I-7001; Case C-13/00 *Ireland v Commission (Berne Convention)* [2002] ECR I-2953; Case C 53/96 *Hermès* [1998] ECR I-3603; Cases C-300/98 and C-392/98 *Dior and Others* [2000] ECR I-11307. Cf. S. Mardsen, 'Invoking Direct Application and Effect of International Treaties by the European Court of Justice: Implications for International Environmental Law in the European Union' [2011] 60 International and Comparative Law Quarterly 750.

71 Case C-459/ 03 *Commission vs. Ireland (MOX Plant)*, para. 64–67.

72 Ibid, Opinion of Advocate General Maduro, para. 36.

the Convention', within the terms of the ERTA judgment.[73] Furthermore, the CJEU held that

> within the specific context of the Convention, a finding that there has been a transfer to the [Union] of areas of shared competence is contingent on the existence of [Union] rules within the areas covered by the Convention provisions in issue, irrespective of what may otherwise be the scope and nature of those rules.[74]

Therefore, insofar as there is Union legislation on an area covered by the UNCLOS, that area falls within Union competence, whether exclusive or shared, and the CJEU's exclusive jurisdiction.

Leaving aside the issue of whether this particular analysis is the best way to reach a conclusion on the jurisdiction of the Court,[75] the CJEU's approach illustrates some of the main questions identified in previous pages. The discussion about the interpretation of the declaration regarding the nature of the competence on the protection of the environment casts much doubt over the legal certainty that a declaration must provide to third parties.[76] If Ireland and the EU institutions do not agree on what the declaration says about the distribution of competences, it is difficult to expect that from third parties to a mixed agreement. The *MOX Plant* case shows on one hand, as AG Maduro said, the lack of certainty of declarations of competence. On the other, the case shows the CJEU's eagerness to use the declaration of competence to deal with complex issues concerning the vertical division of competences in the EU and some of the issues (like the jurisdiction of the Court) linked to it.

4.3.2 The Crucial Importance of the Declaration of Competence? The LZ Case

The approach towards the declaration of competence made to UNCLOS adopted by the CJEU in the *MOX Plant* case contrasts with the approach that it took to the declaration of competence made to the Aarhus Convention in the *Lesoochranárske zoskupenie VLK v Ministerstvo zivotného prostredia Slovenskej republiky* case (LZ case).[77]

[73] Ibid, para. 105. [74] Ibid, para. 108.

[75] For a critical analysis of the approach developed by the CJEU in relation to the division of competences, see: M Cremona, 'Defending the Community Interest: The Duties of Cooperation and Compliance' in M. Cremona and B. De Witte, *EU Foreign Relations Law: Constitutional Fundamentals* (Hart 2008); P. Koutrakos, (n 35).

[76] R. Churchill and J. Scott 'The *Mox Plant* Litigation: The First Half-Life' [2004] 53(3) International and Comparative Law Quarterly 666.

[77] Case C-240/09 *Lesoochranárske zoskupenie VLK v Ministerstvo zivotného prostredia Slovenskej republik (LZ) [2011] ECR* I-01255.

The case concerns a preliminary reference made by the Slovak Supreme Court on the direct effect of article 9 (3) Aarhus Convention. Article 9 (3) of the Aahus Convention provides, inter alia, 'that each Party shall ensure that... members of the public have access to administrative or judicial procedures to challenge acts and omissions by private persons and public authorities which contravene provisions of its national law relating to the environment'. Lesoochranárske zoskupenie VLK (LZ), an environmental association, argued that by not allowing it to participate in various administrative procedures on the granting of permissions to hunt brown bears, the Slovak Republic had breached article 9 (3) of the Aarhus Convention. Given the fact that the Aarhus Convention was a mixed agreement, the question of the CJEU's jurisdiction on article 9 (3) of the Aarhus Convention was raised during the proceedings.

According to the declaration of competence:

> the legal instruments in force do not cover fully the implementation of the obligations resulting from Article 9 (3) of the Convention as they relate to administrative and judicial procedures to challenge acts and omissions by private persons and public authorities other than the institutions of the European [Union]... and that, consequently, its Member States are responsible for the performance of these obligations at the time of approval of the Convention by the European [Union] and will remain so unless and until the [Union], in the exercise of its powers under the [Treaties], adopts provisions of [Union] law covering the implementation of those obligations.[78]

In other words, Member States retain their competence (and resposibility) to ensure that members of the public have access to their national procedures on environmental issues. The declaration thus establishes a sort of parallel competence on issues having to do with article 9 (3): the EU is responsible for making sure that EU institutions comply with this provision,[79] while the Member States are responsible for making sure that their national institutions comply with this provision.[80] Therefore, in an scenario like the *LZ* case, the CJEU would not have jurisdiction over the

78 Council Decision 2005/370/EC of 17 February 2005 on the conclusion, on behalf of the European Community, of the Convention on access to information, public participation in decision-making and access to justice in environmental matters [2005] OJ L 124, 3.

79 The Union has transposed that obligation in Regulation (EC) 1367/2006 of the European Parliament and of the Council of 6 September 2006 on the application of the provisions of the Aarhus Convention on Access to Information, Public Participation in Decision-Making and Access to Justice in Environmental Matters to Community Institutions and bodies [2006] OJ L 264, 13–19.

80 Cf. Case C-240/09 *LZ*, Opinion of AG Sharpston para. 77.

issue, since the EU has no competence to make sure national institutions abide with article 9 (3).

AG Sharpston shared this view in her Opinion,[81] arguing that the declaration was of *crucial importance* to establish the jurisdiction of the Court. Furthemore, according to the AG, the obligations at stake in the case (i.e. the obligation to allow LZ to intervene in a national procedure on hunting licences) were not within the sphere that lies within the scope of EU law.[82] While Sharpston was following the Court's use of the declaration of competence in the *MOX Plant* case, the Court slightly departed from its previous approach. Like in the *MOX Plant* case,[83] the Court continued to link its jurisdiction to the exercise of competence by the EU.[84] Though, unlike in the *MOX Plant* case, the Court dismissed what the declaration of competence said regarding article 9 (3), and the view of AG Sharpston on the declaration. The declaration made to the Aarhus Convention was not a useful reference base. Instead of engaging with the discussion on the intepration of the declaration of competence, the Court took a broader view, basing its jurisdiction on the explicit external competence on environmental issues[85] and the exercise of an internal shared competence on the protection of certain species.[86]

The Court's reading (or lack of it) of the declaration of competence in the *LZ* case could create problems as the participation of the EU and its Member States in the Aarhus Convention. According to the Court, article 9 (3) of the Aarhus Convention falls within the scope of EU law since it relates to a field covered in large measure covered by it.[87] In other words, the Court seems to be arguing that article 9 (3) of the Aarhus Convention falls within EU's exclusive competence,[88] even though the declaration of competence provides that unless the Union has adopted legislation on that specific issue, Member States retain their competence on article 9 (3). According to the Court, Member States seems to be no longer competent on issues covered by article 9 (3).

Nevertheless, the EU has yet to adopt legislation implementing article 9 (3) in relation to national procedures. Consequently, according to the declaration, Member States are responsible for issues covered by the EU's exclusive competence. There can be a scenario in which a Member

[81] Ibid, para. 78. [82] Ibid, para. 79.

[83] Case C-459/03 *Commission vs. Ireland (MOX Plant)*, para. 108.

[84] Case C-240/09 *LZ*, para. 32. [85] Ibid, para. 35. [86] Mardsen, (n 70) 755.

[87] Case C-240/09 *LZ*, para. 40. [88] Cf. Opinion 1/03, para. 121. Cf. Eeckhout, (n 7) 108.

State could bear international responsibility for a breach of article 9 (3) of the Aarhus Convention, but could not implement the decision since it is no longer competent to implement article 9 (3) of the Aarhus Convention. This scenario does not seem too hypothetical since in 2011 the EU's compliance with article 9 (3) of the Aarhus Convention was examined by the Compliance Committee of the Aarhus Convention,[89] and made a similar reading of the declaration of competence to that made by AG Sharpston.[90] Consequently, the CJEU's interpretation of the declaration of competence made to the Aarhus Convention could endager the EU's image within the Aarhus Convention bodies.

4.4 Conclusions

In theory, declarations of competence are supposed to give legal certainty to non-EU parties to mixed agreements with regard to where responsibilities reside. By externalizing the internal division of competence, the declarations of competence give an a priori solution to questions of implementation and compliance with mixed agreements. They also provide legal certainty to third parties that neither the EU nor its Member States will try to avoid their responsibility in case of a breach by one hiding behind the other. This is even clearer in those agreements in which the REIO clause establishes the joint and several responsibilities of the REIO and its Member State as a subsidiary mechanism to the declaration of competence. In such agreements, if neither the EU nor a Member State provides an answer as to who is responsible, both will have to answer for their silence on the issue.[91]

Although in theory declarations could provide an easy solution to the different responsibility scenarios which were identified in the introduction, a closer look suggests otherwise. First, the internal division of competence is anything but simple. Competences not only change over time, but also vary depending on the stage of the life-cycle of the agreement (e.g. negotiation, conclusion or implementation). Second, it appears that declarations create more problems than they solve. In terms of content,

89 UN Economic and Social Council, 'Report of the Compliance Committee: Findings and Recommendations with Regard to Communication ACCC/C/2008/32 (Part I) Concerning Compliance by the European Union' (14 April 2011) ECE/MP.PP/C.1/2011/4/Add.1. See Chapter 5.

90 Ibid, para. 58.

91 Cf. J. Heliskoski, (n 3).

they are vague and fail really to clarify when the EU is responsible under each specific mixed agreement.[92] As Olson argues:

> Declarations are not a particularly useful document from the point of view of the EU's Treaty partners. Declarations rarely, if ever, include something which would be far more informative: an article-by-article . . . analysis informing treaty partners clearly and in detail which entity will be exercising which rights and performing which obligations.[93]

Moreover, they need to be constantly updated so as to keep up with the evolution of the EU's powers, but are not.[94] Consequently, after close examination, it is clear that declarations of competence do not answer the question of EU competence to implement mixed agreements but instead create more uncertainty. For instance, what are the legal effects of a declaration which carries outdated legislation?

Having established that declarations of competence as they stand today do not provide legal certainty to third parties, one question arises: is there any other way that the EU and its Member States could provide legal certainty to the other parties to multilateral (mixed) agreements? First, the EU and its Member States should make a special effort during the negotiations of multilateral conventions to assure the other parties that the division of competence is an internal issue that does not affect their compliance with the multilateral convention.[95] Most of the time the obligation to make a declaration of competence is the result of a lack of effective coordination between the EU and its Member States during the negotiation of the agreement.[96] Therefore, most of the problems that the declarations of competence create could be avoided if the EU effectively spoke with one voice during the negotiations of a multilateral convention. Declarations of competence seem to be the price to pay for the lack of coordination during the negotiations.

Second, instead of trying to clarify the complexities surrounding the internal division of competence and its dynamic nature, the EU should

[92] B. De Witte, 'Too Much Constitutional Law in the European Union's Foreign Relations?' in M. Cremona and B. De Witte, *EU Foreign Relations Law: Constitutional Fundamentals* (Hart 2009) 15.

[93] Peter M. Olson, 'Mixity from the Outside: The Perspective of a Treaty Partner' in C. Hillion and P. Koutrakos (eds), *Mixed Agreements in EU Law Revisited: The EU and Its Member States in the World* (Hart 2010) 345.

[94] Hoffmeister, (n 4), 259. [95] Kuijper, (n 19) 225.

[96] Cf. C. Rijken and V. Kronenberger, 'The United Nations Convention against Transnational Organised Crime and the European Union' in V. Kronenberger (ed), *The EU and the International Legal Order: Discord or Harmony?* (T. M. C. Asser Press 2001) 481–517.

stress in its declarations made to international agreements not the fact that it has competence over an issue, but that, presented with a situation in which contracting parties may demand such clarification, the EU will promptly give an univocal response. Perhaps, by laying down clear procedures in the declaration in which a third party can obtain clarification on a particular aspect of the division of competence regarding the agreement, third parties' legal certainty would be effectively safeguarded.

5 The Apportionment of the EU's International Responsibility in International Environmental Law

The International Application of EU Declarations of Competence

5.1 Preliminary Remarks

The previous chapter signalled the main problems that declarations of competence pose when examined closely and that Multilateral Environmental International Agreements (MEIAs) are the most common scenario in which the EU makes a declaration of competence. Moreover, the previous chapter showed also how the Court of Justice of the EU (CJEU) had approached their interpretation and how this application highlighted some of the problems that these declarations entail. By contrast, this chapter examines their international application by providing an overview of the disputes where the EU has been involved and concerning the application of an MEIA with a declaration of competence.

Thus, the present chapter focuses on whether and how the declarations of competence are being applied by international environmental courts. By analysing the existing practice on the issue, it is possible to test the relevance and usefulness of the declarations as way of apportioning the international responsibility of the EU and its Member States. Moreover, it is also possible to better understand how they help in dealing with the EU's international responsibility. This chapter is divided in two parts. In the first part, the chapter focuses on the main aspects of the EU's participation in the UNCLOS. It examines on one side how UNCLOS envisages the EU's participation in the agreement by focusing on Annex IX, and its application. Three disputes are the centre of the section: the international part of the *MOX Plant* case;[1] *Chile v European Union* (the *Swordfish*

[1] *'MOX Plant Case' (Ireland v United Kingdom)* (Order No 3) (2003) 126 ILR 310. For analysis of the internal litigation in relation to the declaration of competence see Chapter 4.

case);[2] and the Request for an Advisory Opinion Submitted by the Sub-Regional Fisheries Commission (SRFC Advisory Opinion).[3]

The second part of the chapter moves its analysis to the Aarhus Convention, which does provide a mechanism by which individuals (mainly environmental NGOs) can bring complaints against the Convention contracting parties. Therefore, the reports of the Aarhus Convention's Compliance Committee (ACCC) should be a fertile ground to observe how an international body applies an EU declaration of competence. Yet, this section shows that declarations of competence are barely mentioned (if at all) within the Aarhus Convention. Moreover, this section shows how the EU's normative control plays a role in how breaches are attributed within this international agreement. The last section draws some conclusions on the actual relevance of the declarations of competence as a useful tool to determine when the EU is internationally responsible.

5.2 Articulating the EU's Participation in UNCLOS

Undoubtedly the EU's participation in UNCLOS constituted a landmark event. It was the first time that the EU and its Member States took part in such an ambitious agreement,[4] though the negotiations that led to EU membership were not easy.[5] First, while there was no doubt that at that time EU Member States had already transferred part of the areas covered by UNCLOS to the EU, the Convention also touched upon traditionally sensitive areas like military issues or borders,[6] where EU Member

2 *Case Concerning the Conservation and Sustainable Exploitation of Swordfish Stocks in the South-Eastern Pacific Ocean (Chile/European Union)* (Order of 16 December 2009) ITLOS Reports 2008/10.

3 *Request for an Advisory Opinion Submitted by the Sub-Regional Fisheries Commission (SRFC)* (Advisory Opinion of 2 April 2015) [nyr].

4 Veronica Frank, *The European Community and Marine Environmental Protection in the International Law of the Sea: Implementing Global Obligations at the Regional Level* (Martinus Nijhoff 2007) p149.

5 For an overview of the role of the EU (then the EEC) and its Member States during the negotiations see: Kenneth R. Simmonds, 'The Community's Participation in the U.N. Law of the Sea Convention' in David O'Keeffe and Henry G. Schermers (eds), *Essays in European Law and Integration* (Kluwer 1982); Albert W. Koer, 'Participation of the European Economic Community in the New Law of the Sea Convention' [1979] 73 American Journal of International Law 426.

6 Tullio Treves, 'The European Community and the Law of the Sea Convention: New Developments' in Enzo Cannizazaro (ed), *The European Union as an Actor in International Relations* (Kluwe Law International 2002) 279.

States had to be present. Second, there was opposition from third States, especially the soviet States, which had traditionally refused to recognize the EU as an international legal person.[7]

Thus, the EU's accession to UNCLOS had two interlinked consequences. On one hand, it was clear that UNCLOS would adopt the shape of a mixed agreement. UNCLOS' broad scope falls within both the EU's powers (e.g. fisheries) and its Member States' exclusive powers (e.g. military issues), as well as shared ones (e.g. environment). On the other hand, from the perspective of third parties, UNCLOS should not only reflect this mixed nature but also the former's legal certainty.[8] Therefore, to reflect the aspirations of the EU, the necessity of having its Member States present, and the concerns of third countries, a compromise solution was adopted in the form of Annex IX. This section examines in a greater detail both the wording and consequences that Annex IX has had over the responsibility of the EU within UNCLOS.

5.2.1 Annex IX of UNCLOS: A Procedural Solution

Annex IX was the price to pay for the EU's accession to UNCLOS.[9] It was the first attempt to open an agreement of such importance to the EU and by extension to any other IO.[10] Consequently, the Annex sought to regulate the four main aspects of the participation of the EU in the UNCLOS: accession, participation, responsibility and dispute settlement.

5.2.1.1 The Accession of IOs to UNCLOS

In contrast to other multilateral agreements which are open only to REIO,[11] according to article 2 Annex IX, UNCLOS is open to signature to any IO, regardless of its geographical nature. However, third parties' pursuit of legal certainty, combined with a functional approach towards the role and international personality of the IO, determined that the accession was to be conditional upon compliance with certain requisites.

[7] Kenneth R. Simmonds, 'The European Economic Community and the New Law of the Sea' [1989] VI Recueil de Cours de la Académie du Droit International 9, 118.

[8] Joni Heliskoski, *Mixed Agreements as a Technique for Organizing the International Relations of the European Community and Its Member States* (Kluwer Law International 2001) 158.

[9] Sonja Boelaert-Suominen, 'The European Community, the European Court of Justice and the Law of the Sea' [2008] 23(4) International Journal of Maritime and Coastal Law 643, 665.

[10] For a list of all the parties see: www.un.org/Depts/los/reference_files/chronological_lists_of_ratifications.htm.

[11] See Chapter 4.

Article 2 Annex IX enshrines two requisites for an IO to accede to UNCLOS. So far the EU is the only IO that has met both and acceded to UNCLOS. This might be due to the fact that Annex IX was designed with the special feature of the EU in mind.[12]

First, a majority of the members of the IO must be signatories to UNCLOS for the IO to accede. On one hand, this requisite can be regarded as an expression of the IO's functional nature insofar as its accession is constrained by the compulsory participation of its Member States. This requisite seems to stem from the fact that during the negotiations of UNCLOS, certain States raised the issue of whether the EU (then the EEC) could effectively implement the Convention without the participation of its Member States. Therefore, a majority of the EU's Member States being also bound by UNCLOS would ensure that if the EU would not live up to its international obligations, somebody else would in any event.

On the other hand, this conditionality on IOs' accession also worked the other way around since it also precluded IO Member States from using the IOs' conferred and limited nature to escape from certain obligations of UNCLOS.[13] It must be borne in mind that UNCLOS did not accept reservations. Thus, if the EU had not acceded to UNCLOS, EU Member States would only be able to comply with those obligations not falling under EU exclusive competence. Thus, they would had been making de facto reservations – i.e. not being bound by certain parts of the agreement – to the different parts of UNCLOS with which they were no longer competent. This possibility of hidden reservations inevitably would have led to a responsibility gap: the EU would have not been responsible since it would not be a party to UNCLOS, and EU Member States would not be in a position to comply with UNCLOS.

The second requisite established by article 2 Annex IX is the deposit of a declaration made by the IO specifying the matters governed by the Convention that have been transferred to the IO. It must be recalled that this declaration is the main expression of the wishes of legal certainty by third parties, and it is expected to solve most of the problems in that regard.[14]

[12] Boelaert-Suominen, (n 9) 665.

[13] Giorgio Gaja, 'The European Community's Participation in the Law of the Sea Convention: Some Incoherences in a Compromise Solution' [1980] 5 Italian Yearbook of International Law 110, 111.

[14] Cf. Peter M. Olson, 'Mixity from the Outside: The Perspective of a Treaty Partner' in Christophe Hillion and Panos Koutraks (eds), *Mixed Agreements Revisited: The EU and Its Member States in the World* (Hart 2010); Heliskoski, (n 8).

5.2.1.2 The Limited Participation of IOs in UNCLOS: The Obligation to Make a Declaration of Competence

Article 4 Annex IX envisages under which terms this participation might take place. Two aspects must be highlighted from the wording of this provision. This article recognizes both the autonomous and limited nature of IOs' legal order. While paragraph (2) rightly identifies IOs' limited legal personality when it states that an IO can be a party 'to the extent that it has competence in accordance with the declarations', paragraphs (3), (4) and (5) ascertain IOs' autonomous nature from its Member States, regardless of whether or not they have also acceded to UNCLOS.[15]

As has been already pointed out,[16] the REIO clauses have yet to find a way to meet both the EU's dynamic nature and third parties' legal certainty. Nevertheless, it must not be forgotten that Annex IX is the first participation clause that envisaged the declarations of competence formula.

Article 5 of Annex IX that envisages the time, subjects and content of the declarations of competence to be made both by the EU and its Member States, aims at providing a certain solution to this problem. The provision enshrines in its paragraph (5) that any UNCLOS' party can request the EU and its Member States to provide information as 'to which has competence in respect to any specific question'. At first sight, inasmuch as it imposes the obligation to state the competence and who exercises it in a certain area covered by UNCLOS, this provision renders the declaration of competence redundant. However, it must be borne in mind that this could be an appropriate way to deal with the dynamic character of EU's competence.[17]

5.2.1.3 IO Responsibility under Annex IX

Article 6 Annex IX establishes that, in those cases where neither the EU nor its Member States provide clarification on who is responsible (or that

[15] Paragraphs 3, 4 and 5 provide as follows: '3. Such an international organization shall exercise the rights and perform the obligations which its member States which are Parties would otherwise have under this Convention, on matters relating to which competence has been transferred to it by those member States. The member States of that international organization shall not exercise competence which they have transferred to it. 4. Participation of such an international organization shall in no case entail an increase of the representation to which its member States which are States Parties would otherwise be entitled, including rights in decision-making. 5. Participation of such an international organization shall in no case confer any rights under this Convention on member States of the organization which are not States Parties to this Convention.'

[16] See Chapter 4.

[17] Cf. Heliskoski, (n 8) 164.

clarification is incomplete) in respect to any specific matter, they will be considered jointly and severally responsible. It appears then that in terms of responsibility the EU and its Member States could no longer be separate subjects. Annex IX considers that in the event of a breach of an international obligation the EU and its Member States could be indistinguishable subjects regardless of who has committed the violation if they do not provide a clarification on the apportionment of the obligation breached.

Yet, this provision remains silent on its relationship with the declaration of competence. To what extent should the EU and its Member States be held jointly responsible if the declaration of competence served its purpose? In relation to this question, it has been argued that the joint and several responsibilities would only arise in case of a failure to provide information on the division of competences. The EU and its Member States would only be jointly and severally liable for the breach of Annex IX.[18] The alleged breach of UNCLOS that led to the third party to ask for a clarification would be attributed following the rules of responsibility. In other words, Annex IX would not establish joint and several responsibility as the general rule of responsibility of IOs and their Member States; it would establish that the failure to provide information as to the divisions of competences would lead to joint and several responsibility.[19] On the contrary, if the obligation to provide information on the division of competence has been met, the responsibility of the EU and/or its Member States stemming from the breach of any other obligation will vary depending on what the declaration of competence says about who has the competence and consequently is responsible.

Articles 5 and 6 of Annex IX provide with a procedural framework within which the doubts as to the questions of attribution can be addressed.[20] Even though Annex IX does not solve the question of allocation of responsibility in mixed situations, 'it foresees an uncomplicated mechanism for

[18] Pierre Klein, *La responsabilité des organisations internationales dans les ordres juridiques internes et en droit de gens* (Université de Bruxelles 1998) 458.

[19] *Request for an advisory opinion submitted by the Sub-Regional Fisheries Commission (SRFC)* para. 174. The ITLOS also seems to be of this view: 'The SRFC Member States may, pursuant to article 6, paragraph 2 of Annex IX to the Convention, request an international organization or its member States which are parties to the Convention for information as to who has responsibility in respect of any specific matter. The organization and the Member States concerned must provide this information. Failure to do so within a reasonable time or the provision of contradictory information results in joint and several liability of the international organization and the Member States concerned.'

[20] Heliskoski, (n 8) 165.

responding to such questions'.[21] Yet, this proceduralization of the EU's responsibility at the same time 'dispenses with the need to address the controversial issue of the scope and nature of the [Union] competence in abstract'[22] and tips the balance in favour of third parties in absence of an agreement between the EU and its Member States.[23]

5.2.1.4 Dispute Settlement

Article 7 of Annex IX has the same underlying rationale as the previous provisions. After recognizing that the EU has full autonomy to choose the judicial fora according to article 287 (3) UNCLOS, restricts its freedom of choice. The Annex foresees that:

> When an international organization and one or more of its member States are joint parties to a dispute, or parties in the same interest, the organization shall be deemed to have accepted the same procedures for the settlement of disputes as the member States.

The scope of the present provision needs some clarification since UNCLOS favours complete apportionment of all obligations between the EU and its Member States. The only cases which could fall under this provision would be either in an article 6 Annex IX situation or in those cases where the EU or the Member States would jointly breach the convention, for instance by aiding or assisting the other one in the commission of the wrongful act. However, this latter situation is not exclusive for an IO and its Member States. The EU could assist or be assisted by a third party in the violation of the agreement and yet there would not be any provision in UNCLOS imposing upon them the obligation to accept the same procedures as the third party it aided. Therefore, this provision would not only have practically no relevance, but it would also be discriminatory as regards the EU and its Member States.[24] Otherwise, it would not be consistent with the scope of Annex IX. If joint responsibility only arises in those cases where the failure to provide information would occur, the possibility of

[21] Moshe Hirsch, *The Responsibility of International Organizations towards Third Parties: Some Basic Principles* (Martinus Nijhoff 1995) 23.

[22] Heliskoski, (n 8) 166. For a more recent analysis of the proceduralization of the EU's responsibility see: Andrés Delgado Casteleiro, 'The International Responsibility of the EU: Between Pragmatism and Proceduralization' [2012] 15 Cambridge Yearbook of European Legal Studies 563.

[23] Hirsch, (n 21) 23.

[24] Arguments supporting the discriminatory nature of Annex IX can be found in: Nanette A. Neuwahl, *Mixed Agreements: Analysis of the Phenomenon and Their Legal Significance* (European University Institute 1988); Simmonds, (n 7). For the other aspects of the Annex which might discriminate against the EU and its Member States, see the previous chapter.

bringing a claim against the EU and its Member States for any other reason beyond their collaboration in the violation of the Convention would not be possible. In other words, the type of dispute which would determine that both the EU and its Member States have to be joint parties to a dispute, is the same type of dispute in which two States with no special relation whatsoever would have to be joint parties to the dispute. However, only IOs and their Member States have to accept the same dispute settlement mechanisms.

Overall, Annex IX struggles in reconciling the desire for autonomy of the EU and the wish for legal certainty of third parties. The Annex does not solve any of the questions regarding the relations between UNCLOS' mixed nature and the responsibility of the EU and its Member States. Instead it creates a procedural framework which avoids solving the question a priori, and moves the solution further down the line.

5.2.2 *The Declarations of Competence*

The drafting of the declaration of competence to UNCLOS was not a trivial issue. The EU had observer status throughout the discussion of UNCLOS. Therefore, from the moment of the signing of the new Convention, its status did change, thus enabling the EU to take part in the discussions in the establishment of the International Tribunal for the Law of the Sea and the International Sea-Bed Authority as a full member.[25]

As a consequence, the EU made a first declaration[26] with that fact in mind. This declaration stated that *a separate decision on formal confirmation* would be taken at a later stage. Thus, as Simmonds pointed out, 'the Declaration was made in the short term with a view to securing participation in the works of the Preparatory Commission'.[27] For that reason the Declaration was considered to be *brief and formal* and to have an *interim character*.[28] In addition, other scholars note that this interim declaration did not satisfy the precise requisites envisaged in Annex IX and that this first declaration implicitly showed the reluctance of the EU to clarify its competence to third parties in the official declaration.[29]

This declaration includes both a list of EU legislation and the general subjects on which the EU has competence that are enshrined in it.

25 Kenneth R. Simmonds, 'The Community's Declaration upon Signature of the UN Convention on the Law of the Sea' [1986] 23 Common Market Law Review 521, 531.

26 The text of this Declaration can be found in ibid 538–540.

27 Simmonds, (n 7) 143. 28 Simmonds, (n 25) 531.

29 Javier Roldán Barbero, 'La CEE y el Convenio sobre Derecho del Mar de 1982: consideraciones sobre la relación entre el Derecho de Comunitario y el Derecho Internacional' [1991] 18(2) Revista de Instituciones Europeas 551.

However, the relationship established between the two parts is not complete. In the part of the declaration where competence is established on the basis of overall subjects, the EU holds that it has competence on the conservation and management of sea fishing resources, and on the regulation for the protection of the maritime environment. The list nevertheless only includes legislation of the latter subject. The reason for this is that the declaration points out in its first part that the EU has exclusive competence over the conservation and management of sea fishing resources. Therefore, it is the responsible subject on this issue, whereas in the regulation for the protection of the maritime environment, the declaration states the competence is partially transferred as it is envisaged in the list of EU legislation of the declaration.

In 1994, a new declaration was annexed to the Agreement on the implementation of Part XI of UNCLOS.[30] This new declaration, concerning the competence of the EU with regard to the matters governed by UNCLOS and the 1994 agreement relating to the implementation of Part IX of the Convention, follows the same pattern as its predecessor with a few slight changes. The first novelty of this new declaration is that, when addressing the competence of the EU in certain fields, it does so by linking that subject to provisions of UNCLOS. For instance, the new declaration states that 'by virtue of its commercial and customs policy, the [Union] has competence in respect of those provisions of Parts X and XI of the Convention and of the Agreement of 28 July 1994 which are related to international trade'. Or when addressing the EU's competence on maritime transport, the declaration holds that, with regard to

> the provisions on maritime transport, safety of shipping and the prevention of marine pollution contained, inter alia, in Parts II, III, V, VII and XII of the Convention, the [Union] has exclusive competence only to the extent that such provisions of the Convention or legal instruments adopted in implementation thereof affect common rules established by the [Union].

This new declaration can be considered an improvement in terms of clarity, although this could be based on the different legal effects that both declarations have.[31] The first declaration was brief and formal and had an interim character; it was a provisional declaration, while the new one did not have any of those features; it was the definitive declaration.

[30] Agreement relating to the implementation of Part XI of the United Nations Convention on the Law of the Sea 10 December 1982 (adopted 28 July 1994, entry into force 28 July 1996) 1836 UNTS 3.

[31] Frank, (n 4) 165.

Furthermore, in 1998, the EU also made a declaration regarding the Straddling Stocks Agreement.[32] Unlike the previous ones, the declaration does not exemplify the EU's competence by referring to legislation. It just states the competence through the reference to general subjects. As a way of example, the declaration recognizes EU exclusive competence internally and externally on the conservation of living marine resources (which also was exclusive at the time of the previous declarations), and the shared competence as to scientific research.

Nevertheless, since those declarations were made, EU competence and legislation have evolved and changed their scope in the areas covered by UNCLOS.[33] Therefore, as has been recognized by the EU, an update of the declarations should be made.[34]

5.3 The EU's International Responsibility within UNCLOS

5.3.1 The MOX Plant Case

The *MOX Plant* case constitutes a good example of how the declaration of competence was not applied when it should have been. The complexity of the case would have called for its application since it revolves around the relations between different agreements covered under the UNCLOS umbrella (UNCLOS itself, the OSPAR Convention and even the EC Treaty).

Ireland considered that the operation of a plant of this kind in Sellafield (in the UK), which would increase the discharge of nuclear waste to the Irish Sea,[35] constituted a breach of the OSPAR Convention and UNCLOS. First, Ireland submitted the dispute to arbitration under the OSPAR Convention. Ireland argued that the UK had breached article 9 of the OSPAR Convention concerning access to environmental information. The Tribunal dismissed Ireland's claims by arguing that the claim did not fall within the scope of article 9 of the Convention.[36]

32 United Nations Agreement for the Implementation of the United Nations Convention on the Law of the Sea of 10 December 1982 relating to the Conservation and Management of Straddling Fish Stocks and Highly Migratory Fish Stocks (adopted 4 August 1995, entry into force 11 December 2001) 2167 UNTS 3.

33 For an overview of this evolution see: Boelaert-Suominen, 'Bolaert, IJMCL'.

34 In a speech the ITLOS EC Commissioner, Borg, mentioned that 'it may also be an opportune moment to consider updating the list of legislation attached to the declaration.' The speech can be found at: http://ec.europa.eu/maritimeaffairs/speeches/speech76_en.html.

35 Robin Churchill and Joanne Scott, 'The *Mox Plant* Litigation: The First Half-Life' [2004] 53(3) International and Comparative Law Quarterly 643, 644.

36 *OSPAR Convention (Ireland v United Kingdom)* (2003) 42 ILM 1118.

In parallel, Ireland also brought a claim against the UK by virtue of Part XV of UNCLOS.[37] Since neither Ireland nor the UK had agreed on the forum where to submit the dispute, by virtue of article 287 (5) UNCLOS, an arbitral tribunal constituted under the rules of Annex VII was the competent body to hear the case. During the oral hearing, the UK raised the issue of the mixed nature of UNCLOS, and the apportionment of its provisions between the EU and its Member States.[38] This is the kind of situation in which a declaration of competence would apply. The arbitral tribunal would have to examine the case in the light of the declaration to ascertain whether the EU or its Member States are competent on the subject area of the dispute. Yet, this was not the case in the present dispute. Instead of using the declaration of competence to determine whether the EU was competent, the arbitral tribunal relied on the answer to a parliamentary question made to the Commission on the issue.[39] Furthermore, the arbitral tribunal recognized that:

> whether, and if so to what extent, all or any provisions of the 1982 Convention fall within the competence of [EU] or its Member States would fall to be decided by the European Court of Justice.[40]

It appears that the arbitral tribunal disregarded the existence of the declaration. Consequently, the arbitral tribunal decided to suspend its proceedings until December 2003 to have a clearer picture of the EU legal position.[41] There is no doubt that, by suspending its proceedings, the arbitral tribunal showed great concern over the issue of competing jurisdictions, and the autonomy of the EU legal order. By linking the issue of competence and jurisdiction, the tribunal avoided the possibility of issuing a decision contradicting the CJEU.[42]

However, the disregard for the declaration of competence is particularly striking. The fact that the arbitral tribunal remained silent on the issue puts forward the question of the international relevance and effectiveness of the declarations. Otherwise, the tribunal would have mentioned the declaration either to terminate the proceedings since Ireland and the UK had no competence on the issue, or to enter into the substance of the issue provided that declaration granted them jurisdiction on the issue.

[37] *PCA, Ireland v United Kingdom ('MOX Plant Case'). Order N° 3. Suspension of proceedings on jurisdiction and merits, and request for further provisional measures.*

[38] Ibid. [39] Ibid. [40] Ibid. [41] Ibid.

[42] For an overview of the issues of competing jurisdictions in the *MOX Plant* case see Churchill and Scott, (n 35).

5.3.2 *Swordfish, Spain, Chile and the EU*

Perhaps the lack of use of the declaration of competence in the first part of the *MOX Plant* litigation was due to the intra-EU nature of the dispute. Ireland and the UK understood that the arbitral tribunal had competence on the issue so it was not necessary to draw attention to the declaration. Given this factor, any analysis of the practice of the declarations of competence, and more specifically of the UNCLOS one would not be complete without the analysis of a 'third State v EU' type of international dispute.

The only case ever to be brought in the framework of the UNCLOS against the EU and/or its Member States was the *Swordfish* case between the EU and Chile.[43] The case concerned the fishing of swordfish, which is a highly migratory species according to Annex I of UNCLOS. This fact implies that, due to its migration patterns, the swordfish moves between the Exclusive Economic Zone (EEZ) of different Coastal States and the high seas.[44] Due to their transnational nature, article 64 UNCLOS provides a general obligation of cooperation between States for the preservation of highly migratory species like the swordfish.[45] This duty of cooperation has determined the creation of regional organizations aimed at managing these stocks.[46] The Framework Agreement for the Conservation of Living Marine Resources on the High Seas of the Southeast Pacific (Galapagos Agreement),[47] signed between Colombia, Ecuador, Peru and Chile, was an attempt at establishing a framework of cooperation in the sense of article 64 of UNCLOS. However, the agreement has yet to enter into force.[48]

[43] *Case concerning the Conservation and Sustainable Exploitation of Swordfish Stocks in the South-Eastern Pacific Ocean (Chile/European Union).*

[44] Robin Churchill and Vaughan Lowe, *The Law of the Sea* (3rd edn, Manchester University Press 1999) 311.

[45] Article 64 UNCLOS: 'The Coastal State and other States whose nationals fish in the region for the highly migratory species listed in Annex I shall cooperate directly or through appropriate international organizations with a view to ensuring conservation and promoting the objective of optimum utilization of such species throughout the region, both within and beyond the exclusive economic zone. In regions for which no appropriate international organization exists, the Coastal State and other States whose nationals harvest these species in the region shall cooperate to establish such an organization and participate in its work.'

[46] Supra, Section 5.2.

[47] Framework Agreement for the Conservation of Living Marine Resources on the High Seas of the Southeast Pacific signed in Santiago de Chile on 14 August 2000.

[48] See article XIX of the Galapagos Agreement. Text of the agreement and ratifications status can be found at: www.ecolex.org/ecolex/ledge/view/RecordDetails;jsessionid=366A8DC0F347B9D9686A77FFCC2FD093?action=i18n.SetLocale&id=TRE-153658&index=treaties&locale=es_ES.

The lack of a multilateral framework to deal with the preservation and management of fishing activities in the high seas of the Southeast Pacific lead Chile to adopt a series of unilateral measures aimed at this objective. In 1990 the Chilean government enacted Decree 293 (1990)[49] which established conservation measures for the swordfish within Chile's EEZ. This decree envisaged that non-compliance with the measures enshrined in it would carry the prohibition to land Chilean ports.[50] This prohibition led the Chilean authorities to deny access to port to Spanish vessels that caught swordfish in Chile's EEZ.[51] It must be signalled that the obligations imposed upon the vessels fishing swordfish in the EEZ were the same measures envisaged in article 62 (2) of UNCLOS.[52] Furthermore, Chile adopted Decree 598 (1999).[53] This decree extended both the prohibition of port access as well as the measures of conservation of the swordfish established for the EEZ to the high seas.[54] The Spanish vessels catching swordfish in the high seas were also denied access to Chilean ports, since, according to Chile, they were not complying with the decree, particularly the obligations of transfer of information to the Coastal State and the presence of observers in the vessels.

Unlike the EEZ for which UNCLOS has laid down precise rules on the actions that Coastal States can and cannot take, UNCLOS proclaims the freedom of the high seas (article 87) and does not foresee any detailed rules on the conservation of living resources. It just establishes that, along with the necessity to cooperate, some limitations to the freedom of fishing in the high seas are imposed.[55] Therefore, in absence of a cooperation framework, it is unclear whether a Coastal State can adopt unilateral

[49] Decreto 293 de 5 de Septiembre de 1990 que establece normas de regulación para la pesquería de Pez Espada o Albacora. BO de 15 de Octubre 1990.

[50] Article 3 of the Decree 293 (1990).

[51] Marcos A. Orellana, 'The Swordfish Dispute between the EU and Chile at the ITLOS and the WTO' [2002] 71(1) Nordic Journal of International Law 55, 60.

[52] Among the conservation measures envisaged in the Decree which are taken from article 62.2 UNCLOS: '(c) . . . the types, sizes and amount of gear; (e) specifying information required of fishing vessels, including catch and effort statistics and vessel position reports; (g) the placing of observers or trainees on board such vessels by the Coastal State; (h) the landing of all or any part of the catch by such vessels in the ports of the Coastal State'.

[53] Decreto 598 de 15 de octubre de 1999 que aplica artículo 165 de la ley general de pesca y acuicultura a la especie pez espada, BO de 25 de Noviembre 1999.

[54] Orellana, (n 51) 61.

[55] Article 116 UNCLOS provides that 'all States have the right for their nationals to engage in fishing on the high seas subject to: . . . b) the rights and duties of Coastal States provided, inter alia, in article 63.2 and articles 64 to 67.'

measures regarding the conservation of highly migratory species in the high seas as Chile did.

5.3.2.1 Parallel Disputes in the WTO and in the ITLOS

As a consequence of the different views concerning the legality of the unilateral measures adopted by Chile regarding the denial of access to port of Spanish vessels fishing swordfish in the Southeast Pacific, two disputes were brought to different international bodies.

On one hand, in April 2000, the EU started, by virtue of article 4 of the Dispute Settlement Understanding (DSU), consultations in the WTO.[56] According to the EU, Chile, by not allowing [Union] fishing vessels, operating in the Southeast Pacific to unload their swordfish in Chilean ports either to land them for warehousing or to tranship them onto other vessels, was in breach of articles V and XI of GATT.

On the other hand, in December 2000, Chile started, by virtue of article 15 of the ITLOS Statute, a special chamber dispute concerning the conservation of swordfish stocks.[57] Chile asked the ITLOS to rule on:

> (a) whether the European Union has complied with its obligations under the Convention, especially articles 116 to 119 thereof, to ensure conservation of swordfish, in the fishing activities undertaken by vessels flying the flag of any of its Member States in the high seas adjacent to Chile's EEZ;
> (b) whether the European Union has complied with its obligations under the Convention, in particular article 64 thereof, to cooperate directly with Chile as a Coastal State for the conservation of swordfish in the high seas adjacent to Chile's EEZ as also to report its catches and other information relevant to this fishery to the competent international organization and to the Coastal State.[58]

Neither of the proceedings ended up with a pronouncement of the judicial bodies. While the WTO dispute has been suspended since 2003,[59] the ITLOS

[56] WTO. Chile – Measures Affecting the Transit and Importing of Swordfish. DS193. Request for Consultations by the European Communities. 19 April 2000.

[57] *Case concerning the Conservation and Sustainable Exploitation of Swordfish Stocks in the South-Eastern Pacific Ocean (Chile/European Union)* (Order 2000/3 of 20 December 2000).

[58] Ibid.

[59] WTO, 'Chile – Measures Affecting the Transit and Importing of Swordfish' (WTO, 2015), www.wto.org/english/tratop_e/dispu_e/cases_e/ds193_e.htm.

dispute was withdrawn from the register in 2009 when Chile and the EU reached an agreement on the issue.[60]

Undoubtedly, the diplomatic solution reached in both mechanisms might be seen as a good solution, given the great amount of risk of normative fragmentation that the dispute entailed.[61] However, the lack of a conflict, and more specifically the lack of a final decision by a judicial body preclude us from examining how the questions of responsibility were dealt with in practice. This absence of judicial resolution addressing questions of responsibility does not imply that those questions did not exist. Indeed, as will be shown, this fact might show that the procedural solutions laid down by the EU to deal with the apportionment of obligations are irrelevant in practice.

5.3.2.2 The Attribution of the Conduct of the Spanish Vessels to the EU

The choice of bringing the EU to the ITLOS might have responded to the fact that Chile understood that the alleged breach of UNCLOS by the Spanish vessels fishing swordfish in the high seas was attributable to the EU. However, how did Chile reach that conclusion?

On one hand, it could be sustained that, by bringing this dispute, Chile somewhat retaliated to the consultations proceedings initiated against it by the EU in the WTO. This could be a plausible explanation given the chain of events previously detailed. Thus, by initiating the WTO disputes, the EU indicated that any breach committed in the area should be attributed to it. Although this could be true in the present dispute, this reasoning concerning the attribution of responsibility between the EU and its Member States depending on whether they have brought a similar dispute could be seen as problematic, to say the least. If this link between bringing a dispute and being responsible were to be accepted as a rule of attribution some problems would arise in the specific context of fisheries. For instance, since a very similar case was brought before the ICJ by Spain against Canada,[62] it could be argued that, in the present case, given that precedent, Chile could have also brought the case against Spain.

60 *Case concerning the Conservation and Sustainable Exploitation of Swordfish Stocks in the South-Eastern Pacific Ocean (Chile/European Union)* 5.

61 Orellana, (n 51); Gabrielle Marceau, 'Conflicts of Norms and Conflicts of Jurisdictions: The Relationship between the WTO Agreement and MEAs and Other Treaties' [2001] 35(6) Journal of World Trade 1081.

62 *Fisheries Jurisdiction (Spain v Canada)* (Judgment) [1998] ICJ Rep 432.

On the other hand, Chile might have brought the EU because it examined the declaration of competence or initiated a procedure under article 6 of Annex IX UNCLOS. In relation to the latter, there is no reference in any of the documents made public by the ITLOS to Annex IX or article 6 whatsoever.[63] Therefore, it could also be presumed that Chile did not find it necessary to invoke article 6 (2) of Annex IX. The fact that article 6 (2) Annex IX is nowhere to be found in the dispute might mean that Chile did not have any doubts concerning who was responsible for the Spanish vessels' behaviour. On one hand, Chile's certainty could be explained, as mentioned earlier, because of the WTO claim the EU brought against Chile. On the other hand, Chile's certainty against whom to bring the claim could be explained by the use of the declaration of competence. Although, like Annex IX, there is no reference to the declaration in any of documents, it could not be excluded that the Chilean legal service might have examined it. However, there is no way to know this for sure.

Nevertheless, it can be examined how the declaration might have been used in the *Swordfish* dispute. The declaration envisages that the EU has exclusive competence over the conservation and management of living marine resources. Furthermore, this competence applies with regard to waters under national fisheries jurisdiction and to the high seas.[64] Therefore, insofar as the EU has exclusive competence over the issue, the conservation and management of living marine resources in the high seas, like swordfish, would be apportioned to the EU. In principle, EU Member States would not be bound as a matter of international law by the provisions of the agreement, but this does not mean that a supposed breach could not be attributed to them. In addition, the declaration of competence to the Straddling Stocks Agreement enshrines that:

> The [Union] enjoys the regulatory competence granted under international law to the flag State of a vessel to determine the conservation and management measures for marine fisheries resources applicable to vessels flying the flag of Member States.[65]

63 All the public documents on the case can be accessed at: www.itlos.org/cgi-bin/cases/case_detail.pl?id=6&lang=en.

64 Agreement relating to the implementation of part XI of the United Nations Convention on the Law of the Sea of 10 December 1982, Official Journal L 215, 20.8.1994, pp. 10–20. Cf. United Nations Agreement for the Implementation of the United Nations Convention on the Law of the Sea of 10 December 1982 relating to the Conservation and Management of Straddling Fish Stocks and Highly Migratory Fish Stocks signed in New York 4 August 1995. Official Journal L 189, 3.7.1998, pp. 17–41.

65 United Nations Agreement for the Implementation of the United Nations Convention on the Law of the Sea of 10 December 1982 relating to the Conservation and

Thus the EU is also competent to ensure that the Spanish vessels comply with UNCLOS in relation to the conservation of swordfish in high seas. However, regardless of what the apportionment of obligations might say, the act that violated the UNCLOS must also be attributable to the EU. Therefore, to what extent can the failure to comply with UNCLOS of Spanish vessels fishing swordfish in the Southeast Pacific be attributed to the EU?

Since the Spanish vessels did not comply with the measures required for the conservation of swordfish, this breach of UNCLOS would fall under EU competence and, *mutatis mutandi*, its duties as a flag State. Thus, as long as the flag State is responsible in international law for its vessels in cases where an act or omission of the vessel is attributable to the flag state,[66] the EU would be responsible if those acts can be attributed to it. Yet, Chile phrased its claim in such a way that the breach of UNCLOS would be the consequence not so much of the Spanish fishermen's action *per se* but of the EU's lack of cooperation to solve the question of the fishing of highly migratory species in the Southeast Pacific.

If Chile had phrased the question by establishing a link between the behaviour of private fishermen in high seas and the breach of UNCLOS by the EU, it could be argued that the attribution of the breach to the EU would have been much more difficult.[67] First, UNCLOS establishes the freedom of the high seas even for fishing (article 87 UNCLOS) so strictly speaking the EU's lack of measures for the protection of the swordfish in the Southeast Pacific would not constitute a breach of UNCLOS.[68] Second, if it were to be assumed that Spanish vessels had breached the UNCLOS, how would their conduct be attributed to the EU?

5.3.3 *The SRFC Advisory Opinion*

5.3.3.1 Background to the Dispute

In principle, international law has not settled the issue of whether the conduct of individuals not exercising any kind of public power or

Management of Straddling Fish Stocks and Highly Migratory Fish Stocks signed in New York 4 August 1995. Official Journal L 189, 3.7.1998, pp. 17–41.

66 Churchill and Lowe, (n 44) 257.

67 Armen Sarvarian, 'EU Accession to the ECHR and the Law of International Responsibility' in Vasiliki Kosta, Nikos Skoutaris and Vassilis P Tzevelekos (eds), *The EU Accession to the ECHR* (Hart 2013) 92.

68 Churchill and Lowe, (n 44) 301.

authority can be attributed to a State or an IO.[69] Undoubtedly, the responsibility of the flag State or an IO for the conduct of vessels flying under their flag raises many interesting questions as regards attribution and responsibility.

Against this background, in 2013, the SRFC requested an advisory to the ITLOS[70] on this issue, among others. More specifically, the SRFC asked the ITLOS to clarify to what extent an IO should be held liable for any illegal fishing conducted by vessels to which fishing licences were by an IO the extent of the responsibility of the latter.[71]

5.3.3.2 The Responsibility of the EU in Relation to the Conduct of Vessels Flying under a Union Flag: The Declaration of Competence as a Starting Point for the Analysis

The ITLOS understood that the relevant definition of an IO would be the one enshrined in Annex IX of UNCLOS.[72] At first sight, while it appears that the Tribunal is embracing a broad understanding of an IO, it must not be forgotten that the definition of an IO, as well as the whole rationale underpinning Annex IX of UNCLOS, had the EU in mind.[73] The ITLOS recognized this fact straight away by narrowing down its analysis of the responsibility of the EU under Annex IX and more specifically to the EU's declaration of competence.[74]

For the ITLOS the EU declaration of competence is the logical starting point for the analysis of the responsibility of the EU. The Tribunal notes

69 See: ILC, 'Report of the International Law Commission on the Work of Its 61st Session' (4 May–5 June and 6 July–7 August 2009) UN Doc A/64/10. Nevertheless, Sarvarian argues that in those situations responsibility should rest in any case with the State and not with the IO since the link between the conduct and the IO would be too remote. Sarvarian, (n 67) 92.

70 *Request for an advisory opinion submitted by the Sub-Regional Fisheries Commission (SRFC).*

71 The question as originally worded by the SRFC was slightly rephrased by the ITLOS. Compare the original wording of 'question 3' ('Where a fishing license is issued to a vessel within the framework of an international agreement with the flag State or with an international agency, shall the State or international agency be held liable for the violation of the fisheries legislation of the Coastal State by the vessel in question?') with the Reading of the Tribunal of that question. (The Tribunal notes in this regard that this question concerns the liability of a flag State or of an international agency for the violation of the fisheries legislation of a Coastal State by a vessel holding a fishing license issued within the framework of an international agreement with that flag State or international agency. In the present case, the expression 'international agency' is considered synonymous with 'international organization'). Ibid.

72 See Section 5.2.1.1. 73 Boelaert-Suominen, (n 9) 665.

74 *Request for an advisory opinion submitted by the Sub-Regional Fisheries Commission (SRFC)* para. 159.

that pursuant to the declaration the EU has an exclusive competence on the conservation and management of sea fishing resources, and that is the only competence relevant in the framework of the advisory opinion.[75] Furthermore, the ITLOS substantiates its argument on the exclusive nature of EU competence on the subject matter of the Advisory Opinion by referring to how the EU has exercised that competence. More specifically, the ITLOS shows how the EU in the framework of the Common Fisheries Policy provides a definition of a 'Union fishing vessel' ('fishing vessel flying the flag of a Member State and registered in the Union').[76]

The *SRFC Advisory Opinion* is so far the only international judicial decision in which a declaration of competence has been referred to. Even though it is a noteworthy event, it should be contextualized. First, the declaration was not referred to in a contradictory dispute but within the request for an advisory opinion. Since there was no specific conduct to place within the competence of the EU, it is difficult to evaluate the effectiveness of the declarations. Moreover, the reference to pieces of legislation absent in the declaration only highlights the shortcomings and inherent risks that current declaration of competence creates. The lack of specific conduct to attribute to the EU should limit any optimistic reading on the use of declarations of competence in international disputes. In any event, the *SRFC Advisory Opinion* shows how declarations of competence seem to relate more to the issue of the apportionment of obligations than to the attribution of conduct.[77] In other words, the existence of the declaration of competence would not *per se* solve the question of the attribution of conduct and the eventual responsibility of the EU.[78] Instead, they should be regarded as a starting point for the analysis of the responsibility of the EU.

5.3.3.3 Competence, Due Diligence and Responsibility

The Tribunal draws a clear line between the responsibility of the EU and its competence. Inasmuch as the EU has exercised its competence (as seen in the declaration of competence), it should bear responsibility for any action

75 Ibid.

76 Ibid. Interestingly, the regulation that enshrines that definition is not in the list of EU legislation attached to the declaration of competence made to UNCLOS. See: Section 2.1.2.

77 See Chapter 2.

78 A similar argument in relation to the link between competences and responsibility in more general terms can be found in Chapter 1.

taken under its umbrella.[79] However, the ITLOS does not seem to clearly establish *prima facie* the extent of that responsibility. In other words, what is the scope of the EU's responsibility in a field covered by its competence? It appears that the ITLOS is not giving a clear answer especially with regard to the responsibility of its Member States. According to the ITLOS:

> [a]n international organization which in a matter of its competence undertakes an obligation, in respect of which compliance depends on the conduct of its Member States, may be held liable if a Member State fails to comply with such obligation and the organization did not meet its obligation of 'due diligence'.[80]

There are at least two possible readings of this statement. First, it could be argued that the ITLOS is not discounting that EU Member State could still be held responsible for the commission of the internationally wrongful act regardless of the exclusive nature of the competence. The distinction drawn between the conduct of the Member State and the conduct of the EU would point in this direction. Inasmuch as the EU met its obligation of due diligence, it would not be responsible. However, that would not exclude the responsibility of the Member State that failed to comply with that obligation. Therefore, it could be argued that the responsibility of the EU would be in any case shared with its Member States.

A second and more logical reading of this statement would be to assume that insofar as the ITLOS has established that the responsibility of a State for the conduct of a fishing vessel with their flag stems from an obligation of due diligence,[81] it would also apply by analogy to the EU. This is confirmed further along the opinion when the Tribunal acknowledges that 'only the international organization may be held liable for any breach of its obligations arising from the fisheries access agreement, and not its Member States'.[82] The EU's responsibility would, according to the ITLOS, arise from its 'due diligence' obligations over a vessel flying the flag of an EU Member State, and would exclude the responsibility of the Member State.[83]

More interestingly, when establishing the link between competence and responsibility, but especially by developing it, the *SRFC Advisory Opinion* adopts a similar approach to that of the EU's normative control as a way to attribute responsibility even in such remote situations.[84] The reference to the EU Common Fisheries Policy and its definition of an Union

[79] *Request for an advisory opinion submitted by the Sub-Regional Fisheries Commission (SRFC)* para. 168.

[80] Ibid. [81] Ibid. [82] Ibid. [83] Ibid. [84] Sarvarian, (n 67) 92.

fishing vessel in the Opinion[85] could be read as the ITLOS considering not only whether the EU has exclusive competence but also whether it has exercised it as regards fishing vessels.

Moreover, in a similar scenario but where an EU shared competence has been exercised, it appears that the ITLOS would also hold the EU solely responsible. This seems to be confirmed by the fact that the Tribunal acknowledges that, the obligations of the flag State become the obligations of the EU when the latter has exercised its exclusive competence in fisheries matters.[86] Although the *SRFC Advisory Opinion* does not deal with the actual practicalities of the EU's responsibility, it shows nevertheless how even in situations in which there might be a declaration of competence, the latter does not completely solve the question of attribution. Furthermore, it also shows how, when faced with a claim against the EU, the ITLOS might be inclined to accept the exclusive responsibility of the EU in cases where it did not exercise its due diligence obligation in ensuring that Union fishing vessels comply with the Law of the Sea. This due diligence obligation, according to the ITLOS, would entail taking all necessary measures, including those of enforcement, to ensure compliance. Thus, a certain parallelism could be drawn between this concept of due diligence and normative control. Inasmuch as the EU ensures, through its rules and their effective application, that Union fishing vessels comply with the Law of the Sea, any breach of the latter would entail the exclusive responsibility of the EU.

5.4 The EU's Responsibility and the Aarhus Convention Compliance Committee

As mentioned in the previous chapter, the Aarhus Convention was concluded by the EU as a mixed agreement on the basis of its shared environmental policy competence as laid down in article 192 TFEU.[87] As opposed to UNCLOS, where there was a mix of different competences, the Aarhus Convention provides an illuminating example of the

85 *Request for an advisory opinion submitted by the Sub-Regional Fisheries Commission (SRFC)* para. 165.

86 Ibid.

87 Council Decision (EU) 2005/370/EC of 17 February 2005 on the conclusion, on behalf of the European Community, of the Convention on access to information, public participation in decision-making and access to justice in environmental matters [2005] OJ L 124/1.

relation between shared competences and the EU's responsibility. Moreover, the EU made a declaration of competence to the Aarhus Convention. Given that the ACCC has dealt with 130 complaints,[88] it could provide useful insights as regards the attribution of conduct to the EU and the effectiveness of the EU's declaration of competence. Yet, though there were more than 100 complaints made against the EU and its Member States to the ACCC, the EU declaration of competence is barely mentioned.

This section is structured in three parts. After a brief explanation of how the ACCC operates, this section surveys all the claims brought against the EU and its Member States within the framework of the ACCC to identify if the declaration of competence made to the Aarhus Convention has ever been mentioned and how the ACCC has approached its analysis. The third section examines whether the ACCC has developed a consistent practice to deal with the attribution of conduct to the EU and its Member States and how it tackles the issue of the EU's normative control.

5.4.1 *A Brief Explanation of the Nature of the ACCC and Its Consequences as Regards the Establishment of the Responsibility of the EU*

Before we enter into the analysis of how the ACCC deals with the EU's responsibility, it is necessary to highlight that the ACCC does not fit exactly within the definition of an international judicial body, unlike the other dispute settlement systems examined in this study. Generally speaking, non-compliance mechanisms enshrined in MEIA are not dispute settlement mechanisms aiming 'to reach an independent judicial verdict by legal analysis and interpretation of facts'.[89] Yet, the ACCC enshrined in the Aarhus Convention has been described as a quasi-judicial body[90] and its recommendations are referred to as jurisprudence.[91] The ACCC's quasi-judicial nature stems from the independent nature of its eight members, as opposed to other non-compliance committees constituted by

88 See later and Section 5.3.2.

89 Nils Goeteyn and Frank Maes, 'Compliance Mechanisms in Multilateral Environmental Agreements: An Effective Way to Improve Compliance?' [2011] 10(4) Chinese Journal of International Law 791.

90 Cesare Pitea, 'The Non-Compliance Procedure of the Aarhus Convention: Between Environmental and Human Rights Control Mechanisms' [2006] 16(1) Italian Yearbook of International Law 85, 115.

91 Veit Koester, 'The Compliance Committee of the Aarhus Convention: An Overview of Procedures and Jurisprudence ' [2007] 37(2–3) Environmental Policy and Law 83, 83.

representatives of the contracting parties,[92] and from the possibility for individuals to make communications to the ACCC regarding compliance with the Aarhus Convention by the contracting parties.[93]

Despite these innovations, the ACCC's non-judicial nature is very well entrenched within its DNA. First, Decision I/7,[94] which established the ACCC, had as its legal basis article 15 of the Aarhus Convention that stresses the non-judicial nature of the ACCC.[95] According to this provision:

> The Meeting of the Parties shall establish, on a consensus basis, optional arrangements of a non-confrontational, non-judicial and consultative nature for reviewing compliance with the provisions of this Convention. These arrangements shall allow for appropriate public involvement and may include the option of considering communications from members of the public on matters related to this Convention.

Second, the procedures before the ACCC are framed accordingly. This is seen in the language used where expressions such as 'non-compliance', 'submission' or 'communication', and 'Party concerned' are preferred to words such as 'breach', 'application' or 'defendant'.[96] Moreover, the ACCC's recommendations and reports are not binding.[97] It is for the Meeting of the Parties to give legal effect to the ACCC's recommendations and adopt the appropriate measures.[98]

Finally and more importantly, in relation to the responsibility of the EU within the Aarhus Convention, the application of the rules of responsibility is conducted in a heterodox fashion, departing from the classical structure of international responsibility.[99] The rationale underpinning the ACCC is quite different from international responsibility's

[92] Pitea, (n 90) 86.

[93] Antoni Pigrau Solé and Susana Borrás Pentinat, 'Diez Años del Convenio de Aarhus sobre acceso a la información, la participación y el acceso a la justicia en materia de medio ambiente' in Antoni Pigrau Solé (ed), *Accesso a la información, participación y acceso a la justicia en materia de medio ambiente, diez años del Convenio de Aarhus* (Atelier 2008) 51.

[94] UN Economic and Social Council, 'Decision I/7: Review of Compliance' (21–23 October 2002) ECE/MP.PP/2/Add.8. Available at: www.unece.org/fileadmin/DAM/env/pp/documents/mop1/ece.mp.pp.2.add.8.e.pdf.

[95] Cf. Pitea, (n 90) 86; Pigrau Solé and Borrás Pentinat, (n 93) 51.

[96] Pitea, (n 90) 86.

[97] Jerzy Jendrośka, 'Aarhus Convention Compliance Committee: Origins, Status and Activities' [2011] 8(4) Journal for Environmental and Planning Law 301, 416.

[98] Pitea, (n 90) 106.

[99] Antonino Alí, 'Non-Compliance Procedures in Multilateral Environmental Agreements: The Interaction between International Law and European Union Law' in Tullio Treves and others (eds), *Non-Compliance Procedures and Mechanisms and the Effectiveness of International Environmental Agreements* (T. M. C. Asser Press 2009) 532.

raison d'être.[100] The ACCC seems to be more concerned with bringing the contracting party back to comply with the Convention than with strictly providing reparations. The main consequence is that the ACCC will take rather pragmatic solutions that might seem to disregard the legal nuance of the law of international responsibility. In any case, even though any conclusions that could be drawn from the works of the ACCC in relation to the responsibility of the EU are adopted within a non-judicial set-up, the case law of the ACCC could nevertheless shed some light on the practical application of declarations of competence and the ACCC's approach to the EU's normative control.

5.4.2 The EU as an Actor in the ACCC: The Declaration of Competence in the ACCC's Reports

Even in a set-up where pragmatic and political solutions might prevail over rules and judicial enforcement, the declaration of competence might still play a relevant role when deciding whether to submit a communication on non-compliance to the EU or to its Member States. Especially given the shared nature of environmental competence, there would plenty of possibilities for the declaration to be used to determine whether the communication correctly targeted the EU and or its Member States.

Since the ACCC began its operations, the ACCC has received 130 communications from the public, with 10 being brought against the EU alone, one against the EU and one Member State, and 94 against EU Member States.[101] By contrast, there are only two submissions between parties and none of them targets the EU or any of its Member States.[102] Given that the EU and its Member States amount to more than 80 per cent of the communications made to ACCC, and that in some of them either the same facts were brought against the EU and one of its Member States

[100] Laura Pineschi, 'Non-Compliance Procedures and the Law of State Responsibility' in Tullio Treves and others (eds), *Non-Compliance Procedures and Mechanisms and the Effectiveness of International Environmental Agreements* (T. M. C. Asser Press 2009) 489.

[101] The list of all communications made by the public as well as the recommendations of the AC CC can be found at: www.unece.org/env/pp/pubcom.html.

[102] UN ESC, 'Findings and Recommendations with Regard to Compliance by Ukraine with the Obligations under the Aarhus Convenition' (14 March 2005) UN Doc ECE/MP.PP/C.1/2005/2/Add.3 (Submission ACCC/S/2014/1 by Romania concerning compliance by Ukraine). Available at: www.unece.org/fileadmin/DAM/env/documents/2005/pp/c.1/ece.mp.pp.c1.2005.2.Add.3.e.pdf; UNECE, 'Submission by Lithuania concerning compliance by Belarus' (25 March 2015) ACCC/S/2015/2.

separately[103] or jointly,[104] a mention of the declaration of competence should eventually arise.

Yet, in the 11 communications brought against the EU, only once is the declaration of competence mentioned.[105] Moreover, in all the concluded proceedings against Member States, there is not a single reference to the declaration of competence. All in all, the existence of just one complaint in which the declaration was referenced could be seen as a proof of their ineffectiveness, especially when reading of certain cases. As will be shown, in certain cases there was potential for the declaration to apply and yet it did not.

5.4.3 EU Responsibility as Established by the ACCC: Shared Competence but Separate Responsibilities

The non-judicial nature of the ACCC becomes especially clear when dealing with EU responsibility. The flexibility in the proceedings as well as its approach to responsibility play an important role when dealing with the attribution of a breach to the EU. Three cases are put forward to show how the ACCC's approach does not take into account the shared nature of environmental competence when establishing the responsibility of the EU and its Member States. The first one considers parallel communications brought against the EU and Lithuania. The second one concerns the joint communication brought against the EU and the UK.[106] The last one deals with the communication brought against the EU where the declaration of competence was mentioned.[107] By examining these three cases, this section will try to show how the ACCC approaches the issue of the EU's responsibility.

[103] UN ESC, 'Report by the Compliance Committee Addendum: Compliance by Lithuania with its Obligations under the Convention (Communication ACCC/C/2006/16)' (4 April 2008) UN Doc ECE/MP.PP/2008/5Add.6; UN ESC, 'Report by the Compliance Committee Addendum: Compliance by the EC with Its Obligations under the Convention (Communication ACCC/C/2006/17)' (2 May 2008) UN Doc ECE/MP.PP/2008/5/Add10.

[104] UN ESC, 'Findings and Recommendations with Regard to Communication ACCC/C/2012/68 Concerning Compliance by the European Union and the United Kingdom of Great Britain and Northern Ireland' (13 January 2014) UN Doc ECE/MP.PP/C.1/2014/5.

[105] UN ESC, 'Finding and Recommendation with Regard to Communication ACCC/C/2010/54 Concerning Compliance by the European Union' (2 October 2012) UN Doc ECE/MP.PP/C.1/2012/12.

[106] ACCC/C/2012/68. [107] ACCC/C/2010/54.

5.4.3.1 Parallel Submissions, Joint Responsibility?

In its reports ACCC/C/2006/16 (Lithuania) and ACCC/C/17 (EU), the ACCC dealt with two parallel complaints brought by an NGO (Association Kazokiskes Community) over the authorization of a landfill in the territory of Kazokiskes, a village in Lithuania. According to the NGO, Lithuania was in non-compliance with the Aarhus Convention, and more specifically its article 6, which concerns the obligation to inform the public during the environmental decision-making procedures that led to the authorization of that landfill. According to the ACCC, inasmuch as its national legislation lacked a clear requirement for the public to be informed in an adequate, timely and effective manner, Lithuania was in non-compliance with the Aarhus Convention.[108] More specifically, Lithuania breached the Aarhus Convention by not allowing the public to be informed on the different stages of the authorization but by limiting it to a single stage, within the Environmental Impact Assessment (EIA).

Similarly, according to the NGO, the EU was also in non-compliance of article 6 Aarhus Convention by not correctly implementing it through the EIA Directive. Yet, unlike with Lithuania, the ACCC found that the EU was in compliance with the Convention. Interestingly, while the ACCC understood the special nature of the EU,[109] it failed to establish how that would influence the EU's responsibility:

> Article 6 of the Convention obliges the Parties to meet the minimum requirements for public participation in decision-making.... While this applies to the Party concerned too, the structure of the European [Union] and its legislation differs from those of all other Parties to the Convention in the sense that while relevant [Union] legislation has been adopted to ensure public participation in various cases of environmental decision-making, it is the duty of its Member States to implement [Union] directives.[110]

When read jointly with the ACCC report concerning Lithuania, it would appear that the ACCC seems to be arguing that, when implementing EU directives in particular, the responsibility rests nevertheless with the Member State. Yet, a closer reading of the report seems to point into another direction, more in line with the responsibility of the EU based on its normative control over its Member States. The ACCC understood that the EIA Directive provided for a mechanism of public participation. Moreover, it found that nothing in EU law prevented the public from

[108] ACCC/C/2006/16, para. 90. [109] Alí, (n 99) 532. [110] ACCC/C/2006/17, para. 44.

being informed throughout all the different stages of the decision-making procedure leading to the authorization of a landfill:

> Bearing in mind the above characteristic features of the [Union] law and the fact that under EIA and IPPC directives public participation is mandatory in case of the two main permitting decisions applicable to landfills covered by Annex I to the Convention, the Committee is of the opinion that as far as application of article 6 of the Convention in relation to multiple permits applicable to landfills is concerned, the [Union] legal framework in principle properly assures achievement of the respective goals of the Convention.[111]

The ACCC does not seem to be discarding that the EU would be in non-compliance in a scenario in which the national legislation would not allow for public participation during the EIA procedure, because the EIA Directive did not provide for it. It could be argued that the fact that the communications discussed previously were filed separately clearly shows how there were two parallel acts and not a single one that needed to be attributed to either the EU or Lithuania. The actions of Lithuania fell outside the scope of the EU's normative control.

5.4.3.2 Joint Proceedings, Separate Responsibilities

By contrast, it could be expected that if the communication has been brought jointly against the EU and one of its Member States, the question of the attribution of non-compliance to the EU and/or the Member State in question could arise. Yet in ACCC/C/2012/68, the issue of attribution was completely absent. In fact, the communication concerned the renewable energy programmes of the EU and the UK respectively and the impact of the latter on two specific projects in Scotland. For the ACCC it was clear that these two claims were separate. More specifically, while it declared the part of the communication against the UK admissible, it established the inadmissibility of the claims against the EU.[112] As the report observes: [g]iven the structure of the EU and its Member States, . . . the communication rather concerns implementation of the Convention by the UK than by the EU.[113]

By adopting its renewable energy plan the UK was not implementing EU legislation, but was acting within the sphere of its shared environmental competence. Therefore, the ACCC seems to understand that insofar as the case does not relate to the implementation of the Convention by the EU, it is not responsible. This report could be seen as delineating the external

[111] ACCC/C/2006/17, para. 45.
[112] ACCC/C/2012/68, para. 75–77.
[113] ACCC/C/2012/68, para. 49.

contours of the EU's normative control. Inasmuch as the action of the UK does not stem from its implementation of EU law, it continues to bear its responsibility for the due implementation of the Aarhus Convention.

5.4.3.3 Declarations of Competence and Normative Control

Generally, discussions on the responsibility of the EU in relation to mixed agreements like the Aarhus Convention tend to focus on whether it is the EU or any of its Member States party to the agreement which should bear the responsibility over a certain breach. In fact, declarations of competence are supposed to address this issue.[114] However, the mixed nature of an agreement does not mean that all EU Member States are parties to the agreement. There are situations in which an EU Member State might decide not to join the EU in a mixed agreement. For example, Ireland only ratified the Aarhus Convention in 2012. Yet, the EU had concluded it in 1998 and it had entered into force in 2005.[115]

In 2010, an individual submitted a communication to the ACCC on the EU's non-compliance because of its failure to properly monitor implementation of EU law related to the Convention by Ireland with respect to Ireland's National Renewable Energy Action Plan (NREAP).[116] The individual alleged that such conduct amounted to a breach of articles 4, 5, 7 and 9 (1) of the Convention.

When analysing the communication, the ACCC mentioned the declaration of competence when determining the extent of the EU's responsibility under the Aarhus Convention. Consequently, the declaration of competence would play a role in identifying if the EU's competence and responsibility covered the actions of Ireland in this particular case. However, the declaration was mentioned in passing[117] and only in relation to

[114] Joni Heliskoski, 'EU Declarations of Competence and International Responsibility' in Malcolm D. Evans and Panos Koutrakos (eds), *The International Responsibility of the European Union International and European Perspectives* (Hart 2013).

[115] ACCC/C/2010/54, para. 74. [116] ACCC/C/2010/54, para. 3.

[117] ACCC/C/2010/54, para. 18. 'Upon approving the Convention, the Party concerned confirmed its declaration made upon signature. It also declared that the legal instruments that it had already enacted to implement the Convention did not cover fully the implementation of the obligations resulting from article 9, paragraph 3, of the Convention, to the extent that they did not relate to acts and omissions of EU institutions under article 2, paragraph 2 (d), and thus Member States would be responsible for the performance of these obligations until the Party concerned, in the exercise of its powers under the Treaty establishing the European Community (which was superseded by the Treaty on the Functioning of the European Union), adopted provisions of EU law covering the implementation of these obligations. The Aarhus Regulation came into effect on 28 June 2007.'

the controversial article 9 (3).[118] Yet, as mentioned previously, the individual was arguing that it was article 9 (1) and not article 9 (3) Aarhus Convention that was the provision being breached. The reference to the declaration of competence could be seen as testimonial. Moreover, its residual role is better understood when the declaration is examined. With the exception of the reference to article 9 (3) Aarhus Convention, the declaration just lists the objectives of the EU's environmental policy. Therefore, the declaration would not have been of that much help in establishing the responsibility of the EU is this particular case, as it is difficult to establish the competence of the EU just based on its objectives.[119]

The ACCC continued its examination of the role of the EU in relation to the NREAP and considered that two issues arise when examining the EU's responsibility: first, whether the EU legal framework is compatible with the Convention; and, second, whether the EU has fulfilled its responsibility to monitor that, in implementing EU law properly, its Member States, including Ireland, meet the obligations resting on them by virtue of the EU being a party to the Convention.[120] Thus, for the ACCC, the responsibility of the EU within the Aarhus Convention rests on two elements: either the EU's regulatory framework is not aligned with the Convention, and/or the EU has not properly controlled the implementation of the Aarhus Convention.[121] These two elements are to certain extent the basic components of the EU's normative control. When the EU has exercised its competence and laid down the regulatory framework through EU legislation the EU is responsible for the actions of its Member States carried out under this normative umbrella.

It appears that when the EU shares its competence with its Member States whenever the former has exercised its competence, it is responsible for the actions of the latter. However, a small caveat is necessary. It is unclear the extent to which the fact that Ireland was not a party to the Convention played a role in the establishment of the EU's responsibility. Had Ireland been a party to the Aarhus Convention at that time, would the EU still bear the sole responsibility over Ireland's NREAP? Given how

[118] On the controversy surrounding this provision: see Chapter 4. Case C-240/09 *Lesoochranárske zoskupenie VLK v Ministerstvo zivotného prostredia Slovenskej republiky* [2011] ECR I-1255; Case C-404/12, C-405/12 *Council and Commission v Stichting Natuur en Milieu and Pesticide Action Network Europe* [nyr] ECR; Jerzy Jendrośka, 'Recent Case-Law of the Aarhus Convention Compliance Committee' [2011] 8(4) Journal for Environmental and Planning Law 375.

[119] See Chapter 4.

[120] ACCC/C/2010/54, para. 76.

[121] Id, para. 85.

in the previous examples the ACCC was not inclined to establish the joint responsibility of the EU and its Member State, it is submitted that it would seem unlikely that in this complaint the EU would have shared its responsibility with Ireland had the latter been a party to the Aarhus Convention when the event took place.

While the quasi-judicial nature of the ACCC leads one to qualify any conclusions on the EU's responsibility under the Aarhus Convention, the reports examined here nevertheless shed some light on the issue. First, they seem to confirm that declaration of competence are not well suited to be applied in practice. Even when mentioned in a report, it is difficult to see their relevance in terms of responsibility. Second, these cases show how the ACCC is confronted with breaches stemming from the EU's normative control, and how so far the responsibility has rested exclusively with the EU. Moreover, while it might seem logical to see at least some discussion on the EU's joint responsibility with its Member States within this Convention that falls clearly within shared competence, the discussion has not arisen yet.

5.5 Conclusions

By examining the international practice on EU declarations of competence, the present chapter has aimed to establish whether they really help in dealing with the articulation of EU responsibility. While the previous chapter raised the issue of the theoretical problems that declarations pose to the apportionment of responsibility between the EU and its Member States, this chapter examined how international courts have applied them. However, as this chapter has shown, there is little international practice in this area, and where there is practice the declarations of competence do not completely solve the question of the attribution of responsibility to the EU.

The lack of international visibility contrasts with its internal relevance in the EU. The *MOX Plant* dispute perfectly exemplifies this contradiction. In the international dispute, the declarations were not mentioned at all by any of the parties. In contrast, in the CJEU case, the parties relied on it to establish the division of competence over the issue.[122]

The declarations of competence do not solve all the problems concerning the responsibility of the EU. The declaration could be (if properly updated and implemented) a useful tool for the apportionment of

[122] See Chapter 4.

international obligations. As the *SRCF Advisory Opinion* demonstrates, declarations of competence would not solve the issue of the EU's responsibility. Instead they would be just a preliminary step in the establishment of the responsibility of the EU; the application of the rules of attribution would still be needed.

Thus, the question of attribution would have to be resolved through other means. The jurisprudence of the ACCC shows the little practical relevance of the declaration of competence made to the Aarhus Convention, and how, in an area falling squarely within shared competence, responsibility is not shared. On the contrary, the ACCC seems to recognize that the special character of the EU plays a role in the attribution of responsibility.[123] Furthermore, according to the ACCC, the special character of the EU entails that it is responsible for the wrongdoings of its Member States when such acts are carried out under its normative control.[124] Though the ACCC cannot be considered an international judicial body, the conclusions it has reached definitely shed some light on the discussions on EU responsibility. It appears that, when faced with questions on the responsibility of the EU even in areas of shared competence, international bodies seem to understand that normative control does not entail the joint responsibility of the EU and its Member States but the sole responsibility of the EU.

[123] ACCC/C/2006/16, para. 90. [124] ACCC/C/2010/54, para. 85.

6 The EU's Normative Control and International Responsibility

The WTO Dispute Settlement System

6.1 Introduction

Unlike mixed agreements with a declaration of competence, the responsibility of the EU in the WTO system is not aprioristically linked to the internal division of competences. The EU has not established any kind of mechanism to make its division of competence clear to third parties that may want to bring a claim against it or its Member States. As a logical consequence of the lack of a mechanism designed to deal with EU responsibility in the WTO, to understand how the EU manages its responsibility in the WTO it is necessary to examine the disputes to which the EU has been party. The practice until now shows the EU being involved (apart from the disputes brought directly against it) in practically all the disputes against any of its Member States in one way or another. While this practice has led to the assumption that the EU is eager to be held responsible in the WTO, this chapter will argue that in most of the cases there is an EU law element which points to the EU's responsibility.[1]

The discussions on the EU's responsibility in the WTO usually mention the position taken by the EU during the LAN dispute.[2] In this case, the

[1] ILC, 'Second Report on Responsibility of International Organizations, by Giorgio Gaja, Special Rapporteur' (2 April 2004) UN Doc A/CN.4/541. Pieter Jan Kuijper and Esa Paasivirta, 'Further Exploring International Responsibility: The European Community and the ILC's Project on Responsibility of International Organizations' [2004] 1 International Organizations Law Review 111, 124. Against Andrés Delgado Casteleiro and Joris Larik, 'The "Odd Couple": The Responsibility of the EU at the WTO' in Panos Koutrakos and Malcolm D. Evans (eds), *The International Responsbility of the European Union European and International Perspectives* (Hart 2013); Eleftheria Neframi, *Les accords mixtes de la Communauté européenne:aspects communautaires et internationaux* (Bruylant 2007) 556.

[2] WTO, *European Communities – Customs Classification of Certain Computer Equipment: Report of the Panel* (22 June 1998) WT/DS62/R, WT/Ds67/R and WT/DS68/R, as modified by The Appellate Body Report WT/DS62/Ab/R, WT/DS67/Ab/R and WT/DS68/Ab/R.

US brought separate panels against the EU, Ireland and the UK regarding, among other things, the tariff treatment of LAN. Though a procedural agreement was reached between the US, the EU, and its two Member States by which the complaints lodged against the latter were merged into a single claim against the EU, the US expressed the common concerns of third parties regarding the responsibility of the EU and Member States in mixed agreements where no declaration of competence has been made. In particular, the US requested that the panel 'specify which of these parties was responsible to the US for this nullification or impairment [of] the value of concessions accruing to the US under the GATT 1994'.[3] As a response to this demand from the US, the EU declared that it was:

> ready to assume the entire international responsibility for all measures in the area of tariff concessions, whether the measure complained about has been taken at the [EU] level or at the level of Member States.[4]

While this statement could be seen as evidence of the EU's alleged eagerness to be held responsible in the WTO, both the panel and the Appellate Body answered neither the EU statement nor the argument by the US on the attribution of conduct. They assumed the EU to be the relevant export market, without entering into the question of the apportionment and attribution of obligations between the EU and its Member States.[5] Therefore, the EU was solely responsible for the customs regulations on LAN equipment, but no reasoning for that was provided. This example, as well as others, has allowed Eeckhout to argue that: '[o]ne would expect issues of responsibility to arise as a consequence of attempts to deny or evade such responsibility. Here the opposite appears to happen'.[6] However, to what extent are the previous statements and assumptions completely true? Is the EU in a race to the top (in contraposition to a race to the bottom) regarding responsibility within the WTO?

On one hand, it could be argued that the EU has an underlying strategy to foster its presence in the WTO. However, would this responsibility preclude a Member State's liability? Does the DSU promote the EU's

3 Ibid. Panel Report para. 3.2.

4 WTO, *European Communities – Customs Classification of Certain Computer Equipment: Oral Pleading of the European Commission to the Panel* (12 June 1997) para. 6; also can be found in: Gaja, (n 1) para. 27.

5 WT/DS62/R, WT/Ds67/R and WT/DS68/R, para. 96.

6 Piet Eeckhout, 'The EU and Its Member States in the WTO – Issues of Responsibility' in Lorand Bartels and Federico Ortino (eds), *Regional Trade Agreements and the WTO Legal System* (Oxford University Press 2006) 449.

responsibility over that of Member States? How do third States react to EU participation in the dispute settlement?

By fostering negotiations and mutually agreed solutions throughout the dispute settlement procedures, the WTO Dispute Settlement System not only favours diplomatic solutions over judicial adjudication but also allows the EU to intervene in any dispute brought against its Member States (as long as the claimant would agree).[7] The EU and the claimant would reach a solution on the substance of the dispute by leaving aside the application of the rules of attribution. WTO member states accept this possibility without any significant objections.[8] Moreover, the procedural design of the Dispute Settlement would also encourage the EU to be targeted as the respondent instead of its Member States.[9] For instance, in terms of retaliation,[10] there is a comparative advantage in starting consultations with the EU rather than with a Member State. If instead of bringing a claim against France on the tariff of cheese products, and

[7] See article 4 of the Dispute Settlement Understanding. For an analysis of the WTO Dispute Settlement Mechanism see: Ernst-Ulrich Petersmann, *The GATT/WTO Dispute Settlement System: International Law, International Organizations and Dispute Settlement* (Kluwer Law International 1997); David Palmeter and Petros C. Mavroidis, *Dispute Settlement in the World Trade Organization: Practice and Procedure* (2nd edn, Cambridge University Press 2004); Xavier Fernández Pons, *La Organización Mundial del Comercio y el Derecho Internacional. Un estudio sobre el sistema de solución de diferencias de la OMC y las normas secundarias de Derecho internacional general* (Marcial Pons 2006); Peter Van Den Bossche, *The Law and Policy of the World Trade Organization: Text, Cases and Materials* (2nd edn, Cambridge University Press 2008); Santiago M. Villapando, 'Attribution of Conduct to the State: How the Rules of State Responsibility May Be Applied within the WTO Dispute Settlement System' [2002] 5(2) *Journal of International Economic Law* 393; Joost Pauwelyn, *Conflict of Norms in Public International Law: How WTO Relates to Other Rules of International Law* (Cambridge University Press 2003); Joost Pauwelyn, 'Enforcement and Countermeasures in the WTO' [2000] 94 American Journal of International Law 335; Irene Blázquez Navarro, *Integración europea y diferencias comerciales de la OMC* (Marcial Pons 2007); Javier Díez-Hotchleitner Rodríguez, 'La Unión Europea ante la Reforma del Sistema de Solución de Diferencias de la OMC' in Juan Manuel Faramiñan Gisbert (ed), *Globalización y Comercio Exterior Actas de las XX Jornadas de la Asociación Española de Profesores de Derecho Internacional y Relaciones Internacionales, 2003* (Boletín Oficial del Estado 2005); Marcella Distefano, *Soluzione delle Controversie nll'OMC e Diritto Internazionale* (CEDAM 2001).

[8] It appears that the reasons behind its objection have more to do with a divide-and-rule strategy than with concern over the actual enforcement of WTO law or the lack of knowledge of the EU's executive federalism. Pieter Jan Kuijper, 'International Responsibility for EU Mixed Agreements' in Christophe Hillion and Panos Koutrakos (eds), *Mixed Agreements Revisited: The EU and Its Member States in the World* (Hart 2010) 214.

[9] Delgado Casteleiro and Larik, (n 1).

[10] Article 22 DSU; Pauwelyn, 'Enforcement and Countermeasures in the WTO' (n 7) 335.

consequently adopting a retaliation measure against cheese products of French origin, a WTO member could bring the same dispute against the EU, the retaliation would not only include French cheese products but also the same products of the other 27 EU members. Therefore, the claimant has a wider range of products on which to adopt retaliatory measures than if it brought the same claim against just one EU Member State.

On the other hand, it could be argued that there is no such eagerness on the part of the EU to be held responsible. Most of the disputes which arrive at the WTO DSM involve the EU in one way or another.[11] Subsequently, it should fall upon the EU to bear responsibility. Indeed, the LAN dispute clearly entails the implementation of the EU's exclusive competence by Member State authorities. Therefore, the position of the EU regarding the claims against Ireland and the UK can be seen as a mere manifestation of the link between competence and responsibility. The EU could be responsible due to the competence involved, as most of the cases cover areas over which the EU has exercised its powers. Thus, perhaps the remaining disputes, the residual ones, are moved by the inertia created by the practice developed in the other cases.

This chapter aims to examine whether there is actual eagerness on the part of the EU to be held responsible within the WTO, and whether this approach (or lack of it) is a useful and effective way to manage EU responsibility. Section 6.2 focuses on the EU competences involved in the WTO. This issue is of significant relevance since the main argument concerning EU responsibility within the WTO is that there is no relation between the allocation of competences at the EU level and EU responsibility. Section 6.3 examines the EU's participation in the WTO Dispute Settlement System. It considers three cases touching on these issues. These cases shed light on which rules of attribution the WTO panels applies to the EU and show that the WTO panels understand that the EU is responsible for any act committed by its Member States when they are implementing EU law. In this regard, the panels accept the EU's responsibility for the actions of its Member States, when such actions are committed because of the EU's normative control over its Member States. Overall, the analysis of these specific disputes shows the current problems and issues which arise regarding EU competence and responsibility not only in the WTO but in general.

[11] Delgado Casteleiro and Larik, (n 1).

6.2 The EU in the WTO: Issues of Competence

Legal relations between the EU and the WTO are significantly determined by the evolving nature of the EU's division of competence. This section will analyse which competences are involved within the WTO and how these competences have evolved over time. Moreover, this section shows how the dichotomy between exclusive and shared competence does not begin to grasp the intricacies of the responsibility and attribution of conduct in the WTO. As it will be shown, while the CCP has expanded its material scope over the years, its exclusive nature has not expanded accordingly. By tracing the evolution of the division of competences as regards the WTO agreements, this section will show how establishing a clear a priori correlation between the exclusive competence of the EU in the field of international trade and the attributing responsibility to the EU is a complicated endeavour.

6.2.1 *From the Succession on GATT 1947 to a Mixed WTO*

EU participation in the GATT/WTO system began with a de facto substitution.[12] Initially, the EU was not a member of the GATT 1947. Yet, its Member States were. Since the EU was not formally bound by the GATT 1947, it could not be responsible for any breach of the GATT 1947 it might commit. Yet, EU Member States were bound and could be held responsible. In principle this should not have been a problem: as it is well known, EU Member States are parties to many international agreements to which the EU is not party because the EU does not have the competence to conclude them. However, since EU Treaties envisaged the progressive transfer of powers in the fields of tariff and trade policy (areas covered by the GATT 1947), the potential for conflict between EU law and GATT 1947 was deemed to arise eventually. It was in *International Fruit Company* where the CJEU dealt with this conflict.[13] This preliminary reference, posed by a Dutch court, as part of the process challenging the implementation of EU regulations on the importation of eating apples, first questioned whether the concept of validity, in the sense of article 267 (ex article 234) TFEU, also entailed validity under international law. Second, the Dutch court

[12] Cf. Alicia Cebada Romero, *La Organización Mundial del Comercio y la Unión Europea* (La Ley 2002) 127; Raas Holdgard, *External Relations Law of the European Community: Legal Reasoning and Legal Discourses* (Wolter Kluwer 2008)

[13] Case 22-24/72 *International Fruit Company* [1972] ECR 1219.

asked whether the challenged measures could be invalid due to their incompatibility with the GATT 1947.[14]

In relation to the validity of Union norms under international law, the Court interpreted article 267 TFEU (ex article 234) in a broad way.[15] In this regard, the CJEU held that:

> the jurisdiction of the Court cannot be limited by grounds on which the validity of the measures may be contested. . . . Since such jurisdiction extends to all grounds capable of invalidating those measures, the Court is obliged to examine whether their validity may be affected by reason of the fact that they are contrary to a rule of international law.[16]

Nonetheless, the Court identified a precondition to be met to examine the validity of a Union measure under international law. The international rule which will be used to assess the validity of the Union measure at stake must be binding on the EU. In the present case, the international rule was the GATT 1947. Logically two possible answers were possible: either the EU was not bound by the GATT 1947 insofar as it was not a party to it, or for other reasons it was bound by the GATT 1947. The CJEU went for the second option and found that the EU was bound by the GATT 1947 regardless of the fact that it had not formally concluded it. How did the CJEU fill the gap between the fact that the EU was not a party to the GATT 1947 but was nevertheless bound by it? For the Court, there were two crucial elements in determining the binding character of the GATT 1947. The first element had an internal nature and concerned the transfer of powers whereas the second element had an external nature and revolved around the exercise of those powers in the international sphere. The CJEU took into account, in establishing the binding character of the GATT 1947 under EU law, the end of the transitional period prior to the completion of the customs union. It was because the Member States had transferred the powers pertaining to the CCP, which included the establishment of a common tariff and trade policy, to the EU that the binding force of the GATT 1947 was carried into the EU legal order. As the CJEU put it:

> The [Union] has assumed the functions inherent in the tariff and trade policy, progressively during the transitional period and in their entirety on the expiry of that period, by virtue of article 111 and [133] of the Treaty. . . . By conferring those powers on the [Union], the Member States showed their wishes to bind it by the obligation entered under the General Agreement.[17]

[14] Ibid. [15] Cf. Panos Koutrakos, *EU International Relations Law* (Hart 2006) 192.
[16] Case 22-24/72 *International Fruit Company* para. 5. [17] Ibid.

Moving to the second element, the EU had exercised the CCP's powers even before the end of the transitional period. The EU had been involved in the negotiation of the Tokyo round and it was participating in the dispute settlement system.[18] The other contracting parties already recognized the EU as a partner in the tariff negotiations and as a party to the agreements of all types concluded within the framework of the GATT 1947.[19] Otherwise put, the EU was already an actor within GATT 1947 even though it had not concluded and was not formally bound by it. Consequently, the Court understood that inasmuch as the Member States had transferred its powers to the EU, which had exercised them, and that third parties accepted that transfer of powers, the EU was bound by the GATT 1947.

With this judgment the Court inextricably linked the CCP and the GATT 1947. By establishing that it was due to the birth of the CCP and the exercise of its external powers within the GATT 1947, the EU had become bound by the latter. The CCP competence would be the relevant competence when concluding international trade agreements within the GATT 1947. Moreover, since the areas covered by GATT 1947 concern tariffs and trade, any implementing measure within the EU would also be adopted by virtue of the CCP competence.

The creation of the WTO supposed a paradigm shift in this regard. On one hand, the extension of the substantive scope of the WTO tested the correlation between the CCP and the WTO.[20] On the other hand, it, logically, entailed a change in the CJEU's approach towards EU participation in the WTO. As *Opinion 1/94* showed, succession was no longer a valid way of examining relations between the EU, its Member States and the WTO. Moreover, the substantive scope of the WTO agreements clearly outgrew the scope of the CCP, not only in relation to the legal basis for the conclusion of the agreement, but also in relation to the policy areas involved in the implementation of the WTO law.[21]

Prior to analysing the EU's competences in issues falling within the WTO, it is important to note the context which gave rise to the opinion. The Maastricht Treaty had failed to codify the existing jurisprudence on the scope and effect of the CCP, which was open to radically different interpretations.[22] Furthermore, the EU and its Member States had put

18 Cebada Romero, (n 12) 128.

19 Case 22-24/72 *International Fruit Company* para. 18.

20 Blázquez Navarro, (n 7) 157.

21 Opinion 1/94 *Re: Competence of the Community to conclude international agreements concerning services and the protection of intellectual property* [1994] ECR I-05267.

22 Marise Cremona, 'EC External Commercial Policy after Amsterdam: Authority and Interpretation within Interconnected Legal Orders' in J. H. H. Weiler (ed), *The EU, the*

aside the issues regarding the division of competences during the negotiations of the Uruguay Round allowing the Commission to act as the sole negotiator.[23] Within this context, the Commission considered that the exclusive competence deriving from the CCP and which traditionally covered all the GATT extended to cover the material scope of the WTO agreements. Thus, pursuant to article 218 (11) TFEU (ex article 300 (6) TEC), the Commission asked the Court to deliver its opinion on the competence involved in the conclusion of the WTO and its annexed agreement. The first question posed by the Commission was in essence asking the Court about the existence and nature of Union competence regarding the WTO agreements. The Commission's second question was looking for clarification on the mixed character of the WTO and the scope of the principle of loyalty.[24]

The analysis given by the Court rightly reduced the questions of the Commission to one simple issue 'whether or not the [Union] has exclusive competence to conclude the WTO agreement and its annexes'.[25] The CJEU answered this question in two steps. First, it analysed the extent to which the explicit exclusive CCP competence covered the WTO agreements. Second, it examined whether there were any other EU competences which might cover those parts of the WTO agreements not falling within the CCP's scope. The Court developed its reasoning following the structure of the WTO. First, it examined EU competence vis-à-vis the Multilateral Agreements on Trade in Goods. The CJEU acknowledged that these agreements fell under the exclusive competence of the Union under article 207 TFEU (ex article 133 (then 113) TEC).[26] This outcome is of special relevance, especially in respect to those issues regarding the Agreement on Agriculture, the SPS agreement or the Subsidies and Countervailing Measures Agreement (SCM Agreement). By subsuming all the Multilateral Agreements on Trade in Goods under the scope of the CCP, the Court identified the divide which may exist between the competences for concluding an international agreement and the competence involved in the implementation of the agreement.[27] In relation to the Agreement on Agriculture, the Court held that:

WTO, and the NAFTA towards a Common Law of International Trade? (Oxford University Press 2000) 9.

[23] Koutrakos, (n 15) 41.

[24] Opinion 1/94 *Re: Competence of the Community to conclude international agreements concerning services and the protection of intellectual property* para. 6.

[25] Ibid. [26] Ibid. [27] See Chapter 4.

> [t]he objective of the Agreement on Agriculture is to establish, on a worldwide basis, 'a fair and market-oriented agricultural trading system' (see the preamble to that Agreement). The fact that the commitments entered into under that Agreement require internal measures to be adopted on the basis of Article 43 of the Treaty does not prevent the international commitments themselves from being entered into pursuant to Article 113 alone.[28]

The CJEU thus recognized that an international agreement could be concluded by exercising a specific competence (CCP) but yet its implementation could require a different competence (Common Agricultural Policy). This becomes specially relevant when compared with the scenario prior to the creation of the WTO. The CCP was the only competence involved in the conclusion and implementation of the GATT 1947. By contrast, with the WTO although the conclusion of the Multilateral Agreements on Trade in Goods may fall within the scope of the CCP and therefore be of exclusive nature, the implementation of those agreements may not fall within the scope of the CCP. Moreover, the implementation could fall within the scope of competence which might be shared in nature. As *Opinion 1/94* shows, the expansion of the WTO did not entail an expansion of the scope of the CCP as to encompass implementing measures. The WTO agreements falling within the CCP during their conclusion would not necessarily be implemented following the same legal basis.[29]

In relation to the Trade Related Intellectual Property Rights Agreement (TRIPS) and the General Agreement on Trade in Services (GATS), the Court established that those agreements did not fall within the scope of the CCP as it stood at that time.[30] This decision has raised much criticism from both sides. On one hand, there has been criticism of the broad notion of the CCP developed by the CJEU to include the Agriculture and SPS agreement in its scope.[31] On the other, it has been argued that this interpretation of the CCP was obsolete inasmuch as the scope of the CCP was reduced to trade in goods.[32]

28 Opinion 1/94 *Re: Competence of the Community to conclude international agreements concerning services and the protection of intellectual property* para. 29 and 32.

29 The relationship between the regulation of susbsidies at the WTO level and states aids at the EU level constitutes a very interesting example in this regard. See Section 5.3.3.3.

30 Opinion 1/94 *Re: Competence of the Community to conclude international agreements concerning services and the protection of intellectual property* para. 71.

31 Piet Eeckhout, *External Relations of the European Union: Legal and Constitutional Foundations* (Oxford University Press 2004) 27; Cremona, (n 22) 13.

32 Blázquez Navarro, (n 7) 155.

Second, having excluded that the GATS and the TRIPS fell outside the scope of the CCP, the CJEU analysed whether there could be an implicit exclusive competence covering those areas. This analysis was done by applying the ERTA principle to the fields covered by the GATS and the TRIPS.[33] In relation to these agreements, the Court established that since in the fields covered by them there was no complete harmonization of the internal rules, no exclusive competence could be implied. Therefore, the GATS and TRIPS were shared competences.[34]

To sum up, following *Opinion 1/94*, mixed participation was the only envisageable formula to deal with EU participation in the WTO. The GATT remained the EU's exclusive competence whereas the GATS and TRIPS were considered to fall within shared competence. *Opinion 1/94* had two consequences as regards the way the relationship between the CCP and the WTO is to be understood. First, the CCP was no longer the only relevant competence for the conclusion of the WTO agreements. Second, even on issues falling within the CCP, the implementation measure might follow the CCP competence. In other words, the competences of the concluding decision do not reflect all the competences or powers that might be involved in the subsequent life of the WTO agreement.

6.2.2 *WTO Competence after Nice*

As Cremona argued when analysing the CCP reform in Amsterdam: '[t]here is no doubt the Court, in *Opinion 1/94*, regards exclusivity as an attribute of the Common Commercial Policy';[35] the Treaty of Amsterdam provided the possibility of extending the scope of the CCP to include the conclusion of international agreements on services or intellectual property (article 133 (5) TEU).[36]

The Treaty of Nice broadened the CCP's material scope even further, but not its exclusive nature. Three new paragraphs[37] were added in order

33 See Chapter 2.

34 Opinion 1/94 *Re: Competence of the Community to conclude international agreements concerning services and the protection of intellectual property* para. 98 and 105.

35 Cremona, (n 22) 21. 36 Ibid.

37 Article 133 TEC: '5. Paragraphs 1 to 4 shall also apply to the negotiation and conclusion of agreements in the fields of trade in services and the commercial aspects of intellectual property, in so far as those agreements are not covered by the said paragraphs and without prejudice to paragraph 6.

'By way of derogation from paragraph 4, the Council shall act unanimously when negotiating and concluding an agreement in one of the fields referred to in the first subparagraph, where that agreement includes provisions for which unanimity is required for the adoption of internal rules or where it relates to a field in which the

extend the scope of the CCP to cover WTO matters while trying to reflect Member States' concerns over the transfer of powers on certain matters.[38]

However, this balance, to say the least, was not as easy as might have been expected. These three new paragraphs have been subject to plenty of criticism[39] and created some problems as regards their interpretation.[40] *Opinion 1/08* showed the problems that they posed in relation to their interpretation.[41]

Leaving aside the complexity of the wording, this provision deepens the divide between the competences involved in the conclusion and the implementation of an agreement. Article 133 TEC goes further than *Opinion 1/94* on this issue.[42] In particular, while *Opinion 1/94* envisaged the possibility

[Union] has not yet exercised the powers conferred upon it by this Treaty by adopting internal rules.

'The Council shall act unanimously with respect to the negotiation and conclusion of a horizontal agreement insofar as it also concerns the preceding subparagraph or the second subparagraph of paragraph 6.

'This paragraph shall not affect the right of the Member States to maintain and conclude agreements with third countries or international organisations in so far as such agreements comply with [Union] law and other relevant international agreements.

'6. An agreement may not be concluded by the Council if it includes provisions which would go beyond the [Union]'s internal powers, in particular by leading to harmonisation of the laws or regulations of the Member States in an area for which this Treaty rules out such harmonisation.

'In this regard, by way of derogation from the first subparagraph of paragraph 5, agreements relating to trade in cultural and audiovisual services, educational services, and social and human health services, shall fall within the shared competence of the [Union] and its Member States. Consequently, in addition to a [Union] decision taken in accordance with the relevant provisions of Article 300, the negotiation of such agreements shall require the common accord of the Member States. Agreements thus negotiated shall be concluded jointly by the [Union] and the Member States.

'The negotiation and conclusion of international agreements in the field of transport shall continue to be governed by the provisions of Title V and Article 300.

'7. Without prejudice to the first subparagraph of paragraph 6, the Council, acting unanimously on a proposal from the Commission and after consulting the European Parliament, may extend the application of paragraphs 1 to 4 to international negotiations and agreements on intellectual property in so far as they are not covered by paragraph 5.'

38 Eeckhout, (n 31) 49.

39 See Christoph W. Herrmann, 'Common Commercial Policy after Nice: Sisyphus Would Have Done a Better Job' [2002] 39(1) Common Market Law Review 7.

40 Opinion 1/08 *Re: GATS* [2009] ECR I-11129.

41 Ibid; cf. Marise Cremona, 'Balancing Union and Member State Interests: Opinion 1/2008, Choice of Legal Base and the Common Commercial Policy under the Treaty of Lisbon' [2010] 35 *European Law Review* 678.

42 Opinion 1/94 *Re: Competence of the Community to conclude international agreements concerning services and the protection of intellectual property* para. 29.

that the implementing measures may not have the same legal basis as the agreement, depending on the legal instrument used to implement the agreement, the Nice reform decouples the internal and external legal basis when they pursue the same objectives. Notwithstanding, Koutrakos disagrees with this view. In his opinion, this article should be read not as further development of *Opinion 1/94* but in light of it. He considers that:

> *where an internal measure was necessary to implement an external measure; they would serve the same objective, their only difference being the former's adoption as matter of necessity in order to enable the EU to comply with its contractual obligations under the latter. In the light of the above, Article 133 (5) (1) TEC could constitute the legal basis of the adoption of internal measures whose aim is to implement agreements concluded under that provision.*[43]

Regardless of the position taken, this discussion over the nature and the legal basis of the implementing measures shows the complexities the EU encounters when implementing WTO obligations. Furthermore, the modification introduced by the Treaty of Nice casts more shadows over the nature of EU competence on the GATS and TRIPS, especially regarding the implementing measure. The Nice reform shows that the CCP's scope is not only a continuously discussed topic in the legal literature but also a cause of inter-institutional conflict.[44]

6.2.3 *Lisbon and the WTO*

The Treaty of Lisbon shed some light on the scope and nature of the CCP and its relationship to the WTO. Article 207 (1) TFEU extended the scope of the CCP to include

> the conclusion of tariff and trade agreements relating to trade in goods and services, and the commercial aspects of intellectual property, foreign direct investment, the achievement of uniformity in measures of liberalisation, export policy and measures to protect trade such as those to be taken in the event of dumping or subsidies.

Thus, as Herrmann highlights, 'an agreement amending the EU's schedule of specific commitments under the [GATS] can now be concluded by the EU alone, an action that previously required agreement by both the EC and its Member States'.[45] With the exception of transport, 'there can be

[43] Koutrakos, (n 15) 63.

[44] Case C-13/07 *Commission v Council (Vietnam Accession) [nyr] ECR, Opinion of the Advocate General; Opinion 1/08 Re: GATS.*

[45] Christoph W. Herrmann, 'The Treaty of Lisbon Expands the EU's External Trade and Investment Powers' [2010] 14 ASIL Insight 2.

little doubt that all current WTO matters would come within the scope of the CCP'.[46]

To sum up, all these discussions show both the evolving nature of EU competence in WTO matters and its complex nature. In addition, as can be seen, EU competence has evolved in the direction of broadening the scope of the CCP to include most WTO matters. However, this broadening is limited. First, the enlargement of the scope of the CCP may not entail the broadening of its exclusive nature.[47] Second, even though the CCP was broadened to serve as a legal basis for other acts besides the conclusion of international agreements, *Opinion 1/94* still stands as regards the implementation of agreements based on a different legal basis than that used to conclude the agreement.

All these complexities show how the relation between the EU and the WTO is much more complex nowadays, where multiple competences interact at the different stages of the life-cycle of the WTO agreements. As the next sections will show, the responsibility of the EU in the WTO is influenced by multiple factors, ranging from the systemic design of the WTO Dispute Settlement System to the expertise that the EU has developed on these issues, or to the fact that the disputes in one way or another relate to EU law.

6.3 The EU in the WTO Dispute Settlement System

6.3.1 EU Participation in the WTO

Unlike in the case of the GATT, where the EU had to substitute its Member States, the EU was an original member of the WTO. It has been already noted that the EU took part in the Uruguay Round negotiations as a single entity represented by the Commission.[48] Hence, the outcome of the negotiations should have taken into consideration the complexities surrounding the participation of the EU and its Member States in mixed agreements and more precisely in the dispute settlement system established pursuant to those agreements.

In the previous chapters it has been shown how the other parties to mixed agreements might demand some clarification of the division of competence or procedural mechanisms to settle the question of the apportionment of responsibility within the agreement between the EU and its Member States. This was not the case in the WTO: the WTO agreement does

[46] Eeckhout, (n 31) 55. [47] Opinion 1/08 *Re: GATS*. [48] Section 6.2.1.

not impose any obligations concerning this issue upon the EU. The reason for this may derive partly from the fact that the EU had already been participating in the GATT, and partly from the role of the Commission as the sole negotiator for the EU and its Member States. The Commission, as can be easily seen in *Opinion 1/94*, was not envisaging mixity as a possibility.[49] It appears that the Commission had in mind the sole participation of the EU in the WTO, so it conducted the negotiations in those terms.

This section analyses how the mixed character of the WTO agreements is reflected in the disputes brought against the EU and its Member States, and therefore begins with an examination of how the WTO agreements take the EU into account. Once the legal framework for EU participation in the dispute settlement has been established, it then analyses how practice concerning the EU, and more specifically its role as respondent to those claims, takes into account the mixed character of the WTO, by analysing three case studies. Thus, this section shows that contrary to what the ILC argued during the codification of article 8 ARIO,[50] the EU is not eager to be held responsible, and the WTO panels have understood that the EU is responsible for any act committed under its normative control. In other words, the EU is responsible under the WTO insofar as a Member State breaches WTO law when implementing EU law.

6.3.1.1 The Regional Economic International Organization (REIO) Clause

Like other multilateral agreements, the WTO envisages a REIO clause, but with a broader scope. Article XII allows the participation of 'separate customs territory possessing full autonomy in the conduct of its external commercial relations and of the other matters provided for in this Agreement and the Multilateral Trade Agreements'. The use of this term 'separate' aims to allow not only international organizations but also territories with a problematic status under international law (e.g. Chinese Taipei or Hong Kong, China) to become members of the WTO.

Although this definition perfectly suits the EU, the EU falls outside the scope since it is an original member of the WTO. In this sense, article XI provides that:

> The contracting parties to GATT 1947 as of the date of entry into force of this Agreement, and the European Communities, which accept this Agreement

[49] Notwithstanding, some EU Member States would have to conclude the WTO agreement, because the EU Treaties do not apply on certain territories of those States.

[50] See Chapter 3.

and the Multilateral Trade Agreements and for which Schedules of Concessions and Commitments are annexed to GATT 1994 and for which Schedules of Specific Commitments are annexed to GATS shall become original Members of the WTO.

As well as being the only WTO member explicitly mentioned in the WTO agreement, the EU became a member without having to show that it met the requirements of Article XII. While this has been criticized for not demanding a declaration of competence either from the customs territories or the EU, the comparison of the EU to an original member shows the efficiency of the Commission's negotiation: not only was it clearly pushing for the EU's exclusive participation in the WTO, but it was also pushing for the legal recognition of its de facto position in the GATT.[51]

6.3.1.2 The EU and the Dispute Settlement System: Applying WTO Responsibility Rules to Mixed Situations

The Commission's aspiration for exclusive EU participation in the WTO is not only reflected in its status as an original member and the absence of any special membership requirement for customs territories, but also in the lack of any special reference to the customs territories besides the question of the nationality of the members of a panel of a dispute on which a customs union takes part.[52]

The rules of attribution in the WTO Dispute Settlement are based on the concept of territoriality. Article 4 (2) DSU envisages that the consultations that WTO members may bring against one another must concern 'measures affecting the operation of any covered agreement taken within the territory' of the latter. The provision establishes a rule of attribution based on territory. A WTO member can be brought to consultations, and subsequently may be held responsible, for any breach of the WTO committed in its territory. It could be considered that article 4 (2) DSU establishes the general rule of attribution within the WTO. Still though, most of the literature regarding responsibility within the WTO obviates this rule when approaching the question of attribution.[53]

Notwithstanding, the WTO Dispute Settlement has followed this territorial approach towards attribution. For instance, the panel report in

[51] Cebada Romero, (n 12) 136. [52] Article 8(3) note 6 DSU.

[53] E.g. Villapando, (n 7) 393; Fernández Pons, (n 7) 268; Eva Steinberger, 'The WTO Treaty as a Mixed Agreement: Problems with EC's and the EC Member States' Membership of the WTO' [2006]17(4) European Journal of International Law 837, 849.

the *Turkey–Textiles* dispute constitutes a good illustration.[54] The dispute concerned the implementation of quantitative restrictions on the importation of textile products to Turkey from India. Suffice it to say that the implementation of those quantitative restrictions was being done by the Turkish authorities on Turkish territory. In addition, according to Turkey, 'the measures at issue stemmed from the Turkey-[EU] customs union'.[55] Therefore the dispute should have also been brought, as Turkey asserted, against the EU. On the contrary, India argued that:

> it was not possible to bring a complaint against the European Communities with respect to the measures at issue, since these had not been taken by the European Communities nor were they legally attributable to the European Communities because the territorial scope of its obligations under the WTO Agreement did not extend to the customs territory of Turkey.[56]

The panel had to decide between three possibilities concerning who had adopted these quantitative measures: (1) they are Turkey's measures; (2) the EU's measures (since the measure involved applying the EU Common Custom Tariff in Turkish territory); (3) the Turkey-EU customs union's measures (which was not a party to the WTO). Therefore, one of the questions at stake was whether the rules enshrined in article 4 (2) of the DSU can be considered the general rule of attribution within the WTO.[57]

The panel first approached the possible attribution of the measure to Turkey. In this regard, the panel held that:

> the measures were implemented through formal action by Turkey and that the measures were published by Turkey in its Official Gazette. . . . In other words, the measures under examination were enacted, implemented and are now applied, by the Turkish government and do not impose any obligation on any other national or supranational authorities. Thus, on their face, the measures at issue appear to be measures taken by Turkey and enforceable on Turkish territory only.[58]

The panel took a territorial approach towards the attribution of the measure at issue. Furthermore, the panel supported its approach when addressing whether the restriction was attributable to the EU. In this regard, the panel followed the argument posed by the EU that the contested measure was 'not enforceable in Turkey as an EU measure as such'.[59] So, on one hand, the measures at issue could not be considered to be EU

[54] WTO, *Turkey – Restrictions on Imports of Textile and Clothing Products: Report of the Panel* (31 June 1999) WT/DS34/R.
[55] Ibid at para. 3.1. [56] Ibid at para. 3.3. [57] Ibid at para. 1.2.
[58] Ibid at para. 9.36. [59] Ibid at para. 9.39.

measures; on the other, since 'Turkey itself was ensuring the surveillance of such quotas at its borders, and that the European Communities and Turkey [had] their respective systems of border control', the measure could not be attributed solely to the EU.[60]

Finally, Turkey had also argued that the fact that this measure had been taken within the framework of a customs union evidenced that 'a fundamental change in the relationship between them and in their relationship with other WTO members' had occurred.[61] The response given by the panel to this argument was that since the customs union was not a WTO member, it did 'not have any autonomous legal standing for the purpose of WTO law and therefore its dispute settlement procedures'.[62] Thus, each party of the customs union was responsible for the implementing measures adopted within its own territory.[63]

As can be extracted from this case, the general rule of attribution within the WTO is based on territoriality: each WTO member is responsible for any measure taken by itself within its territory. Moreover, the WTO panel stressed that customs unions must have legal standing in the WTO (i.e. be a WTO member) for a conduct to be attributed to it.

It is only when the customs union (or an original member like the EU) is party to the WTO that the attribution of conduct based on where the conduct was performed becomes a more complicated. Since the EU and its Member States share the territory in which their respective laws apply, according to article 4 DSU, a breach of the WTO agreements can be attributed either to the EU or to the EU Member States where the breach took place. However, unlike other multilateral agreements, where a procedural solution was envisaged in an annexed declaration, the WTO remains silent on how to attribute a wrongful act when the territory is shared.[64] There is no special rule of attribution envisaged in the DSU in that respect. Hence, to know when the EU is responsible and when its Member States are, it is necessary to examine the WTO disputes brought against the EU and/or its Member States. The rules used by the panels in those cases will shed some light on whether the special rule of attribution

[60] Ibid at para. 9.39. [61] Ibid at para. 9.34. [62] Ibid at para. 9.41.

[63] In addition, the panel based its reasoning on the international practice regarding the legal personality of the customs union. It understood that the lack of 'any legislative body which would have the constitutional authority to enact laws and regulations that would be, as such, applicable to the territory of the customs union' was an essential feature of the customs union's legal personality (para. 9.4.) Cf. Fernández Pons, (n 7) 269.

[64] E.g. the Energy Charter Treaty. See Chapter 7.

is being applied to the EU within the WTO and what the outcome of that rule is.

6.3.2 From Functional Attribution to Normative Control: EU Responsibility in the WTO in Three Case Studies

This section examines how the WTO Dispute Settlement organs have approached the argument put forward by the EU on the functional attribution of the breaches committed by Member State authorities during the implementation of EU law. It does so by examining three different cases concerning the EU's executive federalism and the role of its Member States in relation to the responsibility of the EU. The first case focuses on a traditional scenario of executive federalism: customs implementation. The second case examines a more complex scenario such as the implementation of directives. Finally, the third case analyses an even more complex situation of EU law implementation: state aid decisions.

6.3.2.1 Pure Executive Federalism and the WTO: Selected Customs Matters

Situations like the LAN dispute should be read as exceptions to the way complaints are brought against the EU within the WTO.[65] Normally, third States would start consultations with the EU depending upon whether the measure which causing the breach of a WTO obligation had been adopted by the EU. In this regard, the *Selected Customs Matters* case[66] constitutes a good example by which to examine how WTO bodies approach the EU's executive federalism and EU responsibility for the implementation of WTO law. The dispute concerns the implementation of the Customs Code by EU Member States, an area which falls within exclusive competence, so in principle, there is no doubt that Member State organs are acting as Union bodies. Both a panel and the Appellate Body also got the opportunity to analyse how the EU's multi-level system of implementation complies with WTO law.

(a) Facts and arguments on the alleged breach of WTO law by the EU customs system

In September 2004, the US requested consultations with the EU concerning the alleged non-uniform manner in which the EU administers its laws,

65 Delgado Casteleiro and Larik, (n 1).

66 WTO, *European Communities – Selected Customs Matters: Report of the Panel* (16 June 2006) WT/DS315/R, as modified by the Appellate Body WT/DS315/AB/R.

regulations, decisions and rulings, as well as the failure of the European Union to institute judicial, arbitral or administrative tribunals or procedures for the purpose, inter alia, of the prompt review and correction of administrative action relating to customs matters. The US considered that the 'Union Customs Code',[67] the 'Implementing Regulation',[68] the 'Common Customs Tariff',[69] the 'Taric' and other measures were not being applied in a uniform way.[70] Consequently, it submitted that a breach of article X:3 (a) of the GATT had occurred. This article envisages that:

> Each contracting party shall administer in a uniform, impartial and reasonable manner all its laws, regulations, decisions and rulings of the kind described in paragraph 1 of this Article.[71]

Furthermore, the US argued that there was a breach of article X:3 (b) GATT insofar as, in its view, the EU did not provide for the review and correction of administrative action relating to customs matters in the manner prescribed in that provision.[72] In a nutshell, the US was challenging, in

[67] Council Regulation (EC) 2913/1992 of 12 October 1992 establishing the [Union] Customs Code, [1996] OJ L321, p. 23.

[68] Commission Regulation (EC) 2454/93 of 2 July 1993 laying down provisions for the implementation of Council Regulation (EC) No 2913/92 establishing the [Union] Customs Code [1993] OJ L253, pp. 1–766.

[69] Council Regulation (EC) 2658/87 of 23 July 1987 on the tariff and statistical nomenclature and on the Common Customs Tariff [1987] OJ L 256, pp. 1–675.

[70] Integrated Tariff of the European Communities established by virtue of Article 2 of Council Regulation (EEU) No. 2658/87 of 23 July 1987 on *the tariff and statistical nomenclature and on the Common Customs Tariff*. Vid. note 137.

[71] Paragraph 1 provides as follows: 'Laws, regulations, judicial decisions and administrative rulings of general application, made effective by any contracting party, pertaining to the classification or the valuation of products for customs purposes, or to rates of duty, taxes or other charges, or to requirements, restrictions or prohibitions on imports or exports or on the transfer of payments therefore, or affecting their sale, distribution, transportation, insurance, warehousing inspection, exhibition, processing, mixing or other use, shall be published promptly in such a manner as to enable governments and traders to become acquainted with them.'

[72] Article X: 3 (b) GATT reads as follows: 'Each contracting party shall maintain, or institute as soon as practicable, judicial, arbitral or administrative tribunals or procedures for the purpose, inter alia, of the prompt review and correction of administrative action relating to customs matters. Such tribunals or procedures shall be independent of the agencies entrusted with administrative enforcement and their decisions shall be implemented by, and shall govern the practice of, such agencies unless an appeal is lodged with a court or tribunal of superior jurisdiction within the time prescribed for appeals to be lodged by importers; Provided that the central administration of such agency may take steps to obtain a review of the matter in another proceeding if there is good cause to believe that the decision is inconsistent with established principles of law or the actual facts.'

the WTO, the basic foundations of the EU system of implementation: its executive federalism and the role of the national administrations, as well as the judicial system prescribed in the Treaties. More precisely, the US claimed that:

> Instead of administering its basic customs law in a uniform way, the EU administers it in [28] different ways. As administration is the responsibility of each member State, questions of classification and valuation may be subject to as many as [28] different interpretations, and traders are subject to [28] different procedural regimes for bringing goods into free circulation in the EU. The net result is an administration that distorts rather than facilitates trade and that imposes transaction costs that should not exist where administration is uniform.[73]

This argument put forward by the US is not, in principle, challenging any particular measure implemented by EU Member States. It is bringing a claim against the whole system of customs administration. But neither general international law nor WTO law seems to accept that possibility. Likewise, general international law requires a specific act or an omission which gives rise to the wrongful act, and in both articles 4 (2) and 6 (2), the DSU foresees the necessity of identifying the measure which allegedly violates a WTO obligation.[74]

In addition, the US identified certain fields in which the authorities from certain specific EU Member States were not uniformly implementing the GATT as a way of proving its main argument. The US identified three main issues, with some specific examples of the EU's lack of uniformity when implementing its customs law. It first identified disparities in the tariff classification used by the authorities in Denmark, the Netherlands and the UK in relation to network cards for personal computers, drip irrigation products in France and Spain, unisex articles or shorts in Italy and Spain, blackout drapery lining in the UK, Ireland and the Netherlands, Belgium, and Germany, and liquid crystal display flat monitors with a digital video interface in the Netherlands. Second, it did the same in the area of customs valuation involving royalty payments, successive sales and vehicle repair costs covered under warranty. Third, the US argued that the customs procedures were not being implemented in a uniform way in matters concerning audit procedures, penalties, processing under customs control and local clearance procedures.

In relation to the other claim about the violation of article X:3 (b) GATT, the US linked the issue of the lack of uniformity in the administration

[73] WTO. Panel Report. *European Communities – Selected Customs Matters*, para. 4.3.

[74] Article 2 Responsibility of States for Internationally Wrongful Acts, article 3(2) ARIO.

of customs law to the reviewability of the measures.[75] It was the opinion of the US that the CJEU review powers do not qualify as a prompt review mechanism.[76] Furthermore, the US claimed that 'what is left is a patchwork of Member State customs authorities whose work is reviewed by Member State courts, with no EU tribunal or procedure providing prompt review and correction of customs decisions in a way that would bring about uniformity in the administration of EU customs law'.[77]

By contrast, the EU did not see any incompatibility between its customs administration system, including judicial review and the GATT. The EU first argued that the examples given by the US concerning the lack of uniformity were a 'small number of isolated and misleading examples'.[78] Second, the EU went on to describe how its executive federalism works in the area of customs. In this regard, the Commission explained that Union law is typically implemented through the national administrations of the Member States, and that by virtue of the principles of primacy and direct effect, Union law becomes directly binding on national administrations and may be invoked against them. In addition, it argued that article 4 (3) (ex article 10 TEC) TFEU imposed on Member States a duty of cooperation, which also applies to the execution of Union law.[79] Finally, it went on to describe how the EU's judicial system not only provides a prompt review but also controls uniformity.[80] It is clear that neither the US nor the EU raised questions of competence, and it appears that the moment the US decided to target the EU as a whole it put the competence question to one side.

To sum up, the US considered that those supposed GATT breaches were attributable to the EU and not Member States. This can be easily understood, since the principal contention made by the US relates to the lack of uniformity in the implementation of the EU's customs rules. Nonetheless, the US argument implicitly questioned the division of competences between the EU and its Member States since it questioned its effectiveness in an area which is clearly the EU's exclusive competence.

(b) The panel decision

The first question addressed by the panel was whether the claim against the EU's implementation as a whole was possible. As mentioned previously, article 6 (2) DSU requires the identification of the specific measures

[75] WTO. Panel Report. *European Communities – Selected Customs Matters*, para. 4.35.
[76] Ibid para. 4.45. [77] Ibid at para. 4.45. [78] Ibid at para. 4.48.
[79] Ibid at para. 4.73–4.75. [80] Ibid para. 4.323–4.336.

that are violating WTO law. The panel rightly narrowed the scope of the dispute to the specific measures mentioned by the US. The panel held that the 'identification of the areas of customs administration at issue is necessary to specifically identify the "measures at issue".[81] Under this interpretation of article 6 (2) DSU the 'the United States is precluded from challenging the EU system of customs administration as a whole or overall in this dispute';[82] thus, the panel limited the dispute to the specific measures identified by the US in its request.

Concerning the challenged measures: since all of them involved the implementation of EU customs law in individual Member States, the panel must have understood that the dispute could not challenge the whole EU administration system; EU Member States were responsible for this breach of the WTO. Although this may seem rather improbable since the basic argument of the US was that the EU was not implementing its laws in a uniform way, it cannot be excluded. The panel posed some questions regarding the competence and responsibilities involved in the dispute. More precisely, the WTO body posed the following question to the Commission:

> As a matter of EU law, are the European Communities and/or the member States of the European Communities responsible for discharging the obligations contained in articles X:3(a) and X:3(b) GATT 1994?[83]

The EU, through the Commission, answered that question by making a distinction between 'as a matter of EU law' and 'as a matter of international law'.[84] To put it differently, the Commission made a distinction between the internal and external competences involved in the implementation of the GATT. Thus, the Commission pointed out that while both the institutions of the EU and the authorities of the Member States, where each is acting within its sphere of competences, are internally responsible for discharging the obligations of these provisions, 'as a matter of international law, the EU is solely responsible' for these obligations.[85] With this response the Commission was trying to make clear that the EU is the only internationally responsible entity for compliance with articles X:3 (a) and (b) GATT. Consequently, the acts of the national customs authorities should be attributed to the EU.

[81] WTO. Panel Report. *European Communities – Selected Customs Matters*, para. 7.31.
[82] Ibid para. 7.46.
[83] WTO. Panel Report. *European Communities – Selected Customs Matters*. WT/DS315/R, Annex A. Question 41.
[84] Ibid. [85] Ibid.

However, this answer did not seem to satisfy the panel. In the second substantive meeting the panel went on to demand further explanations on this issue from the Commission. The panel wanted to know whether 'the EU shared competence with the Member States in any one or more of the areas of customs administration, and also to clearly explain the delineation between their respective competences in the relevant areas'.[86] Through these questions the panel seemed to be trying to understand whether the actions should be attributed to the EU or its Member States. The panel asserted in its report that the 'administration of the EU customs law is primarily the responsibility of the member States'[87] This statement shows that the panel might not have understood the differentiation made between internal and external competence. However, it could also be accepted that this could be no more than a vague use of the term 'responsibility' by the panel.

Finally, the panel accepted the EU's view that Member State authorities act as EU agents when implementing EU customs law. The panel concluded that:

> the authorities in the member States – including customs authorities designated for that purpose by the member States and independent bodies, such as a judicial authority or an equivalent specialized body – act as organs of the European Communities when they review and correct administrative action taken pursuant to [EU] customs law.[88]

The implementation of EU customs law is not only the perfect example of how the EU's executive federalism works, but also an easy example. Customs are subject to exclusive competence. The lack of EU customs authorities and the implementation by Member State organs leave no doubt about their functional integration into the EU's administration.[89] However, the EU's multi-level system of implementation comprises other situations in which the vertical relationship established by EU law between EU institutions and Member State authorities is not as straightforward as with customs. In one of these more complex situations, would the panel continue to accept that Member State organs are functionally EU organs when implementing EU law?

[86] WTO: Panel Report. *European Communities – Selected Customs Matters*. WT/DS315/R, Annex B. Question 146.

[87] Ibid at para. 7.156.

[88] Ibid at para. 7.553.

[89] See Chapter 1. Cf. Kuijper, (n 8) 214; Robert Schütze, 'From Rome to Lisbon: "Executive Federalism" in the (New) European Union' [2010] 47(5) Common Market Law Review 1385.

To conclude, the *Selected Customs Matters* dispute shows how even in situations where there is no doubt that the EU is exclusively competent, panels may continue to doubt how the division of competences may influence EU responsibility. This case also illustrates how the WTO Dispute Settlement Mechanism has developed its own attribution rules concerning Customs territories. While the ARIO excluded the possibility of functional integration as a general rule for attributing responsibility to an IO, the panels and also the Appellate Body in this case have accepted that possibility.[90]

6.3.2.2 Normative Control, Shared Competence and Responsibility of the EU

The previous case study has shown how the WTO Dispute Bodies follow a functional criterion when examining the responsibility of the EU. If a Member State authority is functionally an EU organ, in principle, any breach committed by it will be attributed to the EU.

Notwithstanding this, given the plurality of legal instruments within Union law, it might sometimes be harder to make the link between the EU norm supposedly being implemented and the actions of Member States. While the implementation of the EU's customs system as laid down in the different regulations does not leave any room for doubt – Member States are functionally acting as EU organs – the same rule might seem more difficult to assume in the case of the implementation of EU directives. The *Biotech* dispute in a way exemplifies the WTO approach to EU directives, and, more specifically, the exceptions laid down in these legal instruments.[91] Furthermore, this dispute illustrates how a WTO panel manages issues of responsibility in an area of internal shared competence.

(a) The challenged EU measures

The dispute has its origins in three complaints brought against the EU in May 2003 by the US, Canada and Argentina. These States considered that the way the EU and its Member States applied their regime for the approval and marketing of biotech products was contrary to the WTO agreements, and more specifically was inconsistent with certain provisions of the SPS agreement, the Agreement on Agriculture, the TBT Agreement and the GATT.

[90] See Chapter 2.

[91] WTO, *European Communities – Measures Affecting The Approval and Marketing of Biotech Products: Report of the Panel* (29 September 2006) WT/DS291/R, WT/DS292/R, and WT/DS292/R.

The panel identified three different categories of measures at issue: 'a) the alleged general EU moratorium on approvals of biotech products (hereafter the 'general EU moratorium'); b) various product-specific EU measures affecting the approval of specific biotech products (hereafter the "product-specific EU measures"); and c) various EU Member State safeguard measures prohibiting the import and/or marketing of specific biotech products (hereafter the "member State safeguard measures")'.[92]

All these measures were directly (a) and (b), or indirectly (c), enshrined in two pieces of EU legislation: Directive 2001/18[93] and Regulation 258/97.[94] The claim was directed against an area falling within the shared competence of the EU and its Member States, since both pieces of legislation have article 95 TFEU as their only legal basis. Nevertheless, having regarded the concept of functional integration when attributing responsibility developed by the WTO panels, in principle, the issue of competence should not be an issue. Any action of an EU Member State taken when implementing EU law would be attributed to the EU.[95]

However, one of the specificities envisaged in the EU regulatory framework for Biotech products is the possibility of the EU's Member States adopting safeguard measures that would allow them to derogate from the EU legal framework.[96] To put it differently, the EU's biotech legal framework permits Member States not to act as EU organs while complying with EU law. Hence, to what extent would a safeguard measure adopted by a Member State be attributed to the EU?

(b) The panel and the attribution of safeguard measures

There are three possible answers to that question. The first could be based on an examination of the actual procedure for the adoption of safeguard measures. Depending on the degree of control exercised by the EU over a Member States' safeguard, the conduct could be attributed either to the EU or the Member State. Both article 12 of the regulation and 23 of the directive provide the possibility of temporarily restricting or prohibiting the trade or sale of a certain biotech product in a Member State when,

92 Ibid para. 7.98.

93 Council Directive 2001/18/EU of 12 March 2001 on the deliberate release into the environment of genetically modified organisms and repealing Council Directive 90/220/EEU [2001] OJ L106, pp. 1–39.

94 Council Regulation (EU) No 258/97 of 27 January 1997 concerning novel foods and novel food ingredients [1997] OJ L43, pp. 1–6.

95 See WTO. Panel Report. *European Communities – Selected Customs Matters.*

96 Article 12 of the regulation and 23 of the directive.

as a result of new information or a reassessment of existing information, there is a potential risk to human health or the environment. The decision to restrict the trade and sale of biotech products has a provisional nature: it must be approved by the Commission and the other Member States through comitology procedures.[97] Therefore, in principle, any safeguard measure adopted by a Member State must be approved by the EU. Hence, a certain degree of normative control over the measure exists. Not only are the requisites for the adoption of the safeguard measure marked by its exceptional nature, but also the EU will control and approve the measure. So, to the extent that a safeguard measure has been approved through the Union procedures, it would fall under the EU's normative control.

A second possibility would be to examine the actual cases which have given rise to the use of the safeguard measure, to see whether, in practice, Member States are free from any control from the EU. In this regard, it should be mentioned that six Member States had resorted to this mechanism, sometimes more than once.[98] However, in none of those cases were the safeguard measures followed by a Union decision approving them. Moreover, as a consequence of the lack of any Union decision, the safeguard measures taken by the Member State did not cease to exist. In this regard, Poli has considered that this use of safeguard measures is illegal and an attempt to dissociate the actions of Member States from EU legislation.[99] However, the Commission remained inactive. Apart from not following the procedure laid down in the directive and in the regulation, it did not open infringement procedures against the Member States.[100] Obviously, in practice Member States were free from the EU's normative control. Nevertheless, the fact that they were not subject to EU control in this particular case is clearly imputable to the EU. It is because of an omission by the Commission that EU Member States might not be complying with the WTO. In this regard, it is clear that the permanent safeguard measures of EU Member States are a direct consequence of the lack of enforcement of the procedure which controls this kind of measure in matters concerning Biotech products. Thus, any breach of a WTO obligation derived from a Member State's safeguard measure that the EU has not approved or challenged within the period given in the directive and

[97] Sara Poli, *La controversia sugli organismi geneticamente modificati tra obblighi OMC e competenza comunitaria* (Editorialie Scientifica 2008) 53.

[98] Austria, France, Germany, Greece, Italy and Luxembourg.

[99] Poli, (n 97) 54.

[100] Ibid.

the regulation should, insofar as it is an omission by the EU, be attributed to the EU.

A third possible answer to the question of the attribution of these safeguard measures to the EU would be to disregard any type of legal analysis of the issue and assume that to the extent that the issue has not been contested it is not worth examining. This was the line of reasoning that the panel followed:

> It is important to note that even though the member State safeguard measures were introduced by the relevant member States and are applicable only in the territory of the member States concerned, the European Communities as a whole is the responding party in respect of the member State safeguard measures. This is a direct consequence of the fact that the Complaining Parties have directed their complaints against the European Communities, and not individual EU member States. The European Communities never contested that, for the purposes of this dispute, the challenged member State measures are attributable to it under international law and hence can be considered EU measures. Indeed, it was the European Communities – and it alone – that defended the contested member State safeguard measures before the Panel.[101]

Although the panel clearly identified the problem regarding attribution in this paragraph, it avoided any further analysis. The panel decided on the attribution by assuming that since the EU had not contested the issue, the panel should not enter into it. This approach to attribution, while putting the burden of proof on the respondent, makes the panel's task easier. It appears that the panel would be influenced by the inertia of having two claims which are clearly attributable to the EU and a third that, although also attributable, might require some legal analysis.

Nevertheless, it should be said that the panel backs its reasoning on the previous practice developed by other panels. In particular, it quoted the *Asbestos* case,[102] which examines a similar controversy.[103] The panel considered that to the extent that the EU is the responding party, although the measure at issue was being maintained by one Member State (France), the situations are similar. However, while it is true that in the *Asbestos* case, France had approved a decree banning asbestos in an area of shared competence, it is also a fact that it did so under the normative umbrella of the EU.[104] The French asbestos ban was not an illegal safeguard measure,

[101] WTO Report of the Panel. *Biotech Products*, para. 7.101.

[102] WTO, *European Communities – Measures Affecting Asbestos and Asbestos-Containing Products: Report of the Panel* (18 September 2000) WT/DS135/R.

[103] WTO Panel Report *Biotech Products*, footnote 275.

[104] WTO. Report of the Panel. *Asbestos*, para. 3.33–3.34.

it was a possibility envisaged in the Union legislation. Therefore, the French decree could fall under the EU's normative control and subsequently be attributed to the latter. However, it must be acknowledged that the panel did not enter into these issues: it just assumed that the EU as the respondent party is the one responsible for the conduct. On this last point, in the absence of any attribution test it is true that both disputes are similar.

All in all, the *Biotech* dispute, like *Selected Customs Matters*, shows how the relevant factor which determines the attribution of an action to the EU or to its Member States is the nature of the measure. Where the measure at stake falls within an area within which the EU has legislated, the measure should be attributable to the EU. *Biotech* is also a good example of how a rather complex dispute may not be addressed with thoughtful and intricate legal reasoning on all issues. The question of the attribution of safeguard measures is resolved in a simple way which fails to address all the issue's complexities. Nevertheless, the panel expands its rule of attribution from functional attribution to normative control as the attribution rule. Insofar as the actions of Member States fall within the scope of EU law, they should be attributed to the EU.[105]

In conclusion, it should be said that the Council and the European Parliament adopted a new directive amending Directive 2001/18.[106] By virtue of the principle of subsidiarity, EU Member States can decide whether or not they wish to cultivate GMO crops on their territory.[107] While this possibility of prohibiting the cultivation of GMOs crops in a territory entails derogation from the general authorization regime,[108] this derogation does not comprise the possibility of restricting the import of GMOs as the old moratorium did, and in principle should not affect their trade within the EU.[109]

6.3.2.3 The Limits of Control: Illegal Subsidies to Airbus

Another example of the complex web of relations between the EU and its Member States is the area of aid granted by Member States. Article 107

105 Frank Hoffmeister, 'Litigating against the European Union and Its Member States – Who Responds under the ILC's Draft Articles on International Responsibility of International Organizations?' [2010] 21(3) European Journal of International Law 723, 741.

106 Council Directive (EU) 2015/412 of 11 March 2015 amending Directive 2001/18/EC as regards the possibility for the Member States to restrict or prohibit the cultivation of genetically modified organisms (GMOs) in their territory Text with EEA relevance [2015] OJ L 68/1.

107 Ibid. 108 Ibid. 109 Ibid.

(ex article 87 TEC) TFEU lays down the foundations of the EU's control over the subsidy policies of its Member States. According to this provision:

> any aid granted by a Member State or through State resources in any form whatsoever which distorts or threatens to distort competition by favouring certain undertakings or the production of certain goods shall, in so far as it affects trade between Member States, be incompatible with the internal market.

Furthermore, article 108 (ex article 88 TEC) TFEU empowers the Commission to control the compatibility of the aid systems, used by Member States, with the internal market. However, the Commission's control over State aid is not absolute. The Treaties do not only envisage a series of types of State aid which may be considered compatible with the internal market (article 107 (3) TFEU), but they also allow the Council, following a Commission proposal and after consultation with the European Parliament, to establish areas in which the Commission's control is exempted (article 109 TFEU). For instance, article 107 (3) TFEU establishes that 'aid to promote the execution of an important project of common European interest' may be compatible with the internal market. By way of example, the EU has understood that a project common to European interests would include the construction of Large Civil Aircrafts (LCAs), such as the Airbus 380.[110]

In a nutshell, the Commission controls the extent to which Member States can grant aid to private actors. As a consequence, the Commission adopts decisions declaring the compatibility or incompatibility with the internal market of a certain type of aid granted by a Member State. Member State authorities then have to act accordingly and in those cases where the aid has been declared they have to recover it. Unlike classical executive federalism, in which EU legislation must be implemented by all Member States, in the area of State aid only the Member State granting the aid has to comply with the decision of the Commission.

Consequently, as in *Biotech*, it could be argued that inasmuch as the exceptions are envisaged, either in the Treaties or pieces of EU legislation, the EU is exclusively responsible for any breach of the WTO stemming from any of these norms. However, the *European Communities and Certain Member States – Measures Affecting Trade in Large Civil Aircraft* dispute (Airbus dispute) seems to set some limits to the extent to which the EU can normatively control its Member States.

110 Gustavo Luengo Hernández de Madrid, *Regulation of Subsidies and State Aids and EC Law: Conflicts in International Trade Law* (Kluwer Law International 2007) 354.

(a) State aid and Airbus

Airbus is a subsidiary of the European Aeronautic Defence and Space Company (EADS). EADS was the result of the merger of Aérospatiale-Matra of France, DaimlerChrysler Aerospace AG (DASA) of Germany, and Construcciones Aeronáuticas SA (CASA) of Spain.[111] Over the years, Airbus has benefited from a wide range of aid and subsidies granted by the EU and four Member States (Germany, France, Spain and the UK).

Apart from the aid stemming from the consideration of Airbus as a project of common European interest, the multi-national company has received Research and Development (R&D) aid from both the EU and its Member States.[112] The EU granted Airbus R&D aid through its Framework Programmes, and also through the European Investment Bank. The EU considered that R&D aid granted to Airbus by Member States does not constitute illegal aid in the sense of article 107 TFEU inasmuch as they do not affect trade between Member States,[113] since Airbus is, along with Boeing (of US nationality), one of the only two companies in the world which manufacture LCAs.[114] Member States have also granted a wide variety of financial aid in a wide variety of forms, ranging from soft credit to recoverable aid.[115]

This network of aid granted to the main competitor of Boeing made the US bring a claim against the EU and the Member States that had actively granted aid to Airbus. According to the US, all these measures constituted subsidies prohibited by the SCM Agreement. This agreement falls under the EU's exclusive competence.[116]

(b) Actions and arguments of the parties on the attribution of the measures

The SCM Agreement distinguishes between different types of subsidies depending on the effects that they have on international trade.[117] The

[111] http://en.wikipedia.org/wiki/Airbus.

[112] WTO, *European Communities and Certain Member States – Measures Affecting Trade in Large Civil Aircraft: Report of the Panel* (30 June 2010) WT/DS316/R, para. 2.5.

[113] Luengo Hernández de Madrid, (n 110) 336.

[114] WTO. Panel Report. *European Communities and Certain Member States – Measures Affecting Trade in Large Civil Aircraft*. WT/DS316/R, para. 2.2.

[115] Luengo Hernández de Madrid, (n 110) 497.

[116] Opinion 1/94 *Re: Competence of the Community to conclude international agreements concerning services and the protection of intellectual property* para. 44.

[117] For a comparison between the concept of subsidy in WTO Law and the concept of state aid in EU law see: Luca Rubini, *The Definition of Subsidy and State Aid: WTO and EC Law in Comparative Perspective* (Oxford University Press 2009).

objectives pursued by the SCM Agreement and the objectives pursued by EU State aid are different. While the WTO pursues free trade among its members, the EU not only seeks the creation of an internal market but also political and social integration.[118] Consequently there is a potential for conflict between the SCM Agreement and EU State aid regulation. According to the US, the subsidies given to Airbus, while not compromising the EU's internal market (since there is none in that area), constitute subsidies prohibited by the SCM Agreement, either because: they are expressly prohibited (article 3 SCM Agreement); they have adverse effects on the US (article 5 SCM Agreement); or, more precisely, they have adverse effects on Boeing.[119]

As in the LAN dispute, the US initiated consultations not only with the EU, but with the Member States which had given subsidies to Airbus, i.e. France, Germany, Spain and the UK. Consequently, the EU conducted the defence and spoke on behalf of its Member States.[120] Unlike the LAN dispute, the breach did not concern the implementation *stricto senso* of EU law, but a much more complex issue such as whether State aid granted by Member States to Airbus could be attributed to the EU. It could be argued that inasmuch as the EU Treaties and secondary legislation have established a mechanism for the control of State aid, the EU should be responsible for any aid given by a Member State. Since in principle the aid should have been subject to control by the EU, it is the EU's responsibility to ensure that aid is in conformity with EU and WTO law. In other words, the EU should be internationally responsible for aid given by Member States since they fall under its normative control.[121]

(c) The decision of the panel

The panel did not accept the EU's argument, according to which: 'The violations that are alleged by the United States all relate to matters for which the [EU] bears responsibility in the WTO'.[122] It understood that not only had the EU breached the SCM Agreement but also France, Germany, Spain and the UK.[123] The panel concluded that:

118 Luengo Hernández de Madrid, (n 110) 496.

119 WTO, *European Communities and Certain Member States – Measures Affecting Trade in Large Civil Aircraft: Report of the Panel* (30 June 2010) WT/DS316/R, para. 3.1.

120 Luengo Hernández de Madrid, (n 110) 511.

121 WTO, *European Communities – Measures Affecting Trade in Large Civil Aircraft: First Written Submission by the European Communities* (5 April 2007) WT/DS316, p. 43.

122 Ibid.

123 WTO. Panel Report. *European Communities and Certain Member States – Measures Affecting Trade in Large Civil Aircraft*. WT/DS316/R, para. 8.4.

> To the extent that the [EU], France, Germany, Spain and the United Kingdom have acted inconsistently with the SCM Agreement, they have nullified or impaired benefits accruing to the United States under that Agreement.[124]

Disregarding the EU's argument, the panel approached the dispute in a completely different manner to the way it did in *Biotech*. From the beginning, the panel differentiated between each one of the Member States and their subsidies.[125] Even though the panel did not expressly mention the reasons for this differentiation, the nature of the measures breaching the SCM Agreement favoured this differentiated approach. The analysis of whether each one of these subsidies is against WTO law, and the lack of an express EU norm serving as an umbrella to that particular subsidy, makes it difficult to accept the argument that Member States' subsidies stem from compliance with EU law.

By establishing the joint responsibility of the EU and its Member States in the Airbus dispute, the panel established certain limits to the exclusive responsibility of the EU as a consequence of the normative control it exercises over its Member States. Indeed, the specific subsidies analysed in the dispute do not seem to be under the EU's normative control. First, Member States grant subsidies in respect of their national budgets. Second, there is no EU decision authorizing any of the subsidies given to Airbus. In fact, the EU and its Member States' joint responsibility does not stem from their special relations but from all of the parallel subsidies granted to Airbus. If the action had been brought solely against the subsidies which France, Germany, Spain and the UK granted to Airbus, their sole responsibility in an area which supposedly falls under EU's exclusive competence would have been a possibility.

Even though the SCM Agreement falls under the EU's exclusive competence, Member States can still act outside the scope of EU powers. However, this exposes the extent to which the EU State aid regime can conflict with the SCM Agreement.[126] Given the EU's exclusive competence on the SCM Agreement, its lack of control over any possible subsidy that Member States might grant creates dissonances between the EU and the WTO. As Kuijper and Paasivirta have identified, in scenarios of such complexity, like Airbus, it is more important for EU internal compliance mechanisms to be specially effective.[127]

124 Ibid at para. 8.5. 125 Ibid at 7.3. 126 Luengo Hernández de Madrid, (n 110).

127 Pieter Jan Kuijper and Esa Paasivirta, 'EU International Responsibility and Its Attribution: From the Inside Looking Out' in Panos Koutrakos and Malcolm D. Evans (eds), *The International Responsibility of the European Union European and International Perspectives* (Hart 2013) 63.

Finally, the Airbus dispute can be considered a marginal example if put in context with the other disputes brought against the EU and/or its Member States. It is the only WTO case in which joint responsibility between the EU and its Member States has been recognized. Nevertheless, it should not be excluded that this might start a path towards joint responsibility in the WTO in those cases in which the EU does not exercise normative control over the actions of its Member States.

6.4 Conclusions

Although the EU seems to be eager to participate in any dispute brought against it or against its Member States, it is not being held responsible for acts which cannot be attributed to it. In this regard, the panels have developed a consistent jurisprudence on the criteria by which to attribute an action to the EU: whenever the acts which may violate the WTO have been adopted to implement EU norms, the act is attributable to the EU. A common thread emerges in WTO case law: the EU is responsible for the acts of its Member States in a scenario in which the EU exercises normative control over its Member States.[128]

As has been pointed out, contrary to the ILC, which considered that normative control cannot be considered as the general rule of attribution, the WTO Dispute Settlement System has established it as a rule of attribution to deal with breaches by the EU and its Member States. In this regard, this fact shows how the ILC might initially have misread EU practice in the WTO and understood that it was based on the will of the Commission to play a prominent role in the dispute settlement system and not on the actual reasoning of the WTO bodies. Furthermore, normative control as a way of attributing conduct provides us with a harmonious solution to the question of the responsibility of the EU and its Member States vis-à-vis third States. Nevertheless, the WTO Dispute Settlement bodies have implicitly set some limits to the attribution of conduct to the EU when it exercises normative control. Although in the Biotech dispute, the panel seems to accept a broad understanding of the EU's normative control, in the Airbus dispute the panel places a limit on that possibility. There must be a specific EU legal framework with which Member States must comply with for the EU's responsibility to arise. In the absence of such a framework, Member States would continue to be responsible for their acts, even in those agreements which fall under the EU's exclusive competence.

[128] Hoffmeister, (n 105).

Moreover, the EU has taken advantage of the fact that it has many years of experience of dealing with disputes in the GATT/WTO, so the panels are familiar with the EU. Nevertheless, this familiarity leads to situations where the EU is allowed a greater role than it actually deserves. Especially in cases involving its Member States in the TRIPS area, where apart from assisting its Member States, it appears to push for a mutually agreed solution that diminishes their role in the dispute settlement system.[129]

[129] Delgado Casteleiro and Larik, (n 1).

7 Normative Control in the EU and the Responsibility of Member States

An Analysis of the Responsibility of the EU in International Investment Law

7.1 Introduction

The previous chapter showed how, in the context of the WTO Dispute Settlement System, the EU ended up being responsible in any dispute brought against an EU Member State over an issue of EU law. By participating in those disputes, the EU can raise the issue of its normative control over its Member States when they are implementing EU law, which leads to the attribution to the EU of the challenged Member States' actions. However, there are other international agreements in which the institutional design may not foster EU participation and/or responsibility: either because the institutional design of the dispute settlement system is not as flexible as the WTO one, or due to the fact that the EU is not a party to the agreement even though its Member States are. For instance, this is the case of most of the international investment agreements, both bilateral and multilateral.[1] Yet, regardless of these problems, recent developments in investment arbitration case law seem to recognize normative control as a rule of attribution of responsibility to the EU.

This gradual acceptance of the responsibility of the EU for the acts of its Member States when implementing EU law in international investment law has emerged in parallel to the new EU competence in this area. With the entry into force of the Lisbon Treaty in 2009, FDI became an EU exclusive competence; accordingly, the EU institutions have been preparing the legal instruments which will develop a new European international investment policy. Among the topics that are drawing special interest are the issues of the responsibility and participation in investment arbitration of the EU.

[1] See Section 7.2.

Although the issue of the EU's responsibility is not new, it has nevertheless just recently come to the forefront of the debate on the future FDI policy of the EU. On one hand, the exclusive nature of the EU's FDI policy has created some uncertainties in relation to the scope of this new exclusive competence.[2] While there seems to be agreement as to the definition of FDI,[3] the specific scope of the EU's FDI competence and the impact that it will have in the EU's treaty-making practice has yet to be clarified.[4] As a way of example, even though the EU has passed legislation laying down the consequences and establishing procedures to deal with possible incompatibilities between EU law and Member States BITS concluded with third countries, the status of those BITS concluded between EU Member States is unclear.[5] While some authors argue that intra-EU BITS, inasmuch as they contain a dispute settlement clause, are necessarily incompatible with EU law[6] others submit that new FDI competence does not affect EU Member States' powers with regard to intra-EU investment protection.[7]

In addition, further developments within arbitration proceeding blur even more the picture of the EU's responsibility in international investment law. EU Member States have invoked EU law as a way to challenge the jurisdiction of arbitral tribunals and avoid their responsibilities towards foreign investors.[8] Also, investors continue to target EU Member States in international arbitration proceedings which should have been brought

[2] Eileen Denza, 'Responsibility of the European Union in the Context of Investment' in Panos Koutrakos and Malcolm D. Evans (eds), *The International Responsbility of the European Union European and International Perspectives* (Hart 2013) 225. See Chapter 1.

[3] Ibid; Piet Eeckhout, *EU External Relations Law* (2nd edn, Oxford University Press 2011) 62; Jan Ceyssens, 'Towards a Common Foreign Investment Policy? – Foreign Investment in the European Constitution' [2005] 32(3) *Legal Issues of Economic Integration* 259.

[4] Panos Koutrakos, 'Foreign Direct Investment Law in a State of Flux' [2013] 5 European Law Review 599; Angelos Dimopoulos, *EU Foreign Investment Law* (Oxford University Press 2011) 43.

[5] The EU has so far adopted a regulation on the validity of intra-EU Bilateral Investment Treaties see: Council Regulation (EU) 1219/2012 of the European Parliament and Council of 12 December 2012 establishing transitional arrangements for bilateral investment agreements between Member States and third countries [2012] OJ L351/40.

[6] Angelos Dimopoulos, 'The Validity and Applicability of International Investment Agreements between EU Member States under EU and International Law' [2011] 48(1) Common Market Law Review 63, 90.

[7] Hanno Wehland, 'Intra-EU Investment Agreements and Arbitration: Is European Community Law an Obstacle?' [2009] 58(2) International and Comparative Law Quarterly 297, 320.

[8] *Eastern Sugar BV (Netherlands) v The Czech Republic* (Partial Award) SCC Case No. 088/2004 (27 March 2007); *Achmea BV (formerly known as Eureko BV) v The Slovak Republic* (Final Award) PCA Case 2008-13 (7 December 2012).

against the European Union.[9] The European Commission has reacted to this kind of forum shopping by expressing its unease through *amicus curiae* briefs to those proceedings. In its opinion those claims should be brought against it in the CJEU and not in investment arbitration tribunals against EU Member States.[10] It understands that whenever there is an action brought against an EU Member States which was implementing EU law, it should be the EU to bear responsibility. Moreover, the Commission is bringing State aid proceedings against Member States since it considers that paying investment awards amounts to illegal State aid.[11] It therefore appears that dispute settlement issues and more specifically issues of responsibility are now at the centre of the debate on the EU FDI competence.

It is against this backdrop of uncertainty in the progressive shaping of the EU's investment policy, that the recent practice in international investment can shed some light on how the new international investment agreements will tackle the issue of responsibility. This chapter does that by exploring the EU's responsibility in the field of international investment law. It argues that a clear rule of attribution based on the EU's normative control would help in easing most of the concerns raised by the investors regarding legal certainty while safeguarding the division of competences between the EU and its Member States.

The chapter is structured in four parts. After the introduction, the chapter analyses how investment tribunals have, so far, approached the issue of the responsibility of the EU and whether there is some kind of common approach to the issue. The chapter maps investment disputes where there is an EU element present to determine how investment arbitration deals with the EU's normative control. Based on the findings of the previous section, the third section critically discusses EU Regulation concerning financial responsibility linked to investor-state arbitration,[12] as well as the investor-state dispute settlement clauses contained in the new EU Free Trade Agreements. The aim of the section is to examine how these new measures, put forward by the EU institutions, deal with the issue of

[9] AES Summit Generation Limited and AES-Tisza Erömü Kft v The Republic of Hungary (Award) ICSID Case No. ARB/07/22 (23 September 2010); Electrabel S.A. v Republic of Hungary (Decision) ICSID Case No. ARB/07/19 (30 November 2010).

[10] Ibid.

[11] Case T-704/15 *Micula a.o. v Commission* [nyr] ECR, action brought on 28 November 2015.

[12] Council Regulation (EU) No 912/2014 of 23 July 2014 establishing a framework for managing financial responsibility linked to investor-to-state dispute settlement tribunals established by international agreements to which the European Union is party [2014] OJ L257.

the EU's responsibility and the investor's legal certainty. Do these measures strike the right balance between the EU and investors' interests? The fourth section provides some conclusions on the future role of the EU in investor-state dispute settlement.

7.2 International Investment Disputes with an EU Element: Mapping How EU Law Interacts with International Investment Law

In recent years there has been a surge of investment disputes in which EU law has played a role. There are multiple reasons for that surge. First, even before the entry into force of the Lisbon Treaty, the EU had already extended its tentacles to cover this area.[13] The CJEU ruled in 2009 that certain aspects of some of the BITS signed by Austria, Sweden, and Finland were incompatible with EU law and more specifically with its provisions on the free movement of capitals.[14] Second, prior to the fifth EU enlargement wave, many of the former Socialist countries designed very appealing investment policies so as to attract foreign investors. However, once these States acceded to the EU, many of those investment policies could be considered illegal under EU State aid rules. For instance, Hungary established investment programmes which granted exclusive access to the energy markets to those companies interested in investing in the Hungarian energy sector. These programmes were investigated by the European Commission which decided that they violated EU State aid rules.[15]

Third, the State's regulatory autonomy has been subject to a higher degree of scrutiny by investment tribunals. The extent to which the power to regulate can amount to an illegal expropriation under international investment law is now a common debate among international lawyers.[16] Consequently, it is inevitable that, as investors become more litigious over the control which the State exercises over its activity through regulation,

[13] Eileen Denza, 'Bilateral Investment Treaties and EU Rules on Free Transfer: Comment on Commission v Austria, Commission v Sweden and Commission v Finland' [2010] 35(2) European Law Review 263, 263.

[14] Case C- 205/06 *Commission v Austria* [2009] ECR I-1301; Case *C-249/06 Commission v Sweden* [2009] ECR I-3317; Case C-118/07 *Commission v Finland* [2009] ECR I-10889. See: Angelos Dimopoulos, 'The BITs Cases: Practical and Doctrinal Implications' in Javier Díez-Hotchleitner Rodríguez and others (eds), *Recent Trends in the Case Law of the Court of Justice of the European Union* (La Ley 2012); Denza, (n 13).

[15] See note 9.

[16] Catherine Titi, *The Right to Regulate in International Investment Law* (Hart 2014).

and the EU continues to expand its competences in detriment of its Member States, disputes in which EU law is a factor to take into account are going to become more common. For instance, it cannot be excluded that, in a similar vein as it has happened in Australia,[17] the EU tobacco packaging directive could be challenged by foreign investors.[18]

Fourth, as a consequence of the Eurozone crisis, EU Member States had to take measures to avoid defaulting on their debt payments. Even so, those measures impinged on the rights of foreign investors. Greece debt swap or Cyprus nationalization of its most troubled banks led to cases being brought to ICSID by individuals who have allegedly suffered a loss because of those measures. In these cases, the main question that arises is the extent to which the EU should be responsible for helping these Member States in implementing the contested measures.

Within this context, it submitted that the current practice in investment tribunals might shed some light on the extent to which the EU is responsible under international law. So far, the cases in which an EU element has surfaced can be classified in three groups. In the first group of cases, EU law appears as an argument of the respondent State to invoke the invalidity of the Intra-EU BIT under which the case was brought in the first place. The second group revolves around actions brought against Member States over conflicts between specific investment attraction policies and EU State aid rules. The third group concerns actions brought against EU Member States' over decisions not taken under the EU's normative control but which, nonetheless, were negotiated with the EU.

7.2.1 EU Law as an Argument against the Validity of BITs: Any Responsibility of the EU?

In the first group of cases, the respondent used EU law as way to challenge the validity of the intra-EU BITs under which the dispute was brought. However, unlike the BITs cases,[19] these cases were not decided by the CJEU but by investment tribunals applying the Stockholm Chamber of Commerce (*Eastern Sugar v Czech Republic*)[20] or the UNCITRAL rules

[17] *Philip Morris Asia Limited v The Commonwealth of Australia* (Award on Jurisdiction and Admissibility) PCA Case 2012-12 (15 December 2015).

[18] Council Directive 2014/40/EU of 3 April 2014 on the approximation of the laws, regulations and administrative provisions of the Member States concerning the manufacture, presentation and sale of tobacco and related products and repealing Directive 2001/37/EC [2014] OJ L127/1.

[19] See note 14.

[20] *Eastern Sugar BV v Czech Republic* (Partial Award) SCC Case 088/2004 (27 March 2007); *Rupert Joseph Binder v Czech Republic* (Award on Jurisdiction) Not Published (6 June 2007).

(*Eureko*).[21] Moreover, the respondent challenged the validity of the BIT from the moment they acceded to the EU due to the fact that EU law has primacy over them. Leaving aside the interesting questions of the validity of intra-EU BITS[22] and whether accession to the EU has automatically terminated the previous intra-EU BIT,[23] can these cases tell us anything about the responsibility of the EU and its Member States in the field of international investment law?

For instance, in *Eureko v Slovakia*, it is unclear whether, besides the alleged conflict between the EU Treaties and Netherlands-Slovakia BIT, the breach would give rise to the EU's responsibility. The Slovak government introduced a series of legislative measures which modified the health insurance market. First, it would be difficult to argue that the competence to regulate the health insurance market falls within the EU's FDI competence. Second, those legislatives measures were not adopted to comply with any EU obligation, either primary or secondary. There was no EU measure which the Slovakian government was complying with by adopting the challenged measures. In fact, Eureko had also lodged a complaint to the European Commission over the same measures[24] which led to the opening of an infringement procedure against the Slovak Republic, which was pending at the time the arbitral award was granted.[25] Had the European Commission adopted a decision establishing that Slovakia's actions in the health insurance market were in accordance with EU law, the EU might perhaps bear some responsibility for the Slovakia's actions. Insofar as the measures implemented by the Slovak government did not stem from a piece of EU legislation, it would be quite difficult to envisage why the EU should bear any kind of responsibility for those measures.

It seems difficult to imagine how in a similar scenario, but with the EU being bound by the same obligations as Slovakia, the EU would be responsible. This case shows, among other things, that there are situations in which, even though the EU has (exclusive) competence on FDI, Member States' responsibility in international investment law will continue to arise. In a hypothetical mixed investment agreement, actions such as

[21] *Eureko BV (The Netherlands) vs. The Slovak Republic* (Award on Jurisdiction) PCA Case 2008-13 (26 October 2010); *Achmea BV v The Slovak Republic (formerly Eureko BV v The Slovak Republic)* (Final Award) PCA Case 2008-13 (7 December 2012).

[22] See Dimopoulos, (n 6).

[23] August Reinisch, 'Articles 30 and 59 of the Vienna Convention on the Law of Treaties in Action: The Decisions on Jurisdiction in the Eastern Sugar and Eureko Investment Arbitrations' [2012] 39(2) Legal Issues of Economic Integration 157.

[24] *Eureko BV (The Netherlands) v The Slovak Republic* [2010] PCA CAse N°2008-13 para. 55.

[25] Ibid 55.

those assessed in *Eureko v Slovakia* would continue to be attributed to Slovakia and not to the EU.[26]

7.2.2 *The EU's Normative Control and the Attribution of Conduct to EU Member States: The Example of the Energy Charter Treaty*

In the second group of cases, EU Member States do not argue the automatic termination of the agreement that contains the obligation which supports the investment claim. Instead, they face legal action for the implementation of an EU State aid decision. The constitutional design of the EU State aid policy establishes the obligation on the Member State which granted those illegal subsidies to abolish them and even recover them from the investor.[27] Obviously, there will be cases in which the scope of those obligations and the extent to which they impinge on foreign investors' rights will eventually be brought against the EU in international arbitration courts. So far, those cases have only been brought against EU Member States complying with EU State aid norms.

The nature of the relationship that the EU and its Member States have in the field of State aid is especially present in two recent disputes brought to ICSID by virtue of one of the few multilateral investment agreements that exists: the Energy Charter Treaty (ECT). The ECT is a mixed agreement to which both the EU and its Member States are parties. Among the many features of the ECT, its mechanism to settle disputes between investors and contracting parties figures prominently.[28] In this regard, the ECT is (along with NAFTA) one of the two only multilateral agreements which envisage a mechanism for investor-state

[26] Jan Asmus Bischoff, 'Just a Little Bit of "Mixity"? The EU's Role in the Field of International Investment Protection Law' [2011] 48(5) Common Market Law Review 1526, Bischoff argues that 'the competences of the EU in the field of investment protection are mixed and do not cover all aspects of international investment law. Future EU BITs – assuming they govern all issues covered by contemporary BITs – can only be concluded as mixed agreements'. For an opposing view see: Ramón Vidal Puig, 'The Scope of the New Exclusive Competence of the European Union with Regard to Foreign Direct Investment' [2013] 40(2) Legal Issues of Economic Integration 133.

[27] Article 108.2 TFEU provides that 'if, after giving notice to the parties concerned to submit their comments, the Commission finds that aid granted by a State or through State resources is not compatible with the internal market having regard to Article 107, or that such aid is being misused, it shall decide that the State concerned shall abolish or alter such aid within a period of time to be determined by the Commission.'

[28] Esther Zapater Duque, *La Unión Europea y la Cooperación Energética Internacional* (Dykinson 2002) 349. Cf. Jan Paulsson, 'Arbitration without Privity' in Thomas W. Wälde (ed), *The Energy Charter Treaty: An East-West Gateway for Investment and Trade* (Kluwer Law International 1996).

disputes.[29] Article 26 ECT enshrines a wide range of mechanisms for the investor to solve its dispute with a contracting party to the ECT. Investors can bring claims to national courts, ICSID, arbitration under UNCITRAL rules or arbitral proceedings under the Arbitration Institute of the Stockholm Chamber of Commerce.

AES[30] and Electrabel brought two different disputes to ICSID concerning the decision of the Hungarian government to terminate the Power Purchase Agreements (PPAs) they had signed with these companies before Hungary became an EU Member.[31] The PPAs set a list of prices to be paid by Hungary for the electricity produced by AES and Electrabel until a given date. The PPAs guaranteed the generators a return on investment without any commercial risk.[32] Notwithstanding, Hungary's accession to the EU changed the applicable rules regarding energy. In 2005 the Commission opened an infringement procedure against Hungary for this mechanism of energy investment. The Commission was of the view that the PPAs were restricting competition in the energy sector. Therefore, in June 2008 after a three year investigation, it adopted a decision which established that the obligation to purchase energy by virtue of the PPAs constitutes State aid incompatible with the common market, which must be repaid by its recipients.[33]

Electrabel decided to sue Hungary over the termination of the PPAs, disregarding the EU element of the dispute. Even though the EU is not a party to ICSID,[34] it is nevertheless a party to the ECT. Pursuant to article 26.3.b (ii) ECT[35] the EU made a declaration which establishes its practices

[29] For a comparative analysis of both multilateral agreement see: Lawrence L. Herman, 'NAFTA and ECT: Divergent Approaches with a Core of Harmony' [1997] 15(2) Journal of Energy and Natural Resources Law 129.

[30] *AES Summit Generation Limited and AES-Tisza Erőmű Kft. v Republic of Hungary* (Award) ICSID Case ARB/07/22 (23 September 2010).

[31] *Electrabel S.A. v Republic of Hungary* (Decision on Jurisdiction) ICSID Case ARB/07/19 (30 November 2012).

[32] Markus Burgstaller, 'European Law and Investment Treaties' [2009] 26(2) Journal of International Arbitration 181, 212.

[33] Council Decision (EC) 2009/609/EC of 4 June 2008 on the State aid C 41/05 awarded by Hungary through Power Purchase Agreements (notified under document C(2008) 2223) [2009] OJ L225, p. 53.

[34] On the feasibility of the EU becoming a contracting party of ICSID see: Markus Burgstaller, 'Investor-State Arbitration in EU International Investment Agreements with Third States' [2012] 39(2) Legal Issues of Economic Integration 207; also, Christian Tiejte, Emily Sipiorsk and Grit Topfër, *Responsibility in Investor- State-Arbitration in the EU – Managing Financial Responsibility Linked to Investor-State Dispute Settlement Tribunals Established by EU's International Investment Agreements* (2012).

[35] 'For the sake of transparency, each Contracting Party . . . shall provide a written statement of its policies, practices and conditions in this regard to the Secretariat no

and conditions with regard to dispute settlement.[36] This declaration must not be mistaken with a declaration of competences since it does not clarify the vertical division of competences in the EU.[37] Instead, the declaration was designed to assist investors in understanding how the EU relates to the ECT. As regards its dispute settlement provisions, the declaration mentions not only the issue of jurisdiction, but more importantly it lays down a procedure to assist investors in identifying the right subject to target when bringing a claim against the EU and/or its Member States. The declaration provides, inter alia, that:

> the European Communities and their Member States have both concluded the Energy Charter Treaty and are thus internationally responsible for the fulfilment of the obligations contained therein, in accordance with their respective competences.
>
> The Communities and the Member States will, if necessary, determine among them who is the respondent party to arbitration proceedings initiated by an Investor of another Contracting Party. In such case, upon the request of the Investor, the Communities and the Member States concerned will make such determination within a period of 30 days....
>
> ... Given that the Communities' legal system provides for means of such action, the European Communities have not given their unconditional consent to the submission of a dispute to international arbitration or conciliation.
>
> As far as international arbitration is concerned, it should be stated that the provisions of the ICSID Convention do not allow the European Communities to become parties to it. The provisions of the ICSID Additional Facility also do not allow the Communities to make use of them. Any arbitral award against the European Communities will be implemented by the Communities' institutions, in accordance with their obligation under Article 26(8) of the Energy Charter Treaty.[38]

From the procedural history of *Electrabel v Hungary*, it can be seen that the mechanism enshrined in the EU's declaration to the ECT was unknown to the claimant and respondent, and their legal experts.[39] Furthermore,

later than the date of the deposit of its instrument of ratification, acceptance or approval in accordance with Article 39 or the deposit of its instrument of accession.'

36 Statement submitted by the European Communities to the Secretariat of the Energy Charter Treaty pursuant to Article 26. (3) (b) (ii) of the Energy Charter Treaty [1994] OJ L336, p. 115.

37 See Chapter 4.

38 Statement submitted by the European Communities to the Secretariat of the Energy Charter Treaty pursuant to Article 26. (3) (b) (ii) of the Energy Charter Treaty [1994] OJ L336, p. 115.

39 *Electrabel S.A. v Republic of Hungary* (Decision on Jurisdiction) ICSID Case ARB/07/19 (30 November 2012) para. 3.20.

as the Commission highlighted in its *amicus curiae* brief, had the claimant resorted to the procedure envisaged in the declaration, 'the Commission and Hungary could have jointly assisted it in the determination of the respective competences and choice of the correct respondent party' and that, in failing to do so, 'the Claimant took the risk to bring a case against the wrong respondent or before the wrong forum'.[40]

The arbitral tribunal partially accepted the Commission's view. Although confirming its jurisdiction over the issue (a matter that the Commission challenged), it recognized that dispute did not relate to the acts or omissions of Hungary.[41] The Tribunal considered that Electrabel's claim revolved primarily on the legal effect of the Commission's State aid decision. In the Tribunal's view, that decision required Hungary, under EU law, to terminate the PPAs.[42] Moreover, the Court recognized that in such a scenario it would be for the EU to be liable, not Hungary:

> Where Hungary is required to act in compliance with a legally binding decision of an EU institution, recognized as such under the ECT, it cannot (by itself) entail international responsibility for Hungary. Under international law, Hungary can be responsible only for its own wrongful acts. The Tribunal considers that it would be absurd if Hungary could be liable under the ECT for doing precisely that which it was ordered to do by a supranational authority whose decisions the ECT itself recognises as legally binding on Hungary.[43]

The arbitral tribunal thus recognized, if and to the extent that an EU act required Hungary, under EU law, to prematurely terminate the PPAs, that act by the EU cannot give rise to liability for Hungary under the ECT.[44] In other words, the ICISD tribunal acknowledged that those Member State's actions adopted under the EU's normative control entail the exclusive responsibility of the EU and not of the Member State implementing them. Yet, the ICSID tribunal was not as straightforward on the foundations of the EU's responsibility for its normative control over Hungary as it might have been expected.

The arbitral tribunal based its decision by drawing an analogy between the EU's normative control and article 6 of the ASR.[45] By implementing the decision, the arbitral court seemed to recognize the existence of a functional link between the EU and its Member States when the latter

[40] Ibid. [41] Ibid. [42] Ibid. [43] Ibid. [44] Ibid.

[45] 'The conduct of an organ placed at the disposal of a State by another State shall be considered an act of the former State under international law if the organ is acting in the exercise of elements of the governmental authority of the State at whose disposal it is placed.'

implement EU law.[46] The ICSID Tribunal rightly identifies that Hungarian organs are EU organs from a functional perspective.[47] Yet, there is a small inconsistency with its argumentation. The threshold of functional integration under article 6 ASR is higher than that between the EU and its Member States. According to the commentary to that provision: 'Not only must the organ be appointed to perform functions appertaining to the State at whose disposal it is placed, but in performing the functions entrusted to it by the beneficiary State, the organ must also act in conjunction with the machinery of that State and under its exclusive direction and control, rather than on instructions from the sending State'.[48] However, as explained earlier, the EU does not exerts this level of direction or control on its Member States, not even when they have to comply with a decision directly addressed to them.[49] This is certainly true in the case of the decision at the centre of this dispute. The decision only establishes an obligation on Hungary to recover the illegal aid. It does not address the relevant Hungarian organ to recover the aid, or the means to recover it. Therefore, even though the ICSID Tribunal correctly understood the nature of the relation between the EU and Hungary in this area, it failed to find an international legal basis which would support its argumentation. While the functional link embedded in article 6 ASR resonates with the *dédoublement fonctionnel* of the Member States' organs, it is not designed to apply to cases like *Electrabel v Hungary*. It is submitted that this case shows that the EU's normative control is progressively being accepted within the field of international investment law.

To sum up, arbitral tribunals have not adopted a single approach to the responsibility of the EU. Instead, investment arbitration tribunals correctly base the attribution of the wrongful act on the specific acts which gave rise to those issues. Whereas in *Eureko v Slovakia* or *Eastern Sugar v Czech Republic*, the attribution of the Member State's conduct to the EU based on a clear rule is quite difficult to envisage, that rule becomes especially clear in *AES v Hungary* and *Electrabel v Hungary*. The EU is responsible for the actions of its Member States when they are acting under the EU's normative control. However, even though there is a gradual acceptance of the responsibility of the EU for its normative control, the international

[46] Commentary 4 to article 6 ASR highlights the necessity of functional link: '*what is crucial for the purposes of article 6 is the establishment of a functional link between the organ in question and the structure or authority of the receiving State.*'

[47] Cf. Robert Schütze, *From Dual to Cooperative Federalism: The Changing Structure of European Law*, vol 391 (Oxford University Press 2009) 99.

[48] Commentary 2 to article 6 ASR.

[49] See Chapter 3.

legal foundations in which it rests are still not as developed as they should be. The use of article 6 ASR instead of article 64 ARIO shows how international judges and arbitrators have not given careful consideration to the topic of the EU's responsibility. With the unveiling of the new EU FDI competence, the EU's normative control will become an ineludible question in many investment arbitration proceedings.

7.2.3 Sharing Responsibility in International Investment Law

As explained earlier the EU does not only interact with its Member States through normative control. The following section looks into situations in which the Member States' organs do not functionally decouple themselves to implement EU law. Instead, they interact with the EU as formally equal international subjects, either because they were not EU Member States at that time or because their relationship is not governed by traditional EU law. In these scenarios, if a Member State commits an internationally wrongful act, the question of the shared responsibility of the EU will inevitably arise. Two examples in that regard will be brought forward in this section: accession negotiations and the extent to which the EU should bear responsibility for the actions of a candidate country aligning its regulations with the *acquis communautaire*, and, the ongoing claims concerning public debt restructuring after the financial crisis negotiated between the so-called Troika (European Commission, European Central Bank and the International Monetary Fund) and EU Member States like Greece and Cyprus.

7.2.3.1 Member States' Responsibility for Negotiating Their Accession to the EU: *Micula v Romania*

The issue of the shared responsibility of the EU with a (at that time) candidate country arose in *Micula v Romania*.[50] The case revolved around an investment attraction policy for less favoured areas in Romania. By virtue of this policy companies investing in these regions benefited from exemptions on customs duties and taxes while receiving preferential subsidies.[51] However, in 2005, prior to its accession to the EU, Romania withdrew the legislation covering these investment incentives. According to Romania, these modifications were done to adapt its legislation to the EU *acquis*.

[50] *Ioan Micula, Viorel Micula, and others v Romania* (Award) ICSID Case ARB/05/20 (11 December 2013); *Ioan Micula, Viorel Micula and others v Romania* (Decision on Admissibility and Jurisdiction) ICSID Case ARB/05/20 (24 September 2008) 48.

[51] *Ioan Micula, Viorel Micula and others v Romania, Case No. ARB/05/20, Decision on Admissibility and Jurisdiction* para. 31.

Romania submitted, inter alia, that an exemption from customs duties and taxes would be considered State aid incompatible with the internal market, in the context of EU competition policy and, therefore, inconsistent with Romania's obligations under European Law.[52] Yet, there was no decision of the European Commission declaring the incentives as illegal aid. Micula was one of the companies which suffered a loss because of Romania's decision to withdraw those incentives. Accordingly, it sued Romania in ICSID under the Romania-Sweden BIT.

As part of the facts, Romania put forward different EU documents concerning Romania's EU accession procedure. For instance, in a Common position from 28 May 2003, the EU recalled:

> that all fiscal aid provisions, (for example those included in the VAT Law; the Law on customs duties exemptions – including benefits for transactions undertaken by firms located in . . . disadvantaged areas . . .) should be subject to the approval by the Competition Council.[53] In cases where the Competition Council assesses the respective measures to be incompatible with the State aid rules, the EU invites Romania to either end the measures or to align them with the acquis. The EU invites Romania to bring all incompatible aid measures in line with the acquis without delay and to continue to provide information on the progress made towards this goal.[54]

With EU documents such as this, Romania sought to prove, inter alia, that the measures were, to a certain extent, imposed by the EU as a condition in Romania's accession process. However, it was not the European Commission, or any other EU institution for that matter, which identified and determined which measures were incompatible with State aid rules. It was a Romanian body who decided on the incompatibility with the EU *acquis* of such measures.

Moreover, given how EU accession negotiations work and the extent to which conditionality plays a role in it, the question of the extent to which the EU could bear some responsibility over breaches stemming from the accession process seems like an interesting question to ask.[55] Though, in this specific case, the relation is not as straightforward as Romania claimed. The Romanian government took the measures which amounted to a violation of the Romania-Sweden BITS, as part of what they considered to be the necessary steps towards EU accession. In fact the EU in a 2004

[52] Ibid. [53] A Romanian public organ.

[54] *Ioan Micula, Viorel Micula, and others v Romania, ICSID Case No. ARB/05/20, Award* para. 235.

[55] For an overview of how the enlargement of the EU works see: Marise Cremona (ed), *The Enlargement of the European Union* (Oxford University Press 2003).

Common Position accepted to establish transitional arrangements with respect to less favoured areas which meant that investors like Micula could continue to benefit from the tax incentives as long as the less favoured areas continued to exist, under certain conditions, and were limited to 2008, 2009 or 2010.[56] These transitional arrangements did not stop the Romanian government from withdrawing the incentives granted to Micula. According to ICSID, by withdrawing those incentives, Romania was responsible under the Romania-Sweden BIT.[57]

It is difficult to envisage how the EU should bear responsibility in this scenario: the breach is clearly attributable to Romania, and it would be difficult to argue the violation should be attributed to the EU instead. By contrast, had the EU expressly declared those incentives contrary to the internal market and forbade any kind of transitional arrangement, the EU should bear some responsibility jointly with Romania.[58] Shared responsibility in this scenario would be determined from the fact that Romania was not yet a member of the EU. The relationship that the EU and a candidate country have is not embedded with the same internal compliance mechanisms as the relationship between the EU and its Member States when they are complying with EU Stated aid regulations. Therefore, there is the possibility that the conduct of the EU could fall within article 14 ARIO concerning direction and control. If the EU would have established that those incentives did not have to be withdrawn and did that with the knowledge that Romania would be breaching a binding international obligation, the possibility of applying article 14 might apply. However, as explained earlier, that provision provides a rather narrow conception of control that would be difficult to apply to the present scenario.[59] All in all, it appears that, as it stands, international law is not equipped with the necessary tools to establish the responsibility of the EU (or in that respect any other international subject engaging in that kind of scenarios).

Still, in a case such as *Micula v Romania*, where the EU would bear no responsibility whatsoever under international law since it did not exercise any kind of normative control over Romania, the EU would still be able to influence Romania's compliance with the arbitral award. In this respect, Romania's compliance with the ICISID decision can affect the binding obligations that it has now assumed under EU law. In fact,

[56] *Ioan Micula, Viorel Micula, and others v Romania, ICSID Case No. ARB/05/20, Award* para. 243.

[57] Ibid. [58] See Chapter 3.

[59] Christian Dominicé, 'Attribution of Conduct to Mutiple States and the Implication of a State in the Act of Another State' in James Crawford and others (eds), *The Law of International Responsibility* (Oxford University Press 2010) 288.

the Commission considered that the compensation awarded to Micula was an illegal aid and launched an investigation on the matter.[60] Since the ICSID's decision was taken after Romania's accession to the EU, the award would be subject to EU law. Moreover, the CJEU has established that, even though annulment of, or refusal to recognize, an award should be possible only in exceptional circumstances,[61] it is nevertheless possible for the award not to be recognized by EU Courts whenever the said award would contravene EU public policy (like competition policy).[62] The Commission has already made quite clear that *Micula v Romania* might be one of these awards.[63]

Overall, this case shows that the EU can interact with other international subjects (soon to be EU Member States) outside the framework of its normative control. Even though the EU continues to hold a certain degree of influence over the actions of those subjects through conditionality, it bears no responsibility over the actions of the State committing the wrongful act.[64] At the same time, while the EU is not responsible for Romania's action, it can still significantly determine the effectiveness of the arbitral award. Inasmuch as the award can contravene basic public policy principles of the EU, the Commission and the CJEU can stop the award from taking effect within the EU realm. To put it differently, the fact that Romania was outside of the reach of the EU's normative control does not mean that the EU did not intervene in the commission of the wrongful act. Though articles 14–17 ARIO establish a high threshold for the rules of responsibility to apply, the EU should bear some kind of responsibility in these scenarios.[65] Undoubtedly, the actions of Romania are influenced to a certain extent by its accession negotiations with the EU, and yet the latter bears no responsibility.

7.2.3.2 Shared Responsibility and the Eurozone Crisis

Currently Greece is facing a series of cases in ICSID concerning the debt restructuring programme, while Cyprus is also being brought to ICSID over its takeover of Laiki (Cyprus Popular Bank). In *Poštová banka v Greece*, a Slovak bank brought an action against the debt restructuring programme

60 Case T-646/14 *Micula a.o. v Commission*.

61 Case C-126/97 *Eco Swiss China Time Ltd v Benetton International NV* [1999] ECR I-3055 para. 35.

62 Ibid. 63 *T-646/14 Micula a.o. v Commission*.

64 On conditionality and responsibility, see: August Reinisch, 'Aid or Assistance and Direction and Control between States and International Organizations in the Commission of Internationally Wrongful Acts' [2010] 7(1) International Organizations Law Review 63, 68.

65 See Chapter 3.

negotiated by Greece and the European Commission.[66] According to the claimant, the design of debt restructuring retroactively and unilaterally 'amended the terms of the bonds by inserting a collective action clause', which permitted the 'imposition of new terms upon bondholders against their consent if a supermajority of other bondholders consented'.[67] Even though the ICSID award considered that the ICSID Court lacked jurisdiction *ratio materiae* inasmuch as Poštová's investment in Greece did not amount to a protected investment in the sense of article 1 (1) of the Greek-Slovak BIT, the award nevertheless raises some questions worth exploring regarding the different ways in which the EU interacts with its Member States.[68]

In this scenario, rather than a situation of vertical normative control, it appears that the relationship between Greece and the EU could be considered of horizontal nature. To put it differently, Greek organs were not functionally decoupling to implement a piece of EU law. The EU was interacting with a Member State outside its traditional framework: EU constitutional principles such as primacy, direct effect and state liability would not apply to the MoU signed by the Commission with Greece.[69] Therefore, the question arises as to whether the EU could be internationally responsible nevertheless.

Whereas Greece would bear responsibility over the collective action clause by virtue of article 4 ASR, the responsibility of the EU, by contrast, would not be such a straightforward exercise. Still, it could be argued that the EU would be responsible not because the wrongful act would be attributable to it, but because Chapter IV of the ARIO could cover the factual scenario. As in *Micula v Romania*, there is a case to be made for shared responsibility. The MoU enshrined a programme of financial assistance to Greece dependent on a restructuring of the sovereign bonds held by private investors. According to the MoU, the financial funding that the Commission made available to Greece was dependent on the implementation of the debt restructuring programme. The agreed restructure entailed a swap of old bonds by new bonds of lesser value (also known as a 'haircut') to reduce Greece's public debt to sustainable levels. To meet this target, private bond holders had to face a reduction of 53.4 per cent of

66 *Poštová banka, a.s. and ISTROKAPITAL SE v Hellenic Republic (Award)* ICSID Case ARB/13/8 (9 April 2015).

67 UNCTAD, *Recent Developments in Investor-State Dispute Settlement (ISDS)* (UNCTAD 2014) 6.

68 *Poštová banka, a.s. and ISTROKAPITAL SE v Hellenic Republic* para. 371.

69 'Memorandum of Understanding between the European Commission Acting on Behalf of the Euro Member States and the Hellenic Republic' (1 March 2012), http://ec.europa.eu/economy_finance/eu_borrower/mou/2012-03-01-greece-mou_en.pdf.

their value.[70] The collective action clause was introduced so the majority of the private sector would agree to such a big haircut. Hence, could it be argued that the Commission was aiding and assisting Greece to implement its collective action clause? To answer this question, the causal link between the collective action clause and the conditionality will play a fundamental role. In relation to causality, the ILC has established that 'the aid or assistance must be given with a view to facilitating the commission of the wrongful act, and must actually do so'.[71] It understands that the aid given must be 'significant',[72] which would entail a substantial involvement in the commission of the wrongful act.[73]

Consequently, to ascertain whether the Commission aided or assisted Greece in committing the wrongful act, a significant causal link to determine the commission of the wrongful act between the conditionality and the collective action clause would be needed. In other words, it is necessary to examine to what extent the Commission's assistance was dependent on the debt restructuring (causal link), and whether it was somehow a determinant factor in the commission of the wrongful act (substantial involvement). Even though Greece and the Commission agreed that investors should suffer a haircut of 53.4 per cent, the MoU remains silent as to the way to achieve that target. While the Commission linked its financial assistance to the implementation of the debt restructuring programme it did not establish as a precondition that a collective action clause was necessary. Moreover, the MoU links part of the financial assistance to the payment of the bondholders suffering the haircut. In other words, the assistance of the Commission is designed to help Greece pay its debtors. In the absence of the Commission's financial assistance, the haircut that investors would have had to suffer would have been far bigger than the one they had already suffered. Therefore, even though there is significant causal link between the debt restructuring programme and the financial assistance, it would be difficult to argue that assistance was substantial to the commission of the wrongful act. On the contrary, it appears that the Commission's assistance was aimed at reducing the impact of Greece's debt restructuring.

[70] Public bond holders, i.e. the European Central Bank and the Member States' Central Banks, were excluded from the swap. See Eurogroup, 'Eurogroup Statement on Greece' (21 February 2012), www.eurozone.europa.eu/media/368205/statement_on_greece_21_february_2012.pdf.

[71] Commentary 5 to article 16 ASR. See: Helmut Philipp Aust, *Complicity and the Law of State Responsibility* (Cambridge University Press 2011) 210; James Crawford, *State Responsibility: The General Part* (Cambridge University Press 2013) 406.

[72] Commentary 4 to article 14 ARIO. See Crawford, (n 71) 403.

[73] Ibid.

Moreover, it is interesting to note that the Commission concluded the MoU not on behalf of the EU, but on behalf of the Euro Area Member States.[74] For that reason, it could be argued that it should be those Euro Area Member States instead of the EU, who bear a hypothetical shared responsibility over Greece's implementation of a collective action clause. Since the EU did not sign the MoU with Greece, it is even clearer that the principles which inform the EU's normative control over its Member States would not come into play in the present dispute. In this regard, it could be argued that the Commission would be acting in a similar vein to a State organ placed at the disposal of another State. This is a possibility that the CJEU has accepted inasmuch as the tasks attributed to the Commission do not modify the essential character of the powers conferred on it by the Treaties.[75] In the *Pringle v Ireland* case, the CJEU concluded that 'EU Member States are entitled, in areas which do not fall under the exclusive competence of the Union, to entrust tasks to the institutions, outside the framework of the Union'.[76] Hence, when analysed through the prism of the law of international responsibility, it could be argued that, when negotiating and concluding on behalf of the Euro Area Member States, the Commission is acting in the sense of article 6 ASR.[77] Consequently it should be the Euro Area Member States and not the EU sharing the responsibility with Greece.

In *Marfin v Cyprus* (still pending),[78] the issue of shared responsibility could also play a crucial role. In this case, the Marfin Investment Group argues that Cyprus's takeover of Laiki in 2012, which increased Cyprus's stake in the bank to 84 per cent, and included changes in the governing board of Laiki, violated the Cyprus-Greece BIT. The actions of the Cypriot government took to stabilize Laiki were part of set of measures included in a MoU negotiated by the Cypriot government with the Troika.[79] Marfin alleges that the government unlawfully diluted its stake in the bank and mismanaged the bailout, among many other things.[80]

While these facts raise the same kind of questions concerning the EU's shared responsibility as in *Poštová banka v Greece*, the statement of the

74 On the EU's treaty-making powers, see Chapter 1.

75 Case C-370/12 *Pringle v Ireland* [nyr] ECR para. 162. 76 Ibid. 77 See note 46.

78 *Marfin Investment Group v The Republic of Cyprus* (Notice of Dispute) ICSID Case ARB/13/27 (23 January 2013).

79 See: Eurogroup, 'Eurogroup Statement on Cyprus' (25 March 2013), www.eurozone.europa.eu/media/404933/EG%20EG%20Statement%20on%20CY%2025%2003%202013.pdf.

80 UNCTAD 5.

Minister of Finance of Cyprus concerning the context of the negotiations of the MoU could shed some light as to the nature of the relationship established between the Troika and Cyprus. In his statement, the Minister of Finance seemed to imply that, when negotiating the MoU, Cyprus acted under pressure from the Troika. In one of the answers put forward by the Cypriot Minister of Finance to the European Parliament's enquiry on the activities of the Troika, he mentioned that the negotiations on different aspects of the application of the bail-in instrument on bank deposits was made under duress.[81] By using this term, the Minister of Finance seems to be suggesting that Cyprus was coerced into concluding the MoU, which included the measures at the heart of *Marfin v Cyprus*.

Even though political and economic coercion may amount to coercion in the sense of article 18 ASR and 16 ARIO, it seems unlikely that the duress suffered by the Cypriot Government to conclude the MoU would meet the threshold set by the ILC.[82] First, the ILC has narrowly defined the scope of coercion.[83] Nothing less than conduct which forces the will of the coerced State would meet the ILC's threshold. Moreover, the coerced State would have no effective choice but to comply with the wishes of the coercing State.[84] In this regard, the practice as to what is to be considered is rather scant and mostly focused on coercion exercised through the threat or use of armed forces.[85]

In any case, even if the economic and political context in which Cyprus found itself gave the government no option but to accept the conditions set in the MoU, a crucial aspect to coercion would be the causal link between Cyprus's actions and what the MoU enshrines on the national takeover of Laiki. In other words, it is necessary to consider to what extent did the Troika, by linking its financial assistance to Cyprus to the government takeover of Laiki, coerce the latter into violating the rights of Marfin under the Cyprus-Greece BIT. A close examination of the conclusions of the Eurogroup on this issue shows that, while it called for the immediate resolution of Laiki, it remained silent as to how proceed with the resolution of the bank.[86] Likewise, the MoU remains silent on how the resolution

[81] See 'Questionnaire Sent by European Parliament to Minister of Finance of Cyprus' (14 January 2014), www.europarl.europa.eu/document/activities/cont/201401/20140114ATT77319/20140114ATT77319EN.pdf.

[82] Crawford, (n 71) 403.

[83] Commentary 3 to article 18 ASR.

[84] Commentary 2 to article 18 ASR.

[85] Commentary 7 to article 18 ASR.

[86] See: 'Annex to Eurogroup Statement on Cyprus' (25 March 2013), www.eurozone.europa.eu/media/404933/EG%20EG%20Statement%20on%20CY%2025%2003%202013.pdf.

of Laiki should go forward.[87] It appears that the Troika had no opinion as to the details of the nationalization and resolution of Laiki inasmuch as it was done rapidly. Therefore, given the high threshold imposed by ILC for coercion to apply, it is submitted that it appears unlikely that the Troika coerced Cyprus into violating Marfin's rights under the Cyprus-Greece BIT.

By contrast, if it was to be understood that the Troika should bear some responsibility on the nationalization of Laiki, Cyprus would be able to successfully to put forward that a circumstance precluding wrongfulness applied to its conduct.[88] The ILC equates coercion to *force majeure*.[89] Therefore, insofar as Cyprus was coerced into violating the Cyprus-Greek BIT, it will bear no responsibility over its actions, regardless of whether they are attributable to it.[90]

As has been explained earlier, the EU also interacts with its Member States outside the realm of its normative control. It appears that the more horizontal the relation between the EU and its Member States is, the less likely it is that the former will bear responsibility. However, one question remains; should the EU nevertheless be responsible in these scenarios where there is not a relationship of normative control? So far, by adopting narrow conceptions of rules of responsibility besides attribution, the law of international responsibility seems to be reluctant to accept that shared responsibility. However, it cannot be excluded that in the near future situations like the ones described previously could lead to the shared responsibility of the EU and the Member States.

7.3 EU Responsibility and the Future of EU Investment Policy

So far this chapter has analysed how international investment tribunals deal with the responsibility of the EU; this section examines how the future EU international investment policy will deal with the issue of

87 'Memorandum of Understanding on Specific Economic Policy Conditionality between the European Commission, the European Central Bank and the International Monetary Fund and Cyprus, signed on the 12 of April 2013' (29 August 2013), www.imf.org/external/np/loi/2013/cyp/082913.pdf.

88 Commentary 2 to article 18 ASR. See Chapter 3.

89 Ibid.

90 It must also be mentioned that, even though the measures which lead to the violation of the Cyprus-Greece BIT might be solely attributable to Cyprus, Cyprus might nevertheless avoid being held responsible. Besides *force majeure*, the law of international responsibility recognizes other circumstances precluding wrongfulness. Unlike coercion, these other circumstances per se are not linked to issues of attribution and shared responsibility and rely more on the context leading to the commission of the international wrongful act. Crawford, (n 71) 274.

the EU's responsibility. As a result of the exclusive nature of investment competence, since 2010 the Commission has been designing a comprehensive policy in this regard. Moreover, it has also been preparing the legal instruments which will develop the new European international investment policy.[91] Within this new policy, the Commission needed to address the issue of the EU's international responsibility. As has been explained, the EU's responsibility has become a relevant topic since the current arrangements have been proven not to deal with the different interests in an effective way, both in bilateral (intra-EU BITS) and multilateral (ECT) settings.[92]

Against this backdrop, the Commission stressed that the 'issue of the international responsibility between the EU and the Member States in EU investment agreements needs to be addressed'.[93] Still, the proposal did not address the attribution of wrongful acts or any specific rules which could apply to the EU and/or its Member States. Instead, the policy document addressed the issue through the EU's participation in future investment disputes. According to the Commission Communication, '[g]iven the exclusive external competence, [the EU] will also be the sole defendant regarding any measure taken by a Member State which affects investments by third country nationals or companies falling within the scope of the agreement concerned', and pointed out that further rules on responsibility would be tackled in future legislation and its treaty-making practice.[94] Within this context, this section aims to examine how the current EU treaty-making practice in the field of investment law approaches the issue of responsibility of the EU, as well as the EU legislation dealing with the financial responsibility in this area.

7.3.1 EU Investment Treaty-Making Practice and EU Responsibility

Within the design of the EU's comprehensive investment policy, the European Commission recognized that investor-state arbitration 'is such an established feature of investment agreements that its absence would in

[91] European Commission, 'Communication from the Commission to the Council, the European Parliament, the European Economic and Social Committee and the Committee of the Regions. Towards a Comprehensive European International Investment policy' COM (2010) 343 final.

[92] See previous section.

[93] European Commission, 'Communication from the Commission to the Council, the European Parliament, the European Economic and Social Committee and the Committee of the Regions. Towards a Comprehensive European international Investment policy' COM (2010) 343 final, p. 10.

[94] Ibid.

fact discourage investors and make a host economy less attractive than others'.[95] Yet, it seems rather unlikely that the EU would be able to join ICSID in the foreseeable future.[96] Accordingly, the EU will have to design its own dispute settlement provisions and mechanisms to be negotiated and included in its international agreements with an investment element.[97]

Since the entry into force of Lisbon, the EU has concluded two Free Trade Agreements (FTAs)[98] and one Association Agreement,[99] and it is at the moment negotiating more than a dozen agreements with investment chapters embedded in them.[100] Countries such as Canada, Singapore, China or the US are among the current EU negotiating partners with the EU. For instance, the FTA concluded with South Korea included the most comprehensive investment provisions when compared with previous EU trade agreements, but it did not include investor-state dispute settlement provisions.[101] An example of those provisions can be found in the EU-Canada FTA (hereinafter CETA).[102] It is nevertheless expected that, given the little flexibility that the EU has when negotiating international agreements, a similar formula as that enshrined in CETA will be reproduced in the next generation of EU FTAs.[103]

95 Ibid 10. 96 Burgstaller, (n 34).

97 Bischoff, (n 26) 1568. It should be noted however that Burgstaller raises a very interesting issue concerning the compatibility of such clauses with EU law and more specifically with the CJEU's case law on international courts, Burgstaller, (n 34) 221.

98 Free Trade Agreement between the European Union and its Member States, of the one part, and the Republic of Korea, of the other part [2011] OJ L 127; Trade Agreement between the European Union and its Member States, of the one part, and Colombia and Peru, of the other part [2012] OJ L 354; EU-Canada Comprehensive Economic and Trade Agreement (not yet published); EU Singapore Free Trade Agreement (not yet published).

99 Agreement establishing an Association between the European Union and its Member States, on one hand, and Central America on the other [2012] OJ L 346.

100 European Commission, 'The EU's Bilateral Trade and Investment Agreements – Where Are We?' (EC Memo, 3 December 2013), http://trade.ec.europa.eu/doclib/docs/2012/november/tradoc_150129.pdf.

101 Chien-Hui Wu, 'Foreign Direct Investment as Common Commercial Policy: EU External Economic Competence after Lisbon' in James Cardwell (ed), *EU External Relations Law and Policy in the Post-Lisbon Era* (T. M. C. Asser Press 2012) 396. Cf. James Harrison, 'The Legal Framework for Investment Protection between the European Union and Korea: Towards a Level Playing Field for Investors?' in James Harrison (ed), *The European Union and South Korea: The Legal Framework for Strengthening Trade, Economic and Political Relations* (Edinburgh University Press 2013) 109.

102 EU–Canada Comprehensive Economic and Trade Agreement.

103 Peter M. Olson, 'Mixity from the Outside: The Perspective of a Treaty Partner' in Christophe Hillion and Panos Koutrakos (eds), *Mixed Agreements Revisited: The EU and Its Member States in the World* (Hart 2010) 339.

CETA provides a procedure aimed at helping the investor target the correct respondent when dealing with a treatment afforded by the EU or its Member States. Prior to initiating arbitration, CETA envisages that the claimant shall deliver a notice to the EU requesting a determination of the respondent.[104] Unlike the ECT, the agreement imposes an obligation to consult the EU before lodging the dispute. By establishing the compulsory nature of the investor's duty to consult the EU before deciding whom to target, CETA aims to achieve two things. First, it wants avoid the wrong targeting of EU Member States in scenarios in which it should be the EU bearing the responsibility. Second, by establishing a prior obligation to consult, "divide and rule" tactics like those used by the US in the WTO will no longer be possible.[105] Moreover, it appears that the EU wants to keep the attribution of conduct an internal decision. The rule does not shed any light on how the decision of the EU to act as a respondent will be made. The reasons behind the decision of the EU to act as a respondent are unclear. Would the EU act as a respondent because it wants to acknowledge the responsibility as its own, even though it might not be?[106] Which factors will guide that decision? Moreover, the *ad hoc* nature of the responsibility in that situation will entail a greater difficulty (if not impossibility) of advancing normative claims based on those solutions. To what extent would the EU be bound to follow previous decisions to act as a respondent?[107]

The uncertainty and lack of transparency informing that provision contrast with the two different rules of attribution that could apply if the EU does not inform of its decision within 50 days. The attribution of the conduct will be done depending on where the measure which infringes the investor's right under CETA stemmed from:

- where the measures are exclusively measures of an EU Member State, the Member State shall be the respondent;
- where the measures include measures of the EU, the EU shall be the respondent.[108]

While these two rules of attribution will apply in the absence of an EU response within the established period, it is unclear whether they will inform the EU's decision to act as respondent if it responds within 50 days.

[104] Article 8.21 (1) CETA. [105] See Chapter 6. [106] See article 9 ARIO.

[107] Andrés Delgado Casteleiro, 'The International Responsibility of the EU: Between Pragmatism and Proceduralization' [2012] 15 Cambridge Yearbook of European Legal Studies 563, 576.

[108] Article 8.21 (4) CETA.

Moreover, CETA's current wording seems to exclude the possibility of joint responsibility of the EU and its Member States, regardless of the nature of the measures at stake. Inasmuch as one of the measures challenged by the investor includes an EU measure, it should be for the EU to act as a sole respondent.[109] Having one respondent will inevitably make things easier for the investor challenging a wide range of intertwined measures both stemming from the EU and its Member States, even though it might raise some concerns from the perspective of EU Member States. In principle, the EU could be acting as sole respondent and having to defend a Member State policy which falls completely outside of its competence. While this might not be an issue given previous WTO practice,[110] Member States might want to be more involved in how the EU will defend their interest while at the same time defend its own, even in situations in which they might be contradictory.[111]

CETA also remains silent as to what would constitute an "EU measure". Does CETA accept that those measures adopted by EU Member States under the EU's normative control are "EU measures"? Or instead, does it adopt a restrictive view by which only the measures adopted by EU organs *stricto sensu* are EU measures?

In general, although the current rules of attribution in CETA provide certainty to investors concerning the responsibility of the EU, they still leave too many questions unanswered. For instance, it is unclear what elements will be balanced when deciding whether to act or not as respondent? If the rules envisaged in article 8.21 paragraph 4 will be applied regardless, why establish the 50-day period for the EU to decide? Would a Member State regulation adopted under the EU's normative control be considered an "EU measure"? Furthermore, given that disputes brought against the EU could not be settled under the ICSID Convention, Canadian investors would in principle have less means available to challenge an EU measure which negatively affects their rights.[112]

[109] Cf. Andrés Delgado Casteleiro, 'EU Declarations of Competence to Multilateral Agreements: A Useful Reference Base?' [2012] 17(4) European Foreign Affairs Review 491.

[110] See Chapter 5.

[111] For an analysis of this issue but in relation to the ECHR, see: Delgado Casteleiro, (n 107).

[112] Article 8-23 reads: '2. A claim may be submitted under the following arbitration rules:

(a) the ICSID Convention;
(b) the ICSID Additional Facility Rules where the conditions for proceedings pursuant to paragraph (a) do not apply;
(c) the UNCITRAL Arbitration Rules; or

any other arbitration rules on agreement of the disputing parties.'

Therefore, it seems that the responsibility of the EU under CETA while identifying the main problems that investors face when litigating against the EU, it does not address them in a straightforward fashion.[113] Article 8.21 as it currently stands is designed to point an investor to the correct respondent, Despite the aim of legal certainty which informs this provision, the lack of transparency on how the decision will be taken, and the vagueness of the rules have the potential of creating the opposite result: *ad hoc* and opaque responses to questions on the EU's responsibility in international investment law. In a nutshell, the flexible rule of attribution enshrined in CETA seems to be designed to protect the strategic interests of the EU rather than providing certainty to investors.

7.3.2 Managing Financial Responsibility Linked to Investor-State Dispute Settlement Tribunal

In addition to the new investor-state arbitration provisions, the EU published a regulation intended to regulate financial responsibility linked to investor-state dispute settlement tribunals (the Regulation).[114] This Regulation lays down the internal legal framework in which a solution to the question of who will bear the financial burden of a breach of international investment obligation.[115] It also provides a procedure that aims to allow the EU to participate in an investment dispute and the allocation of internal financial responsibility once the dispute has finished. However, it seems unclear how this Regulation will relate to the EU's international responsibility in this area. The Regulation makes a distinction that might be considered artificial between the EU's international responsibility and its financial responsibility.[116] The explanatory memorandum to the Regulation proposal puts forward the idea that 'while . . . the Union bears, in principle, international responsibility for the breach of any provision within the Union's competence, it is possible, as a matter of Union law, to

113 Frank Hoffmeister, 'Litigating against the European Union and Its Member States – Who Responds under the ILC's Draft Articles on International Responsibility of International Organizations?' [2010] 21(3) European Journal of International Law 723.

114 'Proposal for a Regulation of the European Parliament and of the Council establishing a framework for managing financial responsibility linked to investor-state dispute settlement tribunals established by international agreements to which the European Union is party' COM (2012) 335 final.

115 For an overview of the different issues, see: Angelos Dimopoulos, 'The Involvement of the EU in Investor-State Dispute Settlement: A Question of Responsibilities' [2014] 51 (6) Common Market Law Review 16.

116 Tiejte, Sipiorsk and Topfër, (n 34) 20.

provide for the allocation of financial responsibility between the Union and the Member States'.[117]

The artificiality of this distinction between international and financial responsibility is clearly seen in article 3 of the Regulation. Article 3(1) reads as follows:

> 1. Financial responsibility arising from a dispute under an agreement shall be apportioned according to the following criteria:
>   (a) the Union shall bear the financial responsibility arising from treatment afforded by the institutions, bodies or agencies of the Union;
>   (b) the Member State concerned shall bear the financial responsibility arising from treatment afforded by that Member State, except where such treatment was required by the law of the Union.

Notwithstanding point (b) of the first subparagraph, where the Member State concerned is required to act pursuant to the law of the Union to remedy the inconsistency with the law of the Union of a prior act, that Member State shall be financially responsible unless the adoption of such prior act was required by the law of the Union.

Whenever an EU organ commits a wrongful act, it is for the EU to bear responsibility. Likewise, breaches committed by EU Member States' organs should be attributed to the Member States, unless they were acting under the EU's normative control. Given the exclusive nature of FDI, these rules of attribution respond to the fact that EU Member States would not be allowed to act in the field of FDI unless the EU empowered them to do so.[118]

So far, this provision very much resembles the rule of attribution enshrined in article 8.21 of CETA, but taking into account what the ICISID court held in *Electrabel v Hungary* concerning the responsibility of the EU. However, article 3 also contains another rule of attribution. Paragraph 3 envisages that, under certain circumstances, EU Member States might also bear financial responsibility. These circumstances boil down to a single issue: EU Member States will bear financial responsibility if they want to. Therefore, the proposal does not make a clear choice towards the EU's sole responsibility or the joint responsibility of the EU and its Member States.

[117] 'Proposal for a Regulation of the European Parliament and of the Council establishing a framework for managing financial responsibility linked to investor-state dispute settlement tribunals established by international agreements to which the European Union is party' COM (2012) 335 final, 5. This distinction is also reflected, although not as clearly, in the introduction to the regulation. See '*whereas (5)*'.

[118] For a more in-depth critique of the provisions, see: Tiejte, Sipiorsk and Topfër, (n 34) 19.

Instead, it leaves to them to decide depending on the circumstances of the dispute.

Even though the proposal lays down rules as to the allocation of responsibility, the proposal also allows the EU and the Member States to override these rules and modify the allocation of responsibility depending on the specific case. On the other hand, the uncertainty that the variable responsibility would entail is diminished to a certain extent by the different procedures enshrined in the Regulation. The Regulation assumes that, by laying down procedural rules on the participation, third parties' legal certainty is safeguarded.[119] Transparency in how the decisions as to the participation of the EU and its Member States are taken should satisfy the third parties' concerns. This is especially clear in article 18, which provides for a procedure which would allow the third party to get its award even when there is no agreement between the EU and its Member States as to who bears the financial responsibility. Despite this procedure, the legal certainty of other third parties is not completely safeguarded with these procedural strategies. Since each case can be approached in very different ways, depending on how the EU and its Member States decide to approach the dispute, third parties will have difficulties in trying to predict how their dispute will turn out.

Overall, the Regulation is a mixture of pragmatism and proceduralization aimed at safeguarding the legal certainty of third parties while at the same time taking into account the complexities underpinning the division of competences and the autonomy of EU law. However, would not a clear rule of attribution like the one contained in article 3(1) of the Regulation have tackled the problems in a similar fashion while adding even more legal certainty? In addition, the flexibility in the participation of the EU Member States might create problems as regards the constitutional identity of the EU legal order. Given the exclusive nature of the FDI, how can a Member State incur a responsibility if in principle it is not allowed to act in this area unless the EU has authorized it?

Furthermore, when read jointly with investor-state provisions like article 8.21 of CETA, the exact scope of this proposal seems a little be unclear. Is this the procedure under which the EU will decide who will act as respondent in an investment case under CETA? If so, why not enshrine directly in the agreement? While the Regulation should be welcomed as an example of transparency in the procedure leading to the attribution of a wrongful act, the overall context in which it is going to develop might

[119] Cf. Jan Kleinheisterkamp, 'Financial Responsibility in European International Investment Policy' [2014] 63(2) International and Comparative Law Quarterly 449.

call for further clarity. A complete correspondence between the provisions of the Regulation and the investor-state dispute settlement provisions in the international agreements might add to that. An explicit and clear recognition of the EU's normative control as rule of attribution following what the ICSID Tribunal did in *Electrabel v Hungary* most certainly would add certainty as to the commitment of the EU to abide by investment arbitration rulings.

7.4 Conclusions

There is no doubt that the road towards an EU Investment Policy is proving to be a long and bumpy road. So far, uncertainty over the future has been the common feature. The status of EU Member State BITS has yet to be solved.[120] The model of EU BIT has yet to be created.[121] But, especially there is plenty of uncertainty as to how tackle EU investment arbitration.[122]

International arbitration seems to be accepting the EU's normative control as a criterion to attribute responsibility. So far, no EU Member State has been held responsible for actions carried out under the EU's normative control. Instead, ICSID panels like the one in *Electrabel v Hungary* recognize that the EU's normative control should entail the responsibility of the EU and not of the Member State implementing EU law. Moreover, different investment arbitration cases show that the EU can also interact with its Member States outside the realm of normative control. Yet these interactions, according to investment courts, do not entail the shared responsibility of the EU and its Member States. Regardless of the fact that the EU played a fundamental role in influencing its Member States' behaviour, ICISID seems to understand that the link between the EU and its Member States in these scenarios are not as strong as to relocate part of the responsibility to the EU.

Overall, this chapter has shown that the treatment afforded to an investor might be granted by a subject (e.g. a Member State) but the

120 Angelos Dimopoulos and Mavluda Sattorova, 'The Present and Future of EU International Investment Treaties' [2012] 39(2) Legal Issues of Economic Integration 153.

121 Harrison, (n 101); N. Jansen Calamita, 'The Making of Europes International Investment Policy: Uncertain First Steps' [2012] 39(3) Legal Issues of Economic Integration 301.

122 Tiejte, Sipiorsk and Topfër, (n 34). Burgstaller, (n 34); Mavluda Sattorova, 'Return to the Local Remedies Rule in European BITs? Power (Inequalities), Dispute Settlement, and Change in Investment Treaty Law' [2012] 39(2) Legal Issues of Economic Integration 223; Steffen Hindelang, 'Circumventing Primacy of EU Law and the CJEUs Judicial Monopoly by Resorting to Dispute Resolution Mechanisms Provided for in Inter-se Treaties? The Case of Intra-EU Investment Arbitration' [2012] 39(2) Legal Issues of Economic Integration 179.

responsibility might lay with someone else (e.g. the EU). Even though this scenario is not that different from what investors face in a federal state,[123] unlike the latter it appears that both the EU and its Member States will be parties to future international investment agreements.[124] Yet the EU's treaty-making practice does not seem to take such a clear stance on the issue as investment arbitration. The EU should make a special effort to assure investors that they will assist them in determining the correct respondent. So far, the mechanisms laid down to deal with those issues have proven to be not as useful as it might appear.[125] The declaration made to the ECT did not stop AES and Electrabel from targeting the wrong respondent. Against this backdrop, the current rule enshrined in CETA should be welcomed. It provides some guidance as to who will bear responsibility over the treatment afforded to an investor. Nevertheless, the provision leaves some questions unsolved, which might add some degree of uncertainty as to who will bear responsibility. In this regard, although a solution, the proposal for a regulation dealing with financial responsibility stemming from investment disputes makes an artificial differentiation between international and financial responsibility which could create problems once it is implemented.

International investment cases tend to be quite complex given the wide array of measures that they usually entail. The more complex the dispute, the less probable it is that the outcome will satisfy everybody. For these reasons, any rule of responsibility in this area should strive for simplicity and certainty. Moreover, a decision which does not take due account of the rules of responsibility can, especially when speaking about the EU, have very strong constitutional implications. Attributing responsibility to the wrong subject can lead to situations in which not only the constitutional division of competences and the autonomy of EU law might be compromised,[126] but also, the possibility for the investor to get its money back.[127] If the EU wants to be a relevant actor in the field of international investment law it should aim towards simple rules of responsibility to be included in its future international investment agreements.

123 Tiejte, Sipiorsk and Topfër, (n 34) 10.

124 E.g. CETA. Cf. Bischoff, (n 26).

125 Delgado Casteleiro, (n 109).

126 Opinion 2/94 *Re: Accession to the ECHR* [1996] ECR I-1759; Opinion 1/91 *Re: European Economic Area Agreement* [1991] ECR 6079.

127 Case C-126/97 *Eco Swiss China Time Ltd v Benetton International NV* [1999] ECR I-3055.

Conclusions

1 The European Union and International Responsibility

This monograph has analysed the respective international responsibility of the EU and its Member States in the event of a breach of an international obligation that occurs in the course of the implementation of EU law. It has done so from a practical perspective by examining how international bodies attribute an internationally wrongful act to the EU. More precisely, it has shown how different international bodies understand the relationship between the EU and its Member States in relation to their responsibility for a breach of an international agreement which is the direct result of the implementation of EU law.

Chapter 1 began by examining how the EU is bound by the international agreements it has concluded. However, rather than focusing on how international agreements are implemented in the EU, this chapter examined how EU law was implemented. This shift of focus provides greater clarity as to the circumstances under which the EU could breach an international agreement, and consequently sheds some light on the issue of attribution. The chapter showed the legal and institutional mechanisms that inform the implementation of EU law in its Member States. The decentralized implementation of EU law is controlled by the EU through a set of principles (primacy, competence, duty of cooperation) and through institutional procedures (i.e. infringement procedures, judicial control by the CJEU) that highlight member States' lack of autonomy in their compliance with EU law. The chapter concluded with the proposition that rather than focusing on whether the EU has a competence covering the breached agreement to attribute responsibility, it would be wiser to examine the legal grounds under which the acts breaching an international obligation were adopted. If the acts were adopted to comply with an EU norm i.e.

adopted the EU's normative control, there is a case to be made in favour of considering the wrongful act as committed by the EU.

Chapter 2 and 3 examined the extent to which the recent ILC's codification process took the EU's executive federalism into account. In particular, the chapter examined how ARIO could apply to the different situations in which the EU and/or its Member States could incur international responsibility when complying with EU law. The chapter addressed a variety of situations enshrined in the articles that take into account the different facets of the relationship between an IO and its constituent Member States. However, these chapters also raised some doubts about certain provisions, in particular those dealing with the responsibility of the Member States of an IO in relation to acts committed by that IO. More specifically, some serious doubts were raised in relation to article 60 ARIO, both in terms of its wording and its underlying rationale. Article 60 ARIO establishes the responsibility of the Member States of an IO when the IO breaches an international obligation binding on the Member States but not on the IO. The provision relies on rather general concepts (and to a certain extent ones which are difficult to assess) such as the will of the Member State to avoid compliance ("seek to avoid") or circumvention.[1] Given the fact that the EU is not a party to certain agreements in which it has competence, and the fact that Member States are parties to those agreements, article 60 could potentially apply to the EU. Part III identifies an increasing trend in that regard. Moreover, third parties are starting to bring claims against Member States for acts committed when implementing EU law.[2] However, it should be noted that article 60 has not been applied so far.

Chapter 4 analysed the so-called declarations of competence. The chapter provided a systematic overview of the different types of declarations that the EU has used when concluding multilateral mixed agreements. Even though, in theory, the use of a declaration to apportion obligations and responsibility under a mixed agreement between the EU and its Member States might be regarded as a useful tool, practice shows otherwise. The ambiguous wording and the failure to update the declarations combined with the dynamic nature of the EU's division of competence casts

[1] ILC, 'Report of the International Law Commission on the Work of Its 61st Session' (4 May–5 June and 6 July–7 August 2009) UN Doc A/64/10, 163.

[2] *AES Summit Generation Limited and AES-Tisza Erőmű Kft. v Republic of Hungary* (Award) ICSID Case ARB/07/22 (23 September 2010), *Electrabel S.A. v Republic of Hungary* (Decision on Jurisdiction) ICSID Case ARB/07/19 (30 November 2012).

many doubts on the effectiveness and practical relevance of declarations in this regard.

Chapter 5 analysed their international practice (or lack of it) in disputes brought against the EU. The examination of the absence of an application of declaration made to UNCLOS in a Swordfish dispute between the EU and Chile exposes the limited practical relevance of the declarations.[3] Moreover, the dispute shows how Chile, rather than using the declaration, employed other instruments to attribute the actions of Spanish fishermen to the EU. Chile assumed that, as long as the issue at stake was within the EU's exclusive competence, the action should be attributed to the EU and not to Spain.[4] The Swordfish dispute showed how, to a certain extent, there has been a shift from competence to normative control even in situations in which there are instruments designed to solve the issue of the allocation of responsibility by using competence.

This shift towards normative control is more pronounced within the Aarhus Convention Compliance Committee (ACCC). Even though the ACCC is not a judicial body *stricto sensu*, its case law shows how even when only shared competences are involved, there is still room to attribute to the EU conduct committed under its normative control. It appears that international bodies seem to take the position that the EU bears exclusive responsibility in such scenarios.[5]

Chapter 6 confirmed this trend by introducing the example of the WTO Dispute Settlement System and showed how WTO panels have consistently attributed acts committed by EU Member States when implementing EU law to the EU. In other words, the WTO holds the EU responsible for any violation committed under its normative control.

Chapter 7 examined the issue of the EU's normative control and Member States' responsibility by focusing on international investment arbitration. The chapter showed how in this area in which the EU is starting to formulate its policy, the interactions between EU law and international investment law are causing plenty of friction. In recent years, compliance with EU law has become a common argument being put forward by EU Member States. They understand that their violations of international

[3] *Case concerning the Conservation and Sustainable Exploitation of Swordfish Stocks in the South-Eastern Pacific Ocean (Chile/European Union)* (Order of 16 December 2009) ITLOS Reports 2008/10 13.

[4] Frank Hoffmeister, 'Litigating against the European Union and Its Member States – Who Responds under the ILC's Draft Articles on International Responsibility of International Organizations?' [2010] 21(3) European Journal of International Law 723, 738.

[5] Ibid.

investment law stems from a conflict with EU law. While in many of these cases the incompatibility between EU law and international investment law might not be that clear, others raise fundamental questions as regards the responsibility of EU Member States when implementing EU law, especially in relation to the recovery of illegal state aids. So far EU Member States have not been held responsible for conducts, which fall within the EU's normative control. On the contrary, the chapter shows how even in this scenario where bringing a case against the EU is not a possibility, the responsibility of the EU for actions committed under its normative control is taken into consideration.[6]

2 Towards a Theory of Normative Control as a Means of Attributing Responsibility

2.1 *How Special Is the EU? Normative Control as a Special Rule of Attribution*

During the ILC's codification process, the EU argued that the ARIO should take the special features of the EU into account. Those special features mainly related to the EU's normative control. It has been argued that this normative control rests on a set of principles that limit the autonomy of Member States when they are implementing EU law. Member States' *dédoublement fonctionnel* has consequences on the way EU Member States can act. They are subject to a different set of principles depending on whether they are acting under the scope of EU law or not. Therefore it seems logical that the EU argued in favour of that special situation being taken into account in relation to the issue of responsibility. However, this raises a question: how special are the relations between the EU and its Member States? In other words, to what extent could normative control be used as a criterion with which to attribute exclusive responsibility to other IOs besides the EU?

Even though (as is the case with any other IO) the EU needs its Member States to implement its law, the mechanisms of control aimed at ensuring the effective and uniform implementation more closely resemble the "checks and balances" of federal states than the mechanisms of other IOs. Member States administrations must implement EU law by

6 *Electrabel S.A. v Republic of Hungary* (Decision on Jurisdiction) ICSID Case ARB/07/19 (30 November 2012).

virtue of the obligation enshrined in article 291 TFEU. Furthermore, the principle of primacy, determines that whenever there is an EU norm, Member States must comply with EU law. The principle of direct effect provides for an effective mechanism to ensure that the primacy principle is enforced in the Member States.[7] Finally, the duty of cooperation safeguards the primacy of EU law by establishing the obligation of effective implementation.[8] These principles combined with the judicial control envisaged in the Treaties constitute the basis of the EU's normative control over its Member States' actions when implementing EU law. In this respect, international bodies have recognized that situations where normative control is exercised by the EU, the conduct of its Member States should be attributed to the EU and not the Member State which carries out the internationally wrongful act.

Consequently, inasmuch as an IO interacts with its Member States in an analogous way as the EU does, normative control could be used as a rule with which to attribute the responsibility of a wrongful act to the IO and not to the Member States which committed it.[9] Traditionally it has been argued that the normative control exercised by an IO over its Member States does not amount to a concept of control as strong as the 'effective' control envisaged in article 6 of the ARIO (attribution of acts of organs placed at the disposal of an IO).[10] This monograph does not argue that normative control resembles the kind of control that the head of peacekeeping operation exercises over its troops. However, this fact does not preclude an acknowledgement of the fact that normative control, in the EU context, should have some consequences in the international sphere, especially in relation to the attribution of responsibility.

In the same way that EU Member States, as a consequence of the EU's normative control, cannot initiate international disputes over issues falling under the scope of EU law,[11] negotiate or conclude international

[7] Case 106/77 *Amministrazione delle Finanze dello Stato v Simmenthal SpA* [1978] ECR 629 para. 18.

[8] Case C-106/89 *Marleasing SA v La Comercial Internacional de Alimentacion SA* [1990] ECRvI-4135 para. 8.

[9] For the application of the theory of normative control to the UNSC see: Antonios Tzanakopoulos, *Disobeying the Security Council: Countermeasures against Wrongful Sanctions* (Oxford University Press 2011).

[10] Pierre Klein, *La responsabilité des organisations internationales dans les ordres juridiques internes et en droit de gens* (Bruylant, Université de Bruxelles 1998); Pierre Klein, 'The Attribution of Acts to International Organizations' in James Crawford, Alain Pellet and Simon Olleson (eds), *The Law of International Responsbility* (Oxford University Press 2010).

[11] Case C-459/03 *Commission v Ireland (MOX Plant)* [2006] ECR I-4635.

agreements,[12] nor make proposals to bodies set up by a multilateral agreement without the prior consent of the EU, EU Member States should not bear responsibility for the actions committed under the EU's normative control. Instead, the EU should be the responsible subject for the acts of its Member States in their implementation of EU law. The same would apply to any other IO which limited its Member States' powers in an analogous manner.

During the ILC's codification process, the EU proposed different possibilities which could accommodate normative control in the ARIO:

> (1) "Special rules of attribution, so that actions of member States' organs can be attributed to the organization;
> (2) Special rules for responsibility, so that responsibility can be charged to the organization, even if member States' organs were the prime actors of a breach of an obligation borne by the organization;
> (3) Consideration of the possibility that the European [Union] and organizations like it should benefit from a special exception or of a kind of special savings clause for such an organization."[13]

Ultimately, the ILC provided for a special rule of attribution under article 64 ARIO to deal with EU's responsibility stemming from acts committed by its Member States when implementing EU law.[14] This monograph has shown that even though this rule does not already exists in international law, it can be considered to be at an earlier stage of development. As recent disputes have shown, the limits of the EU's normative control have yet to be delineated. For instance, the decision of the WTO panel on the *Airbus* dispute showed how the EU's normative control does not imply that the EU's membership shifts EU Member States' responsibility *per se*.[15] The fact that the EU Member States are members of the EU does not entail that they are no longer responsible for any violation of a mixed agreement that they might commit. EU Member States continue to bear responsibility for those acts that do not implement EU law.

Moreover, even though the EU in its recent treaty-making practice is favouring the recourse to joint responsibility when attributing wrongful acts committed under the EU's normative control, there are no examples in which the EU and its Member States have been held jointly responsible

[12] Case C-266/03 *Commission v Luxembourg (Inland Waterways)* [2005] ECR I-4805; Case C-433/03 *Commission v Germany (Inland Waterways)* [2005] ECR I-6985.

[13] ILC, *Responsibility of International Organizations – Comments and Observations received from Governments and International Organizations* (56th sess, 25 June 2004) UN Doc A/CN.4/545, 6.

[14] ILC, *Report on the Work of Its 51st Session* 173. Cf. Hoffmeister, (n 5) 745.

[15] See Chapter 6.

over actions committed under the EU's normative control.[16] On the contrary, it appears that international bodies are more inclined to recognize the special features of the EU in terms of responsibility than one would initially think. This trend shows how joint responsibility might not be as easy to apply as previously thought.[17]

2.2 The Limits of Normative Control

The exact contours of the EU's normative control as a means of attributing responsibility to the EU are yet to be drawn. For instance, would the EU bear responsibility for those actions committed by a Member States on issues covered by a provision in the Treaties but not legislated for by the EU?

In *Eureko v the Slovak Republic*,[18] the Slovak Republic put forward that, *mutatis mutandi*, by virtue of its EU membership it was no longer bound by the BIT. Moreover, it argued that EU law had rendered the BIT inapplicable.[19] Moreover, there was no EU act covering the Slovak government actions. Therefore, the actions of the Slovak Republic in this case would fall outside the EU's normative control. To a certain extent the Permanent Court of Arbitration acknowledged this fact by dismissing the Slovak Republic's counter-argument.[20]

However, it should also be mentioned that Eureko had itself brought a complaint to the European Commission in 2008.[21] This complaint led to the opening of an infringement procedure against the Slovak Republic, which was pending at the time the arbitral awards was granted.[22] Had the European Commission adopted a decision establishing that Slovakia's actions in the health insurance market were in accordance with EU law, the legislative measures of the Slovak government in that regard would have been under the EU's normative control. Thus, in line with the argument put forward in this monograph, the wrongful act should be attributed to the EU and not to Slovakia. The dispute between Eureko and

[16] See Chapter 7. Cf. Andrés Delgado Casteleiro, 'The International Responsibility of the EU: Between Pragmatism and Proceduralization' [2012/13] 15 Cambridge Yearbook of European Legal Studies 563.

[17] See also how in Opinion 2/13 the CJEU was not completely convinced about the joint responsibility of the EU and one of its Member States as a default rule. Opinion 2/13 *Re: Accession of the European Union to the ECHR* [nyr] ECR, para. 226.

[18] *Achmea B.V. (formerly known as Eureko B.V.) v The Slovak Republic* (Final Award) PCA Case 2008-13 (7 December 2012).

[19] *Eureko BV (The Netherlands) v The Slovak Republic* (Award on Jurisdiction) PCA Case 2008-13 (26 October 2010), para. 19.

[20] Ibid. [21] Ibid. [22] Ibid.

the Slovak Republic shows, among other things, that there are situations in which, even though the EU has competence as long as it has not acted, Member States continue to bear international responsibility.

It appears that international courts and tribunal, while accepting that breaches of international law committed by EU Member States when complying with EU law should be attributed to the EU, are establishing limits to the rule of attribution. These developments show how international courts are trying to solve the underlying tension between the necessity to repair the internationally wrongful act and the problem of dealing with the allocation of powers between the EU and its Member States.

However, these developments also present other questions regarding the EU's nature. On one hand, while a decision like *Micula v Romania*[23] might set limits to the reach of the EU's normative control, it should also be severely criticized for its disregard of the EU's jurisdiction over the issue. This is highlighted by the fact that the Commission has initiated an infringement procedure against Romania over the implementation of the arbitral award.[24] The ICSID did not seem to consider the possibility that, even though the actions could not be attributed to the EU, the issue should be settled within the EU's jurisdiction since the fact of having these issues dealt with by an international court would impinge on the autonomy of EU law and, ultimately, could affect the effectiveness of the decisions adopted by ICSID.[25]

On the other hand, a decision like the WTO *Airbus* case reflects another view of the EU and its relationship with its Member States with regard to international responsibility. While the EU exercises its normative control over its Member States within the area of state aids by authorizing those aids, the EU Treaties expressly provide for certain areas in which the EU does not control its Member States policy as regards state aids.[26] In

[23] *Ioan Micula, Viorel Micula, and others v Romania* (Award) ICSID Case ARB/05/20 (11 December 2013).

[24] Case T-694/15 *Micula v Commission* [nyr] ECR, action brought on 30 November 2015.

[25] Cf. Angelos Dimopoulos, 'The Validity and Applicability of International Investment Agreements between EU Member States under EU and International Law' [2011] 48(1) Common Market Law Review 63, 90; Case C-459/03 *Commission v Ireland (MOX Plant)*; Opinion 1/91 *Re: European Economic Area Agreement* [1991] ECR I-6079; Barbara Brandtner, 'The "Drama" of the EEA Comments on Opinions 1/91 and 1/92' [1992] 3 European Journal of International Law 300.

[26] Luca Rubini, *The Definition of Subsidy and State Aid: WTO and EC Law in Comparative Perspective* (Oxford University Press 2009); Gustavo Luengo Hernández de Madrid, *Regulation of Subsidies and State Aids and EC Law: Conflicts in International Trade Law* (Kluwer Law International 2007).

other words, under certain circumstances, EU Member States can grant subsidies without having to ask the EU to validate their decision. In those situations, it is argued that EU Member States act outside the umbrella of the EU's normative control. However, given that the EU is exclusively competent in relation to the WTO's SCM Agreement, the fact that Member States can adopt measures that, while falling outside the scope of EU law, can breach an agreement that falls within the scope of EU's exclusive competence should be a cause for concern.[27] EU Member States are breaching an international agreement when, in principle, they should not be able to do so, since they do not have the competence to conclude the agreement in the first place. This is an anomaly that is, to a certain extent, inherent to certain mixed agreements[28] and should be handled with the utmost care. The EU should increase its efforts and expand its role in controlling its Member States' state subsidy policies to preclude actions that, while violating an international obligation binding upon the EU, do not violate EU law itself. Otherwise, the EU would be put in a very difficult position in which it could incur responsibility for actions committed by its Member States that would be considered legally valid under the relevant Treaty, but would be simultaneously illegal under the terms of an international agreement binding on the EU.

2.3 Normative Control and Other Areas of EU Law

As was mentioned in the introduction, this monograph focused on disputes brought against either the EU or its Member States by third countries on issues covered by EU law. This selection was based on the fact that, up until this point, this is the only field in which the EU had been held responsible for breaching international law. The analysis of all those disputes supports the idea that the manner in which EU law is implemented combined with the principles and institutional machinery, which assures Member States compliance with EU law, should entail the EU's exclusive international responsibility. Therefore, this monograph reflects a current trend in international law in which the EU bears responsibility for actions carried out under its normative control.

However, the areas of EU law in which the principles, and more specifically the institutional architecture, which ensure Member States'

[27] Opinion 1/94 *Re: Competence of the Community to conclude international agreements concerning services and the protection of intellectual property* [1994] ECR I-5267.

[28] Allan Rosas, 'The European Union and Mixed Agreements' in Allan Dashwood and Cristophe Hillion (eds), *The General Law of EC External Relations* (Sweet and Maxwell 2000).

compliance with EU law are not as strong as they were previously. The most significant example of this is the first pillar: the CFSP. According to article 275 TFEU, the CJEU would not have jurisdiction with respect to the provisions relating to the CFSP nor to acts adopted on the basis of CFSP provision. Therefore, inasmuch as there would not be an internal judicial organ that can ensure the effective compliance of EU Member States with the CFSP acquis, one of the two distinctive features of the EU's normative control would be missing.[29]

Similarly, aside from the lack of judicial control, the current design of the CFSP entails further consequences in relation to the degree of normative control that the EU exercises over its Member States. It is not clear what effects a measure adopted under the CFSP will have. Article 2 TFEU does not subsume the CFSP competence within any of the traditional types of EU competence; as Cremona has argued, the CFSP would be a kind of "*sui generis*" competence or a non-pre-emptive shared competence.[30] Therefore neither the principle of primacy nor the principle of pre-emption would apply to the CFSP.[31]

Consequently, the only principle that would continue to inform the relationship between the EU and its Member States once they had implemented CFSP would be the duty of cooperation. Not only does article 4 (3) TEU apply irrespective of the policy issue, according to the common provisions of the CFSP and more specifically to article 24 (3) TEU, Member States shall support the Union's external and security policy actively and unreservedly in a spirit of loyalty and mutual solidarity and shall comply with the Union's actions in this area. Also by virtue of this provision, Member States shall work together to enhance and develop their mutual political solidarity and shall refrain from any action that is contrary to

29 Yet, it must be signalled that the CJEU seems to be adopting a restrictive view of what would fall within the scope of the CFSP. Therefore, it cannot be excluded that not only the principles informing the EU's normative control but also institutional architecture might gradually permeate into the realm of the CFSP. See as examples: Case C-658/12 *Parliament v Council (Agreement with Mauritius)* [nyr]. Case C-439/13, *Elitaliana v Eulex Kosovo* [nyr] (AG Opinion). Christophe Hillion, 'A Powerless Court? The European Court of Justice and the Common and Foreign Security Policy' in Marise Cremona and Anne Thies (eds), *The European Court of Justice and External Relations Law* (Hart 2014), 47–72.

30 Marise Cremona, 'The Draft Constitutional Treaty: External Relations and External Action' [2003] 40(6) Common Market Law Review 1347, 1353.

31 Declaration no 14 concerning the common foreign and security policy. Cf. Jan Wouters, Dominic Coppens and Bart De Meester, 'The European Union's External Relations after Lisbon' in Stefan Griller and Jacques Ziller (eds), *The Lisbon Treaty European Constitutionalism without a Constitutional Treaty?* (Springer 2008).

the interests of the Union or likely to impair its effectiveness as a cohesive force in international relations. That is to say that EU Member States continue to bear a duty to cooperate with the EU on CFSP issues. Moreover, article 24 (3) TEU provides the Council and the High Representative with the competence to ensure compliance with these principles. Therefore it would be difficult to argue that, as the law stands an action committed by a Member State when complying with a CFSP measure is to be understood as having been committed by the EU by virtue of its normative control.

Therefore, instead of applying a possible rule of attribution based on normative control, it appears that EU Member States would continue to bear responsibility for issues covered by the CFSP, as would the EU which would incur responsibility based not on a rule of attribution but on a rule of responsibility as enshrined in article 17 ARIO.

The fact that certain areas of the EU do not meet the criteria of normative control hints at three ideas on normative control and the European Union. First, even though the EU, when implementing its acquis, more closely resembles a federal state than a classical IO, it continues to be an IO at its heart: established by a treaty; possessed of its own international legal personality; and with States as its constituent members.

Second, there are areas which still remain outside the reach of the EU's normative control. The constitutional design of the CFSP reminds us that regardless of how "federal" the control that the EU exercises over its Member States appears to be, that EU does not have the institutional mechanisms and principles to normatively control its Member States on issues related to CFSP. Yet, especially after *Opinion 2/13*,[32] this could no longer be the case. Be it because the accession to the ECHR might only be a reality if the EU Member States grant the EU jurisdiction over the CFSP, be it because the scope of the CFSP is gradually becoming narrower than it might have appeared at first sight,[33] it cannot be excluded as the EU's normative control within the CFSP tightens, the EU's international responsibility on these issue might start to arise as well.

Finally, inasmuch as rule for attributing a wrongful act to the EU normative control has yet to crystalize, any development on the international responsibility of the EU has the potential of influencing the consolidation of such rule. If the EU, as it shown during the discussion on leading to the

32 Opinion 2/13 *Re: Accession of the European Union to the ECHR*.

33 Case C-658/12 *Parliament v Council (Agreement with Mauritius)*, Case C-439/13, *Elitaliana v Eulex Kosovo* (AG Opinion). Christophe Hillion, (n 29).

ARIO, wants to its normative control recognized as criteria to attributing responsibility under international law, it should make a special effort in controlling its Member States. As long as Member States effectively and uniformly comply with EU law, the case for normative control as rule to attribute responsibility to the EU will further strengthen.

Bibliography

Books

Alvarez, José E., *International Organizations as Law-makers* (Oxford University Press 2005)
Amerasinghe, C. F., *Principles of the Institutional Law of International Organizations* (Cambridge University Press 2005)
Aust, Helmut Philipp, *Complicity and the Law of State Responsibility* (Cambridge University Press 2011)
Blázquez Navarro, Irene, *Integración europea y diferencias comerciales de la OMC* (Marcial Pons 2007)
Brölmann, Catherine, *The Institutional Veil in Public International Law: International Organisations and the Law of Treaties* (Hart 2007)
Brownlie, Ian, *Principles of Public International Law* (7th edn, Oxford University Press 2008)
Cebada Romero, Alicia, *La Organización Mundial del Comercio y la Unión Europea* (La Ley 2002)
Churchill, Robin, and Vaughan Lowe, *The Law of the Sea* (3rd edn, Manchester University Press 1999)
Cortés Martín, José Manuel, *Las Organizaciones Internacionales: Codificación y Desarrollo Progresivo de su Responsabilidad Internacional* (Instituto Andaluz de Administración Pública 2008)
Craig, Paul, *EU Administrative Law* (Oxford University Press 2006)
Craig, Paul, and Gráinne De Búrca, *EU Law: Text, Cases and Materials* (3rd edn, Oxford University Press 2003)
Crawford, James, *State Responsibility: The General Part* (Cambridge University Press 2013)
Cremona, Marise (ed), *The Enlargement of the European Union* (Oxford University Press 2003)
Denza, Eileen, *The Intergovernmental Pillars of the European Union* (Oxford University Press 2002)
Dimopoulos, Angelos, *EU Foreign Investment Law* (Oxford University Press 2011)
Distefano, Marcella, *Soluzione delle Controversie nll'OMC e Diritto Internazionale* (CEDAM 2001)

Eeckhout, Piet, *EU External Relations Law* (2nd edn, Oxford University Press 2011)
External Relations of the European Union: Legal and Constitutional Foundations (Oxford University Press 2004)
Fernández Pons, Xavier, *La Organización Mundial del Comercio y el Derecho Internacional. Un estudio sobre el sistema de solución de diferencias de la OMC y las normas secundarias de Derecho internacional general* (Marcial Pons 2006)
Frank, Veronica, *The European Community and Marine Environmental Protection in the International Law of the Sea: Implementing Global Obligations at the Regional Level* (Martinus Nijhoff 2007)
Groux, Jean, *The European Communities in the International Order* (Commission of the European Communities 1985)
Heliskoski, Joni, *Mixed Agreements as a Technique for Organizing the International Relations of the European Community and Its Member States* (Kluwer Law International 2001)
Hirsch, Moshe, *The Responsibility of International Organizations towards Third Parties: Some Basic Principles* (Martinus Nijhoff 1995)
Holdgard, Raas, *External Relations Law of the European Community: Legal Reasoning and Legal Discourses* (Wolter Kluwer 2008)
Huici Sancho, Laura, *El hecho internacionalmente ilícito de las Organizaciones internacionales* (Bosch 2007)
Jacqué, Jean Paul, *Elements pour un théorie de l'acte juridique en droit international public* (LGDJ 1972)
Klabbers, Jan, *The European Union in International Law* (Pedone 2012)
An Introduction to International Institutional Law (Cambridge University Press 2009)
Treaty Conflict and the European Union (Cambridge University Press 2009)
Klamert, Marcus, *The Principle of Loyalty in EU Law* (Oxford University Press 2013)
Klein, Pierre, *La responsabilité des organisations internationales dans les ordres juridiques internes et en droit de gens* (Bruylant 1998)
Koutrakos, Panos, *EU International Relations Law* (Hart 2006)
EU International Relations Law (2nd edn, Hart 2015)
Krämer, L., *EC Environmental Law* (5th edn, Sweet and Maxwell 2003)
Kuijper, P. J., *Of 'Mixity' and 'Double-Hatting': EU External Relations Law Explained* (Amsterdam University Press 2008)
Luengo Hernández de Madrid, Gustavo, *Regulation of Subsidies and State Aids and EC Law: Conflicts in International Trade Law* (Kluwer Law International 2007)
Macleod, I., I. D. Hendry and S. Hyett, *The External Relations of the European Communities: A Manual of Law and Practice* (Clarendon 1996)
Mendez, Mario, *The Legal Effects of EU Agreements* (Oxford University Press 2013)
Neframi, Eleftheria, *L'action extérieure de l'Union européenne. Fondements, moyens, principes* (LGDJ 2010)
Les Accords Mixtes de la Communauté Européenne: Aspects Communautaires Et Internationaux (Bruylant 2007)
Neuwahl, Nanette A., *Mixed Agreements: Analysis of the Phenomenon and Their Legal Significance* (PhD thesis, European University Institute 1988)

Palmeter, David, and Petros C. Mavroidis, *Dispute Settlement in the World Trade Organization: Practice and Procedure* (2nd edn, Cambridge University Press 2004)

Pauwelyn, Joost, *Conflict of Norms in Public International Law: How WTO Relates to Other Rules of International Law* (Cambridge University Press 2003)

Petersmann, Ernst-Ulrich, *The GATT/WTO Dispute Settlement System: International Law, International Organizations and Dispute Settlement* (Kluwer Law International 1997)

Poli, Sara, *La controversia sugli organismi geneticamente modificati tra obblighi OMC e competenza comunitaria* (Editorialie Scientifica 2008)

Rey Aneiros, Adela, *Una Aproximación a la Responsabilidad Internacional de las Organizaciones Internacionales* (Tirant Lo Blanch 2006)

Rubini, Luca, *The Definition of Subsidy and State Aid: WTO and EC Law in Comparative Perspective* (Oxford University Press 2009)

Sarooshi, Dan, *International Organizations and Their Exercise of Sovereign Powers* (Oxford University Press 2005)

Schermers, Henry G., and Niels M. Blokker, *International Institutional Law: Unity within Diversity* (4th edn, Martinus Nijhoff 2003)

Schütze, Robert, *European Union Law* (Cambridge University Press 2015)

Foreign Affairs and the EU Constitution (Cambridge University Press 2014)

From Dual to Cooperative Federalism: The Changing Structure of European Law, vol 391 (Oxford University Press 2009)

Tiejte, Christian, Emily Sipiorsk and Grit Topfër, *Responsibility in Investor-State-Arbitration in the EU – Managing Financial Responsibility Linked to Investor-State Dispute Settlement Tribunals Established by EU's International Investment Agreements* (European Parliament 2012)

Titi, Catherine, *The Right to Regulate in International Investment Law* (Hart 2014)

Tzanakopoulos, Antonios, *Disobeying the Security Council: Countermeasures against Wrongful Sanctions* (Oxford University Press 2011)

Van Den Bossche, Peter, *The Law and Policy of the World Trade Organization: Text, Cases and Materials* (2nd edn, Cambridge University Press 2008)

Van Vooren, Bart, *EU External Relations Law and the European Neighbourhood Policy: A Paradigm for Coherence* (Routledge 2012)

Van Vooren, Bart, and Ramses A. Wessel, *EU External Relations Law: Text, Cases and Materials* (Cambridge University Press 2014)

Wyatt, Derrick, and Allan Dashwood, *European Union Law* (5th edn, Sweet and Maxwell 2006)

Zapater Duque, Esther, *La Unión Europea y la Cooperación Energética Internacional* (Dykinson 2002)

Zwanenburg, Marten, *Accountability of Peace Support Operations* (Martinus Nijhoff 2005)

Journal Articles and Chapters in Edited Collections

Ahlborn, Christiane, 'The Rules of International Organizations and the Law of International Responsibility' [2011] 8(2) *International Organizations Law Review* 397–482

Alí, Antonino, 'Non-Compliance Procedures in Multilateral Environmental Agreements: The Interaction between International Law and European Union Law' in Tullio Treves and others (eds), *Non-Compliance Procedures and Mechanisms and the Effectiveness of International Environmental Agreements* (T. M. C. Asser Press 2009) 521–534

Alvarez, José E., 'Revisiting the ILC's Draft Rules on International Organization Responsibility' [2011] 105 *Proceedings of the Annual Meeting (American Society of International Law)* 344–348

Amerasinghe, C. F., 'Comments on the ILC's Draft Articles on the Responsibility of International Organizations' [2012] 9 *International Organizations Law Review* 29–31

'Liability to Third Parties of Member States of International Organizations: Practice, Principle and Judicial Precedent' [1991] 85 *American Journal of International Law* 259–280

Azoulai, Loïc, 'The Acquis of the European Union and International Organizations' [2005] 11(2) *European Law Journal* 196–231

Beulay, Marjorie, 'L'Union européenne comme organisation international' in Myriam Benlolo-Carabot, Ulas Candas and Eglantine Cujo (eds), *Union européenne et Droit international* (Pedone 2012) 95–138

Bischoff, Jan Asmus, 'Just a Little Bit of "Mixity"? The EU's Role in the Field of International Investment Protection Law' [2011] 48(5) *Common Market Law Review* 1527–1570

Björklund, Martin, 'Responsibility in the EC for Mixed Agreements' [2001] 70 *Nordic Journal of International Law* 373–402

Blokker, Niels, 'Abuse of the Members: Questions Concerning Draft Article 16 of the Draft Articles on Responsibility of International Organizations' [2010] 7(1) *International Organizations Law Review* 35–48

'The Floor Is to the Authors: Perspectives on the Law of International Organizations as a Separate Field of Study' [2008] 5(1) *International Organizations Law Review* 141–142

'Preparing Articles on Responsibility of International Organizations: Does the International Law Commission Take International Organizations Seriously?' in Jan Klabbers and Asa Wallendahl (eds), *Research Handbook on the Law of International Organizations* (Edward Elgar 2011) 313–341

Boelaert-Suominen, Sonja, 'The European Community, the European Court of Justice and the Law of the Sea' [2008] 23(4) *International Journal of Maritime and Coastal Law* 643–713

Brandtner, Barbara, 'The "Drama" of the EEA Comments on Opinions 1/91 and 1/92' [1992] 3 *European Journal of International Law* 300–328

Brölmann, Catherine, 'International Organizations and Treaties' in Jan Klabbers (ed), *Research Handbook on International Organizations: Contractual Freedom and Institutional Constraint* (Edward Elgar 2011) 285–312

'A Flat Earth? International Organizations in the System of International Law' [2001] 70 *Nordic Journal Of International Law* 319–340

Brownlie, Ian, 'The Responsibility of States for the Acts of International Organizations' in Maurizio Ragazzi (ed), *International Responsibility Today: Essays in Memory of Oscar Schachter* (Martinus Nijhoff 2005) 355–362

Burgstaller, Markus, 'Investor-State Arbitration in EU International Investment Agreements with Third States' [2012] 39(2) *Legal Issues of Economic Integration* 207–221

'European Law and Investment Treaties' [2009] 26(2) *Journal of International Arbitration* 181–216

Calamita, N. Jansen, 'The Making of Europe's International Investment Policy: Uncertain First Steps' [2012] 39(3) *Legal Issues of Economic Integration* 301–329

Ceyssens, Jan, 'Towards a Common Foreign Investment Policy? – Foreign Investment in the European Constitution' [2005] 32(3) *Legal Issues of Economic Integration* 259–291

Churchill, R., and J. Scott 'The *MOX Plant* Litigation: The First Half-Life' [2004] 53(3) *International and Comparative Law Quarterly* 643–676

Clapham, Andrew, 'The European Union before the European Court of Human Rights' in Laurence Boisson de Chazournes, Cesare Romano and Ruth Mackenzie (eds), *International Organizations and International Dispute Settlement: Trends and Prospects* (Trasnantional 2002), 73–88

Collins, Richard, and Nigel D. White, 'Moving beyond the Autonomy-Accountability Dichotomy: Reflections on Institutional Independence in the International Legal Order' [2010] 7(1) *International Organizations Law Review* 1–8

Condorelli, Luigi, and Claus Kress, 'The Rules of Attribution: General Considerations' in James Crawford and others (eds), *The Law of International Responsibility* (Oxford University Press 2010) 221–236

Corten, Olivier, 'La "complicité" dans le Droit de la responsabilité internationale: un concept inutile?' [2011] LVII *Annuaire Française de Droit International* 57–84

Cortés Martín, José Manuel, 'Adhesión al CEDH y Autonomía del Derecho de la Unión: Legitimación pasiva de la Unión y sus miembros y compatibilidad material' [2010] 22 *Revista General de Derecho Europeo* 1–53

'European Exceptionalism in International Law? The European Union and the System of International Responsibility' in Maurizio Ragazzi (ed), *Responsibility of International Organizations: Essays in Memory of Sir Ian Brownlie* (Martinus Nijhoff 2013) 189–200

'The Responsibility of Members due to Wrongful Acts of International Organizations' [2013] 12(4) *Chinese Journal of International Law* 679–722

Cremona, Marise, 'Balancing Union and Member State Interests: Opinion 1/2008, Choice of Legal Base and the Common Commercial Policy under the Treaty of Lisbon' [2010] 35 *European Law Review* 678–694

'Defending the Community Interest: The Duties of Cooperation and Compliance' in M. Cremona and B. De Witte, *EU Foreign Relations Law: Constitutional Fundamentals* (Hart 2008) 125–170

'Disconnection Clauses in EU Law and Practice' in Christophe Hillion and Panos Koutrakos (eds), *Mixed Agreement Revisited* (Hart 2010) 160–186

'The Draft Constitutional Treaty: External Relations and External Action' [2003] 40(6) *Common Market Law Review* 1347–1366

'EC External Commercial Policy after Amsterdam: Authority and Interpretation within Interconnected Legal Orders' in J. H. H. Weiler (ed), *The EU, the WTO, and the NAFTA towards a Common Law of International Trade?* (Oxford University Press 2000) 5–34

External Relations of the EU and the Member States: Competence, Mixed Agreements, International Responsibility, and Effects of International Law (2006) EUI Law Working Paper 2006/22, http://ssrn.com/abstract=963316

'External Relations and External Competence of the European Union: The Emergence of an Integrated Policy' in Paul Craig and Gráinne de Burca (eds), *The Evolution of EU Law* (2nd edn, Oxford University Press 2010) 217–268

Who Can Make Treaties? The European Union' in Duncan B. Hollis (ed), *Oxford Guide to Treaties* (Oxford University Press 2012) 93–124

D'Argent, Pierre, 'La personalité juridique international de l'organisation internationale' in Evelyne Lagrange and Jean-Marc Sorel (eds), *Droit des organisations internationales* (LGDJ 2013) 439–464

Dashwood, Alan, 'Implied External Competence of the EC' in Martti Koskenniemi (ed), *International Law Aspects of the European Union* (Kluwer Law International 1998) 113–123

'Mixity in the Era of the Lisbon Treaty' in Christophe Hillion and Panos Koutrakos (eds), *Mixed Agreements Revisited The EU and Its Member States in the World* (Hart 2010) 351–366

Dashwood, Alan, and Joni Helikoski, 'The Classic Authorities Revisited' in Alan Dashwood and Christophe Hillion (eds), *The General Law of EC External Relations* (Sweet and Maxwell 2000) 3–19

D'Aspremont, Jean, 'Abuse of the Legal Personality of International Organizations and the Responsibility of Member States' [2007] 4 *International Organizations Law Review* 91–119

'The Articles on the Responsibility of International Organizations: Magnifying the Fissures in the Law of International Responsibility' [2012] 9 *International Organizations Law Review* 15–28

Delgado Casteleiro, Andrés, 'EU Declarations of Competence to Multilateral Agreements: A Useful Reference Base?' [2012] 17(4) *European Foreign Affairs Review* 491–510

'The International Responsibility of the EU: Between Pragmatism and Proceduralization' [2012] 15 *Cambridge Yearbook of European Legal Studies* 563–586

'Opinion 1/13: On the Scope of the EU's Exclusive Competence after the Lisbon Treaty' [2015] 51 *Revista de Derecho Comunitario Europeo* 669–684

'United We Stand: The EU and Its Member States in the Strasbourg Court' in Vasiliki Kosta, Nikos Skoutaris and Vassilis P. Tzevelekos (eds), *The EU Accession to the ECHR* (Hart 2014) 105–120

Delgado Casteleiro, Andrés, and Joris Larik, 'The 'Odd Couple': The Responsibility of the EU at the WTO' in Panos Koutrakos and Malcolm D. Evans (eds), *The International Responsibility of the European Union European and International Perspectives* (Hart 2013) 233–255

Denza, Eileen, 'Bilateral Investment Treaties and EU Rules on Free Transfer: Comment on Commission v Austria, Commission v Sweden and Commission v Finland' [2010] 35(2) *European Law Review* 263–274

'Responsibility of the European Union in the Context of Investment' in Panos Koutrakos and Malcolm D. Evans (eds), *The International Responsbility of the European Union European and International Perspectives* (Hart 2013) 215–232

De Witte, Bruno, 'The Emergence of European System of Public International Law: The EU and Its Member States as Strange Subjects' in Jan Wouters, André Nollkaemper and Erika De Wet (eds), *The Europeanisation of International Law* (T. M. C. Asser Press 2009) 39–54

'Too Much Constitutional Law in the European Union's Foreign Relations?' in M. Cremona and B. De Witte (eds), *EU Foreign Relations Law: Constitutional Fundamentals* (Hart 2009) 3–16

Díez-Hotchleitner Rodríguez, Javier, 'La Unión Europea ante la Reforma del Sistema de Solución de Diferencias de la OMC' in Juan Manuel Faramiñan Gisbert (ed), *Globalización y Comercio Exterior Actas de las XX Jornadas de la Asociación Española de Profesores de Derecho Internacional y Relaciones Internacionales, 2003* (Boletín Oficialdel Estado 2005) 61–88

Dimopoulos, Angelos, 'The BITs Cases: Practical and Doctrinal Implications' in Javier Díez-Hotchleitner Rodríguez and others (eds), *Recent Trends in the Case Law of the Court of Justice of the European Union* (La Ley 2012) 737–758

'The Involvement of the EU in Investor-State Dispute Settlement: A Question of Responsibilities' [2014] 51(6) *Common Market Law Review* 1671–1720

'The Validity and Applicability of International Investment Agreements between EU Member States under EU and International Law' [2011] 48(1) *Common Market Law Review* 63–93

Dominicé, Christian, 'Attribution of Conduct to Multiple States and the Implication of a State in the Act of Another State' in James Crawford and others (eds), *The Law of International Responsibility* (Oxford University Press 2010) 281–290

Dupuy, Pierre Marie, 'The International Law of State Responsibility: Revolution or Evolution?' [1989] 11 *Michigan Journal of International Law* 105–128

Dupuy, René-Jean, 'External Relations of the EU and the Member States Competence, Mixed Agreements, International Responsibility, and Effects of International Law' in *XXII FIDE Congress* (FIDE 2006) 1–35

'Le droit des relations entre les organisations internationales' [1960] 100 *Recueil de Cours de la Académie du Droit International* 457–589

Dupuy, René-Jean, and Piet Eeckhout, 'The EU and Its Member States in the WTO – Issues of Responsibility' in Lorand Bartels and Federico Ortino (eds), *Regional Trade Agreements and the WTO Legal System* (Oxford University Press 2006) 449–464

Eagleton, Clyde, 'International Organization and the Law of Responsibility' [1950] 76(1) *Recueil de Cours de la Académie du Droit International* 316–424

Ehlermann, C. D., 'Mixed Agreements: A List of Problems' in David O'Keeffe and Henry G. Schermers (eds), *Mixed Agreements* (Kluwer Law and Taxation 1983) 3–21

Feenstra, J. J., 'A Survey of the Mixed Agreements and their Participation Clauses' in D. O'Keeffe and H. G. Schermers (eds.) *Mixed Agreements* (Kluwer Law and Taxation 1983) 207–248

Gaja, Giorgio, 'The European Community's Participation in the Law of the Sea Convention: Some Incoherences in a Compromise Solution' [1980] 5 *Italian Yearbook of International Law* 110–114

'How Does the European Community's International Responsibility Relate to Its Exclusive Competence?' in *Studi di Diritto Internazionale in Onore di Gaetano Arangio-Ruiz*, vol II (Editoriale Scientifica 2004) 747–755

'Some Reflections on the European Community's International Responsibility' in Henry G. Schermers, Ton Heukels and Philip Mead (eds), *Non-Contractual Liability of the European Communities* (Martinus Nijhoff 1988) 169–176

Gattini, Andrea, 'Breach of International Obligations' in André Nollkaemper and Ilias Plakokefalos (eds), *Principles of Shared Responsibility in International Law: An Appraisal of the Art* (Cambridge University Press 2014) 25–59

Goeteyn, Nils, and Frank Maes, 'Compliance Mechanisms in Multilateral Environmental Agreements: An Effective Way to Improve Compliance?' [2011] 10(4) *Chinese Journal of International Law* 791–826

Hancox, Emily, 'The Meaning of "Implementing" EU Law under Article 51(1) of the Charter: Åkerberg Fransson' [2013] 50(5) *Common Market Law Review* 1411–1432

Harrison, James, 'The Legal Framework for Investment Protection between the European Union and Korea: Towards a Level Playing Field for Investors?' in James Harrison (ed), *The European Union and South Korea: The Legal Framework for Strengthening Trade, Economic and Political Relations* (Edinburgh University Press 2013) 102–123

Heliskoski, J., 'EU Declarations of Competence and International Responsibility' in M. D. Evans and P. Koutrakos (eds), *The International Responsibility of the European Union International and European Perspectives* (Hart 2013) 189–214

Herman, Lawrence L., 'NAFTA and ECT: Divergent Approaches with a Core of Harmony' [1997] 15(2) *Journal of Energy and Natural Resources Law* 129–154

Hernández, Gleider I., 'Beyond the Control Paradigm? International Responsibility and the European Union' [2014] 15 *Cambridge Yearbook of European Legal Studies* 643–668

Herrmann, Christoph W., 'Common Commercial Policy After Nice: Sisyphus Would Have Done a Better Job' [2002] 39(1) *Common Market Law Review* 7–29

'The Treaty of Lisbon Expands the EU's External Trade and Investment Powers' [2010] 14 *ASIL Insight* 1–4

Higgins, Rosalyn, 'Report for Institute de Droit International: The Legal Consequences for Member States of the Non-fulfilment by International Organizations of Their Obligations toward Third Parties' in Rosalyn Higgins (ed), *Themes and Theories: Selected Essays, Speeches, and Writings in International Law*, vol 2 (Oxford University Press 2009) 834–866

'The Responsibility of States Members for the Defaults of International Organizations: Continuing the Dialogue' in Rosalyn Higgins (ed), *Themes and*

Theories: Selected Essays, Speeches, and Writings in International Law, vol 2 (Oxford University Press 2009) 920–925

Hillion, Christophe, 'ERTA, ECHR and Open Skies: Laying the Grounds of the EU System of External Relations' in M. Maduro and L. Azoulai, *The Past and Future of EU Law: The Classics of EU Law Revisited on the 50th Anniversary of the Rome Treaty* (Hart 2010) 224–233

'Mixity and Coherence in EU External Relations: The Significance of the "Duty of Cooperation"' in Cristophe Hillion and Panos Koutrakos (eds), *Mixed Agreements Revisited* (Hart 2010) 87–105

Hindelang, Steffen, 'Circumventing Primacy of EU Law and the CJEUs Judicial Monopoly by Resorting to Dispute Resolution Mechanisms Provided for in Inter-se Treaties? The Case of Intra-EU Investment Arbitration' [2012] 39(2) *Legal Issues of Economic Integration* 179–206

Hoffmeister, Frank, 'Curse or Blessing? Mixed Agreements in the Recent Practice of the European Community and Its Member States' in Cristophe Hillion and Panos Koutrakos (eds), *Mixed Agreements in EU Law Revisited: The EU and Its Member States in the World* (Hart 2010) 249–268

'Litigating against the European Union and Its Member States – Who Responds under the ILC's Draft Articles on International Responsibility of International Organizations?' [2010] 21(3) *European Journal of International Law* 723–747

Hyett, Stephen, 'The Duty of Cooperation: A Flexible Concept' in Allan Dashwood and Cristophe Hillion (eds), *The General Law of EC External Relations* (Sweet and Maxwell 2000) 248–253

Jacqué, Jean Paul, 'Communauté européenne et Convention européenne des droits de l'homme' in Louis-Edmond Pettiti, Emmanuel Decaux and Pierre–Henri Imbet (eds), *La Convention européenne des droits de l'homme Commentaire article par article* (Economica 1999) 83–100

Jendrośka, Jerzy, 'Aarhus Convention Compliance Committee: Origins, Status and Activities' [2011] 8(4) *Journal for Environmental and Planning Law* 301–374

'Recent Case-Law of the Aarhus Convention Compliance Committee' [2011] 8(4) *Journal for Environmental and Planning Law* 375–449

Klabbers, Jan, 'The Changing Image of International Organizations' in Jean-Marc Coicaud and Veijo Heiskanen (eds), *The Legitimacy of International Organizations* (United Nations University Press 2001) 221–255

'Contending Approaches to International Organizations: Between Functionalism and Constitutionalism' in Jan Klabbers and Asa Wallendahl (eds), *Research Handbook on the Law of International Organizations* (Edward Elgar 2011) 3–32

'The Emergence of Functionalism in International Institutional Law: Colonial Inspirations' [2014] 25(3) *European Journal of International Law* 645–675

'Safeguarding the Organizational Acquis: The EU's External Practice' [2007] 4(1) *International Organizations Law Review* 57–89

'The Transformation of International Organizations Law' [2015] 26(1) *European Journal of International Law* 9–82

Klein, Pierre, 'The Attribution of Acts to International Organizations' in James Crawford, Alain Pellet and Simon Olleson (eds), *The Law of International Responsbility* (Oxford University Press 2010) 297–315

'Les Articles sur la Responsibilité des Organisations Internationales: Quel Bilan tirer des travux de la CDI?' [2012] LVIII *Annuaire Française de Droit International* 1–27

Kleinheisterkamp, Jan, 'Financial Responsibility in European International Investment Policy' [2014] 63(2) *International and Comparative Law Quarterly* 449–476

Koer, Albert W., 'Participation of the European Economic Community in the New Law of the Sea Convention' [1979] 73 *American Journal of International Law* 426–443

Koester, Veit, 'The Compliance Committee of the Aarhus Convention: An Overview of Procedures and Jurisprudence ' [2007] 37(2–3) *Environmental Policy and Law* 83–96

Konstadinides, Theodore, 'EU Foreign Policy under the Doctrine of Implied Powers: Codification Drawbacks and Constitutional Limitations' [2014] 39(4) *European Law Review* 511–530

Koutrakos, Panos, 'Case C-94/03, Commission v. Council, judgment of the Second Chamber of 10 January 2006, [2006]ECR I-1; Case C-178/03, Commission v. Parliament and Council, judgment of the Second Chamber of 10 January 2006, [2006]ECR I-107' [2007]*Common Market Law Review* 171–194

'Interpretation of Mixed Agreements' in Christophe Hillion and Panos Koutrakos (eds), *Mixed Agreements Revisited: The EU and Its Member States in the World* (Hart 2010) 116–137

'Foreign Direct Investment Law in a State of Flux' [2013] 5 *European Law Review* 599–600

'Legal Basis and Delimitation of Competence in the EU' in M. Cremona and B. De Witte (eds), *EU Foreign Relations Law* (Hart 2008) 171–198

Kuijper, Pieter-Jan, 'Amsterdam Center for International Law: Introduction to the Symposium on Responsibility of International Organizations and of (Member) States. Attributed or Direct Responsibility or Both?' [2010] 7(1) *International Organizations Law Review* 9–33

'International Responsibility for EU mixed agreements' in Christophe Hillion and Panos Koutrakos (eds), *Mixed Agreements Revisited: The EU and Its Member States in the World* (Hart 2010) 208–227

Kuijper, Pieter-Jan, and Esa Paasivirta, 'EU International Responsibility and Its Attribution: From the Inside Looking Out' in Panos Koutrakos and Malcolm D. Evans (eds), *The International Responsibility of the European Union European and International Perspectives* (Hart 2013) 35–74

'Further Exploring International Responsibility: The European Community and the ILC's Project on Responsibility of International Organizations' [2004] 1 *International Organizations Law Review* 111–138

Louis, Jean-Victor, 'La personnalité juridique internationale de la Communauté et de l'Union Européenne' in Jean-Victor Louis and Marianne Dony (eds),

Commentaire J Megret Le Droit de la CE et de l'Union Européenne Relations Exterieures, vol 12 (Université de Bruxelles 2005) 23–56

'L'insertion des accords dans l'ordre juridique de la Communauté et des Etats membres' in Jean-Victor Louis and Marianne Dony (eds), *Commentaire J Megret Le Droit de la CE et de l'Union Européenne Relations Exterieures*, vol 12 (Université de Bruxelles 2005) 113–140

Marceau, Gabrielle, 'Conflicts of Norms and Conflicts of Jurisdictions: The Relationship between the WTO Agreement and MEAs and Other Treaties' [2001] 35(6) *Journal of World Trade* 1081–1131

Mardsen, S., 'Invoking Direct Application and Effect of International Treaties by the European Court of Justice: Implications for International Environmental Law in the European Union' [2011] 60 *International and Comparative Law Quarterly* 737–757

Messineo, Francesco, 'Attribution of Conduct' in André Nollkaemper and Ilias Plakokefalos (eds), *Principles of Shared Responsibility in International Law: An Appraisal of the State of the Art* (Cambridge University Press 2014) 60–97

Milanović, Marko, and Tatjana Papić, 'As Bad as It Gets: The European Court of Human Rights' Behrami and Saramati Decision and General International Law' [2009] 58(2) *International and Comparative Law Quarterly* 267–296

Moreno Molina, Angel Manuel, 'La Administración Pública de los Estados miembros como Administración comunitaria. Referencia a la sitación española' in Luciano Parejo Alfonso and others (eds), *Manual de Derecho Administrativo Comunitario* (Centro de Estudios Ramon Areces 2000) 145–193

Müller, Daniel, 'Union Européenne et Responsabilité International' in Myriam Benlolo-Carabot, Ukas Candas and Eglantine Cujo (eds), *Union Européenne et Droit International En l'honneur de Patrick Dlaillier* (Pedone 2012) 339–380

Murray, Odette, 'Piercing the Corporate Veil: The Responsibility of Member States of an International Organization' [2011] 8(2) *International Organizations Law Review* 291–347

Naert, Frederik, 'The International Responsibility of the Union in the Context of Its CSDP Operations ' in Malcolm D. Evans and Panos Koutrakos (eds), *The International Responsibility of the European Union European and International Perspectives* (Hart 2013) 313–338

Nedeski, Nataša, and André Nollkaemper, 'Responsibility of International Organizations in Connection with Acts of States' [2012] 9(1) *International Organizations Law Review* 33–52

Neframi, Eleftheria, 'The Duty of Loyalty: Rethinking Its Scope through Its Application in the Field of EU External Relations' [2010] 47 *Common Market Law Review* 323–359

'International Responsibility of the European Community and of Member States under Mixed Agreements' in Enzo Cannizzaro (ed), *The European Union as an Actor in International Relations* (Kluwer Law International 2002) 193–205

'Mixed Agreements as a Source of European Union Law' in Enzo Cannizzaro, Paolo Palcehtti and Ramses A. Wessel (eds), *International Law as Law of the European Union* (Martinus Nijhoff 2012) 325–352

Nollkaemper, André, 'Constitutionalization and the Unity of the Law of International Responsibility' [2009] 16(2) *Indiana Journal of Global Studies* 535–563

'Introduction' in André Nollkaemper and Ilias Plakokefalos (eds), *Principles of Shared Responsibility in International Law: An Appraisal of the State of the Art* (Cambridge University Press 2014) 1–24

'Joint Responsibility between the EU and Member States for Non-Performance of Obligations under Multilateral Environmental Agreements' in Elisa Morgera and Gracia Marín Durán (eds), *The EU and International Environmental Law* (Cambridge University Press 2012) 304–346

'The Role of National Courts in Inducing Compliance with International and European Law – A Comparison' in Marise Cremona (ed), *Compliance and Enforcement of EU Law* (Oxford University Press 2012) 157–194

Olson, Peter M., 'Mixity from the Outside: The Perspective of a Treaty Partner', in Christophe Hillion and Panos Koutrakos (eds), *Mixed Agreements Revisited: The EU and Its Member States in the World* (Hart 2010) 331–348

Orellana, Marcos A., 'The Swordfish Dispute between the EU and Chile at the ITLOS and the WTO' [2002] 71(1) *Nordic Journal of International Law* 55–81

Ott, Andrea, and Ramses A. Wessel, 'The EU's External Relations Regime: Multilevel Complexity in an Expanding Union' in Steven Blockmans and Adam Lazowski (eds), *The European Union and Its Neighbours: A Legal Appraisal of the EU's Policies of Stabilisation, Partnership and Integration* (T. M. C. Asser Press 2006) 19–53

Paasivirta, Esa, 'Responsibility of a Member State of an International Organization: Where Will It End? Comments on Article 60 of the ILC Draft on the Responsibility of International Organizations' [2010] 7(1) *International Organizations Law Review* 49–61

Paasivirta, Esa, and Pieter-Jan Kuijper, 'Does One Size Fit All? The European Community and the Responsibility of International Organizations' [2005] XXXVI(I) *Netherlands Yearbook of International Law* 169–226

Pastor Ridruejo, José Antonio, 'La interrelación de los sistemas de protección de los derechos fundamentales' in Enrique Álvarez Conde and Vicente Garrido Mayol (eds), *Comentarios a la Constitución Europea*, vol 2 (Tirant Lo Blanch 2005) 1655–1667

Paulsson, Jan, 'Arbitration without Privity' in Thomas W. Wälde (ed), *The Energy Charter Treaty: An East-West Gateway for Investment and Trade* (Kluwer Law International 1996) 422–442

Pauwelyn, Joost 'Enforcement and Countermeasures in the WTO' [2000] 94 *American Journal of International Law* 307–347

Pellet, Alain, 'Les fondements juridiques internationaux du droit communautaire' [1994] V(2) *Collected Courses of the Academy of European Law* 201–271

Pescatore, Pierre, 'Les Relations extérieures des Communautés européennes' [1961] 103 *Recueil de Cours de la Académie du Droit International* 9–244

Pigrau Solé, Antoni, 'La Responsabilidad Internacional de la Comunidad Europea' in Fernando M. Mariño Menéndez (ed), *Acción exterior de la*

Unión Europea y comunidad internacional (Boletín Oficialdel Estado 1998) 171–217

Pigrau Solé, Antoni, and Susana Borrás Pentinat, 'Diez Años del Convenio de Aarhus sobre acceso a la información, la participación y el acceso a la justicia en materia de medio ambiente' in Antoni Pigrau Solé (ed), *Accesso a la información, participación y acceso a la justicia en materia de medio ambiente, diez años del Convenio de Aarhus* (Atelier 2008) 21–80

Pineschi, Laura, 'Non-Compliance Procedures and the Law of State Responsibility' in Tullio Treves and others (eds), *Non-Compliance Procedures and Mechanisms and the Effectiveness of International Environmental Agreements* (T. M. C. Asser Press 2009) 483–497

Pitea, Cesare, 'The Non-Compliance Procedure of the Aarhus Convention: Between Environmental and Human Rights Control Mechanisms' [2006] 16(1) *Italian Yearbook of International Law* 85–116

Quadri, Rolando, 'Cours général de droit international public' [1964] 113 *Recueil de Cours de la Académie du Droit International* 237–483

Ragazzi, Maurizzio, 'The ILC Draft Articles and International Financial Institutions: Select Considerations' [2011] 105 *Proceedings of the Annual Meeting (American Society of International Law)* 353–356

Reinisch, August, 'Aid or Assistance and Direction and Control between States and International Organizations in the Commission of Internationally Wrongful Acts' [2010] 7(1) *International Organizations Law Review* 63–77

'Articles 30 and 59 of the Vienna Convention on the Law of Treaties in Action: The Decisions on Jurisdiction in the Eastern Sugar and Eureko Investment Arbitrations' [2012] 39(2) *Legal Issues of Economic Integration* 157–177

Rijken, C., and V. Kronenberger, 'The United nations Convention against Transnational Organised Crime and the European Union' in V. Kronenberger (ed), *The EU and the International Legal Order: Discord or Harmony?* (T. M. C. Asser Press 2001) 481–517

Roldán Barbero, Javier, 'La CEE y el Convenio sobre Derecho del Mar de 1982: consideraciones sobre la relación entre el Derecho de Comunitario y el Derecho Internacional' [1991] 2 *Revista de Instituciones Europeas* 551–583

Rosas, Allan, 'The European Court of Justice and Public International Law' in Jan Wouters, André Nollkaemper and Erika De Wet (eds), *The Europeanisation of International Law* (T. M. C. Asser Press 2009) 71–86

'The European Union and Mixed Agreements' in Allan Dashwood and Cristophe Hillion (eds), *The General Law of EC External Relations* (Sweet and Maxwell 2000) 200–220

'International Dispute Settlement: EU Practices and Procedures' [2003] 46 *German Yearbook of International Law* 284–322

'International Responsibility of the EU and the European Court of Justice' in Malcolm D. Evans and Panos Koutrakos (eds), *The International Responsibility of the European Union European and International Perspectives* (Hart 2013) 139–162

Ryngaert, Cedric, 'Oscillating between Embracing and Avoiding Bosphorus: The European Court of Human Rights on Member State Responsibility for Acts of

International Organizations and the Case of the EU' [2014] 39 *European Law Review* 176–192

Sadurska, Romana, and C. M. Chinkin, 'The Collapse of the International Tin Council: A Case of State Responsibility?' [1990] 30 *Virginia Journal of International Law* 845–890

Sarmiento, Daniel, 'Who's Afraid of the Charter? The Court of Justice, National Courts and the New Framework of Fundamental Rights Protection in Europe' (2013) 50(5) *Common Market Law Review* 1267–1304

Sarvarian, Armen, 'EU Accession to the ECHR and the Law of International Responsibility' in Vasiliki Kosta, Nikos Skoutaris and Vassilis P. Tzevelekos (eds), *The EU Accession to the ECHR* (Hart 2013) 87–104

Sattorova, Mavluda, 'Return to the Local Remedies Rule in European BITs? Power (Inequalities), Dispute Settlement, and Change in Investment Treaty Law' [2012] 39(2) *Legal Issues of Economic Integration* 223–247

Schütze, Robert, 'Federalism and Foreign Affairs: Mixity as a (Inter)national Phenomenon' in Christophe Hillion and Panos Koutrakos (eds), *Mixed Agreements Revisited: The EU and Its Member States in the World* (Hart 2010) 57–86

'From Rome to Lisbon: "Executive Federalism" in the (New) European Union' [2010] 47(5) *Common Market Law Review* 1385–1427

'Lisbon and the Federal Order of Competences: A Prospective Analysis' [2008] 33 *European Law Review* 709–722

'On "Federal" Ground: The European Unions as an (inter)National Phenomenon' [2009] 46 *Common Market Law Review* 1069–1105

Seidl-Hohenveldern, Ignaz, 'Les organes des organisations internationales' in René-Jean Dupuy (ed), *Manuel sur les organisations internationales* (Martinus Nijhoff 1988) 81–100

Serena Rossi, Lucia, 'Does the Lisbon Treaty Provide a Clearer Separation of Competences between EU and Member States?' in Andrea Biondi, Piet Eeckhout and Stefanie Ripley (eds), *EU Law after Lisbon* (Oxford University Press 2012) 85–106

Shraga, Daphna, 'The ILC Draft Articles on Responsibility of International Organizations: The Interplay between the Practice and the Rule' [2011] 105 *Proceedings of the Annual Meeting (American Society of International Law)* 351–353

Simma, Bruno, 'Of Planets and the Universe: Self-Contained Regimes in International Law' [2006] 17 *European Journal of International Law* 483–529

Simmonds, Kenneth R., 'The Community's Declaration upon Signature of the UN Convention on the Law of the Sea' [1986] 23 *Common Market Law Review* 521–544

'The Community's Participation in the U.N. Law of the Sea Convention' in David O'Keeffe and Henry G. Schermers (eds), *Essays in European Law and Integration* (Kluwer 1982) 179–191

'The European Economic Community and the New Law of the Sea' [1989] VI *Recueil de Cours de la Académie du Droit International* 11–166

Stein, Eric, 'External Relations of the European Community: Structure and Process' [1991] 1 *Collected Courses of the Academy of European Law* 115–188

Steinberger, Eva, 'The WTO Treaty as a Mixed Agreement: Problems with EC's and the EC Member States' Membership of the WTO' [2006] 17(4) *European Journal of International Law* 837–862

Stern, Brigitte, 'The Elements of an Internationally Wrongful Act' in James Crawford, Alain Pellet and Simon Olleson (eds), *The Law of International Responsibility* (Oxford University Press 2010) 193–220

Talmon, Stefan, 'Responsibility of International Organizations: Does the European Community Require Special Treatment?' in Maurizio Ragazzi (ed), *International Responsibility Today: Essays in Memory of Oscar Schachter* (Martinus Nijhoff 2005) 405–421

Temple Lang, J., 'The Ozone Layer Convention: A New Solution to the Question of Community Participation in "Mixed" International Agreements' [1986] 23 *CML Review* 157–176

Timmermans, Christian, 'EU and International Public Law' [1999] 4 *European Foreign Affairs Review* 181–194

Treves, Tullio, 'The European Community and the Law of the Sea Convention: New Developments' in Enzo Cannizazaro (ed), *The European Union as an Actor in International Relations* (Kluwe Law International 2002) 279–296

Vidal Puig, Ramón, 'The Scope of the New Exclusive Competence of the European Union with Regard to Foreign Direct Investment' [2013] 40(2) *Legal Issues of Economic Integration* 133–162

Villapando, Santiago M., 'Attribution of Conduct to the State: How the Rules of State Responsibility May Be Applied within the WTO Dispute Settlement System' [2002] 5(2) *Journal of International Economic Law* 393–420

Van Vooren, Bart, Steven Blockmans and Jan Wouters, 'The Legal Dimension of Global Governance: What Role for the European Union? An Introduction' in Bart Van Vooren, Steven Blockmans and Jan Wouters (eds), *The EU's Role in Global Governance: The Legal Dimension* (Oxford University Press 2013) 1–4

Wehland, Hanno, 'Intra-EU Investment Agreements and Arbitration: Is European Community Law an Obstacle?' [2009] 58(2) *International and Comparative Law Quarterly* 297–320

Weil, Prosper, 'Le droit international en quête de son identité: cours général de droit international public' (2015) 237 *Recueil de Cours de la Académie du Droit International* 1–370

Weiler, Joseph H. H., 'External Legal Relations of Non-Unitary Actors' in Joseph H. H. Weiler (ed), *The Constitution of Europe: Do the New Clothes Have an Emperor?* (Cambridge University Press 1999) 130–187

'The Transformation of Europe' [1991] 100 *Yale Law Journal* 2045–2583

Wouters, Jan, Dominic Coppens and Bart De Meester, 'The European Union's External Relations after Lisbon' in Stefan Griller and Jacques Ziller (eds), *The Lisbon Treaty European Constitutionalism Without a Constitutional Treaty?* (Springer 2008), 143–180

Wu, Chien-Hui, 'Foreign Direct Investment as Common Commercial Policy: EU External Economic Competence after Lisbon' in James Cardwell (ed),

EU External Relations Law and Policy in the Post-Lisbon Era (T. M. C. Asser Press 2012) 375–399

Yee, Sienho, 'The Responsibility of State Members of an International Organization for Its Conduct as a Result of Membership or Their Normal Conduct Associated with Membership' in Maurizio Ragazzi (ed), *International Responsibility Today: Essays in Memory of Oscar Schachter* (Martinus Nijhoff 2005) 435–454

Index

www.ingramcontent.com/pod-product-compliance
Ingram Content Group UK Ltd.
Pitfield, Milton Keynes, MK11 3LW, UK
UKHW020232281225
466426UK00007B/348
9781107090545